Frommer's

Seattle
day BY day

3rd Edition

by Donald Olson

D0062551

FrommerMedia LLC

Contents

16 Favorite Moments 1

1 The Best Full-Day Tours 7
The Best in One Day 8
The Best in Two Days 12
The Best in Three Days 16

2 The Best Special-Interest Tours 19
Seattle Heritage 20
Seattle for Art Lovers 26
Seattle Film & Theater 30
Seattle for Kids 34
Caffeinated Seattle 38
Architecture & Design 42

3 The Best Neighborhood Walks 49
Pioneer Square 50
Pike Place Market 54
Downtown 60
Capitol Hill 66
Chinatown/International District 70
Wallingford 74
Fremont 78

4 The Best Shopping 81
Shopping Best Bets 82
Seattle Shopping A to Z 87

5 The Best of the Outdoors 97
The Seattle Waterfront 98
Lake Union 102
Hiram M. Chittenden Locks 106
Green Lake Park 108
Washington Park Arboretum 110
Woodland Park 112
Seattle Center 114

6 The Best Dining 117
Dining Best Bets 118
Seattle Restaurants A to Z 123

7 The Best Nightlife 135
Nightlife Best Bets 136
Seattle Nightlife A to Z 139

8 The Best Arts & Entertainment 145
Arts & Entertainment Best Bets 146
Arts & Entertainment A to Z 148

9 The Best Lodging 153
Lodging Best Bets 156
Seattle Hotels A to Z 157

10 The Best Day Trips & Excursions 163
Tacoma 164
San Juan Islands 166
Bellevue 168
Mount Rainier National Park 172
Vancouver, B.C. 174

The Savvy Traveler 177
Before You Go 178
Getting There 180
Getting Around 182
Fast Facts 183
A Brief History 186

Index 189

Published by:

FROMMER MEDIA LLC

Copyright © 2015 by Frommer Media LLC. All rights reserved. No part of this publication may be reproduced, stored in a retrieval system, or transmitted in any form or by any means, electronic, mechanical, photocopying, recording, scanning or otherwise, except as permitted under Sections 107 or 108 of the 1976 United States Copyright Act, without the prior written permission of the Publisher. Requests to the Publisher for permission should be addressed to support@frommermedia.com.

Frommer's is a registered trademark of Arthur Frommer. Frommer Media LLC is not associated with any product or vendor mentioned in this book.

ISBN 978-1-62887-130-2 (paper), 978-1-62887-131-9 (e-book)

Editorial Director: Pauline Frommer
Editor: Lorraine Festa
Production Editor: Heather Wilcox
Photo Editor: Dana K. Davis
Cartographer: Elizabeth Puhl

Front cover photos, left to right: © Denise Lett, © Christopher Boswell, and © Carlos Yudica/Shutterstock.com. Back cover: © Mcarter.

For information on our other products or services, see www.frommers.com.

Frommer Media LLC also publishes its books in a variety of electronic formats. Some content that appears in print may not be available in electronic formats.

Manufactured in China

5   4   3   2   1

About this Guide

Organizing your time. That's what this guide is all about.

Other guides give you long lists of things to see and do and then expect you to fit the pieces together. The Day by Day guides are different. These guides tell you the best of everything, and then they show you how to see it in the smartest, most time-efficient way. Our authors have designed detailed itineraries organized by time, neighborhood, or special interest. And each tour comes with a bulleted map that takes you from stop to stop.

Hoping to explore Seattle's iconic Pike Place Market or tour the city's eerie underground past? Want to try some of the country's finest coffee while strolling through Seattle's hip shopping districts? Whatever your interest or schedule, the Day by Days give you the smartest routes to follow. Not only do we take you to the top attractions, hotels, and restaurants, but we also help you access those special moments that locals get to experience—those "finds" that turn tourists into travelers.

The Day by Days are also your top choice if you're looking for one complete guide for all your travel needs. The best hotels and restaurants for every budget, the greatest shopping values, the wildest nightlife—it's all here.

Why should you trust our judgment? Because our authors personally visit each place they write about. They're an independent lot who say what they think and would never include places they wouldn't recommend to their best friends. They're also open to suggestions from readers. If you'd like to contact them, please send your comments our way at feedback@frommers.com, and we'll pass them on.

Enjoy your Day by Day guide—the most helpful travel companion you can buy. And have the trip of a lifetime.

About the Author

Donald Olson is a travel writer, novelist, and playwright. His travel stories have appeared in "The New York Times," "National Geographic," and other national publications, and he is the author or co-author of several major travel guides, including "Frommer's EasyGuide to Seattle, Portland & the Oregon Coast," "Frommer's EasyGuide to Germany," "Frommer's Germany Day by Day," "Best Day Trips from London," "England For Dummies," "Frommer's Vancouver & Victoria," and "Michelin Pacific Northwest Guide." His three most recent novels were published under the pen name Swan Adamson. His new book, "Pacific Northwest Garden Tour," is published by Timber Press. Donald lives, writes, and gardens in Manhattan and in Portland, Oregon.

An Additional Note

Please be advised that travel information is subject to change at any time—and this is especially true of prices. We therefore suggest that you write or call ahead for confirmation when making your travel plans. The authors, editors, and publisher cannot be held responsible for the experiences of readers while traveling. Your safety is important to us, however, so we encourage you to stay alert and be aware of your surroundings.

Star Ratings, Icons & Abbreviations

Every hotel, restaurant, and attraction listing in this guide has been ranked for quality, value, service, amenities, and special features using a **star-rating system.** Hotels, restaurants, attractions, shopping, and nightlife are rated on a scale of zero stars (recommended) to three stars (exceptional). In addition to the star-rating system, we also use a **kids icon** to point out the best bets for families. Within each tour, we recommend cafes, bars, or restaurants where you can take a break. Each of these stops appears in a shaded box marked with a coffee-cup-shaped bullet ☕.

The following **abbreviations** are used for credit cards:

AE	American Express	DISC	Discover	V	Visa
DC	Diners Club	MC	MasterCard		

Frommers.com

Now that you have this guidebook to help you plan a great trip, visit our website at **www.frommers.com** for additional travel information on more than 4,000 destinations. We update features regularly to give you instant access to the most current trip-planning information available. At Frommers.com, you'll find scoops on the best airfares, lodging rates, and car rental bargains. You can even book your travel online through our reliable travel booking partners. Other popular features include:

- Online updates of our most popular guidebooks
- Vacation sweepstakes and contest giveaways
- Newsletters highlighting the hottest travel trends
- Online travel message boards with featured travel discussions

A Note on Prices

In the "Take a Break" and "Best Bets" sections of this book, we have used a system of dollar signs to show a range of costs for 1 night in a hotel (the price of a double-occupancy room) or the cost of an entree at a restaurant. Use the following table to decipher the dollar signs:

Cost	Hotels	Restaurants
$	under $100	under $10
$$	$100–$200	$10–$20
$$$	$200–$300	$20–$30
$$$$	$300–$400	$30–$40
$$$$$	over $400	over $40

An Invitation to the Reader

In researching this book, we discovered many wonderful places—hotels, restaurants, shops, and more. We're sure you'll find others. Please tell us about them, so we can share the information with your fellow travelers in upcoming editions. If you were disappointed with a recommendation, we'd love to know that, too. Please write to: Contact@FrommerMedia.com

16 Favorite
Moments

16 Favorite Moments

1 Flying fish at Pike Place Market
2 SkyCity restaurant
3 Fremont Troll
4 Underground Tour
5 Ferryboat
6 Climbing salmon
7 Bumbershoot
8 Tillicum Village
9 New Year's Eve at the Needle
10 Elliott Bay Book Company
11 Alki Beach
12 Lake Union kayak rental
13 Capitol Hill
14 Seafair at Alki Beach
15 Monorail
16 Original Starbucks

Previous page: The Seattle skyline, over Elliott Bay.

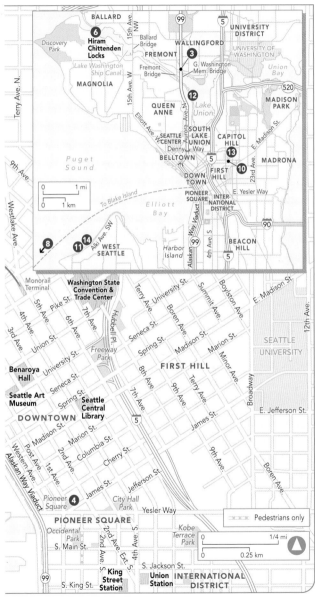

Perched near the edge of the continent, Seattle is a town that has always reached for the future. A land of extremes, the Emerald City is caffeine-driven yet laid-back, practical yet dreamy, soggy yet obsessive about the great outdoors. This pioneer-spirited town is a mix of the old and the new: from the former brothels of the Gold Rush era to the take-your-breath-away architecture of the Central Library. And where else will you find folks planted at a crosswalk in the pouring rain, nary a car in sight, clutching their lattes and waiting patiently for the crossing signal? Seattle is a quirky, endearing town, and here are a few things I like best about it.

1 Dodging the flying fish. Working the crowds just behind Rachel, the giant piggybank that guards Seattle's beloved Pike Place Market, fishmonger-entertainers noisily toss salmon back and forth across the counter. Watch out for the "snapping" monkfish—and the Pike Place Fish Market staffer hiding behind the counter, string in hand, waiting for the next unsuspecting tourist. *See p 54.*

2 Spinning at the Space Needle. On a clear day—or even a cloudy one—head to the Space Needle's SkyCity revolving restaurant for a uniquely Seattle dining experience. A trip to the observation deck is included in the price of your meal.

The Space Needle has become a Seattle icon.

Diners view the Emerald City from every angle as they rotate their way through lunch or dinner. Top off your meal with a fudgy Lunar Orbiter—complete with dry-ice Seattle "fog." *See p 48.*

3 Climbing on the troll. Hunkered under the Aurora Bridge in the funky Fremont neighborhood is a menacing, shaggy-haired troll, clutching a replica Volkswagen Beetle in his gnarly left hand. Ill-tempered he may be, but he's never harmed any of the tourists who scramble up for photo-ops. *See p 78.*

4 Going down under. Seattle wasn't always on the level—at least, not the one folks walk on today. Down below historic Pioneer Square, Underground tour guides will lead you through subterranean passages that were once Seattle streets and relate spicy tales of the city's quirky and occasionally naughty early history. *See p 14.*

5 Riding a ferryboat. Gliding across the Puget Sound is one of the best ways to enjoy this city, which is all about water. The passengers tapping away at their laptops are local commuters, taking advantage of the free Wi-Fi. Grab a scone and a latte on board, then head out on deck and enjoy the view. You can walk aboard or drive your car. *See p 18.*

6 Watching the fish climb. At the Hiram M. Chittenden Locks, see the

The Freemont Troll may look menacing, but he tolerates photo ops.

world's smartest salmon climb the ladders, determined to get from Puget Sound to the lakes and streams where the next generation will begin a journey of its own. Be sure to wave at the boats going up and down in the locks. It's a Seattle tradition. *See p 107.*

⑦ Partying at Bumbershoot. Seattle celebrates summer like nobody's business. The mother of all the non-stop festivals is Bumbershoot, held at Seattle Center on Labor Day weekend to "welcome" back the rainy season. Expect most anything at eclectic Bumbershoot, from stilt-walkers to impromptu parades to sculptures made of "junk." *See p 179.*

⑧ Savoring salmon at Tillicum Village. The local Native Americans greeted Seattle's pioneer families warmly, and you'll get a taste of that hospitality here. As your boat lands, you'll be handed a bowl of steaming clams, then set free to explore Blake Island while salmon roasts in the longhouse. During dinner, enjoy an entertaining show of tribal dances and legends. The high-tech special effects are not exactly traditional, but pretty cool. *See p 25.*

⑨ Ringing in the New Year at the Needle. You've never seen fireworks like these. Exuberant explosions of color "climb" their way up the Needle as festive music booms in the background. Get to Seattle Center around 10:30pm and stake out the highest spot you can find on the west side of the Center House, near the front. Then send someone inside to fetch hot cocoa and popcorn. *See p 179.*

⑩ Curling up with a book at Elliott Bay Book Company. Get lost in Seattle's favorite bookstore, which has packed up its tomes and moved from its longtime Pioneer Square location to great new digs on Capitol Hill. You'll find the same jaw-dropping collection, same knowledgeable staff, and you can still grab a bite at the Elliott Bay Café, which now has two locations. *See p 88.*

⑪ Soaking up the sun at Alki Beach. The Denny Party knew a good thing when they saw it, which is why they made Alki Beach the "Birthplace of Seattle" in 1851. Today, you can gaze across the Puget Sound at the Seattle skyline as you bike, skate or walk along a 2-mile path skirting the sandy beach. Bikes, blades and go-carts are available for rent. Word of warning: The water's chilly! *See p 17.*

Consider scheduling your visit to coincide with Bumbershoot, Seattle's world-famous citywide fest.

No lawn-mowing is necessary at Seattle's famed houseboats.

⓬ Visiting the "neighbors." Rent a kayak and explore the charming floating "neighborhoods" on Lake Union. About 500 Seattleites live on the water, in boats of every size and shape—including the one featured in the movie "Sleepless in Seattle." Just like any "city," there are some upscale areas and others populated by funky little vessels. *See p 103.*

⓭ People-watching on Capitol Hill. The grunge era lives on in this colorful neighborhood, where college students and hangers-on from the '90s still cling to the heyday of Seattle's music scene. Piercings and Mohawks abound, as do funky consignment shops, great little ethnic cafes with student-friendly prices, and some of the best lattes in town. *See p 66.*

⓮ Ogling the pirates. Seafair is a month of merriment and mischief,

kicked off in early July by the Landing of the Pirates at Alki Beach. That's right, pirates. . . as in Vikings, whose blood coursed through the veins of Seattle's largely Scandinavian settlers. Nearly every neighborhood has its own Seafair festival. The zany Torchlight Parade in downtown Seattle is my personal favorite. *See p 178.*

⓯ Riding the monorail. Built for the 1962 World Fair, it's only a mile-long ride, but gliding above downtown is truly a Seattle experience. The monorail starts at Seattle Center and ends on the upper floor of the upscale Westlake Center. In between, you zoom through the center of the bizarre but fascinating Experience Music Project, an innovative museum designed by Frank Gehry and inspired by Seattle native Jimi Hendrix. From the air, the EMP looks like a smashed guitar; from the ground, it's anyone's guess! *See p 63.*

⓰ Sipping lots of lattes. You can't get a better cuppa joe anywhere in the world than right here, where the nation's espresso craze began. Even if you don't know your double-tall-skinny-no-whip from your venti-soy-half-calf, it's fun to make a pilgrimage to the original Starbucks at Pike Place Market. It's standing-room-only, so carry your cup with you as you browse the market stalls. *See p 38.* ●

Glide through the futuristic Experience Music Project on the monorail.

The Best **Full-Day Tours**

The Best in One Day

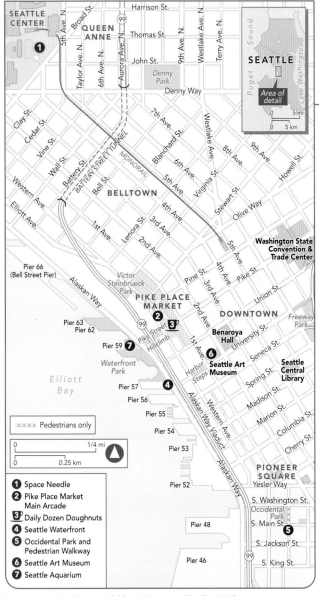

Pedestrians only

```
0                    1/4 mi
0        0.25 km
```

1 Space Needle
2 Pike Place Market Main Arcade
3 Daily Dozen Doughnuts
4 Seattle Waterfront
5 Occidental Park and Pedestrian Walkway
6 Seattle Art Museum
7 Seattle Aquarium

Previous page: Seattle's iconic Public Market sign at Pike Place Market.

One of the most compact big cities in the country, the Emerald City is easy—and just plain fun—to navigate on foot. (Sure you can drive, but parking spots are scarce—and pricey.) This sampler-platter tour roams from one end of town to the other. As you wander, always check out the incline. If it's steep ahead, walk a block further and you'll likely find flatter ground. But don't worry too much about tiring yourself out—there are plenty of places to rest your weary feet while enjoying the eclectic street scene. START: **Monorail or bus 3, 4, 8, 16 or 30 to Seattle Center.**

❶ ★★★ kids Space Needle.
Part retro, part futuristic, more than a touch eccentric, the Needle is the perfect symbol for Seattle. It was built for the World's Fair in 1962 after an artist sketched out a space-age focal point for the event on a place-mat at—where else?—a local coffee shop. Lines for the glass elevator ride up to the observation deck can be long in summertime, but it's worth the wait—just try to not get shoved to the back, or you'll miss the view on the way up. The typical Seattle mist only makes the view from the top that much dreamier. Your ticket to the top includes a free digital download from the Space Needle's photography department. You can also have lunch or dinner at the revolving SkyCity restaurant (reservations highly recommended) and rotate around the town while you dine. *Bonus:* Pick up a dining ticket

on the ground floor, and you won't have to pay to go to the top. ⏱ *1 hr. Summer weekends are busiest. 400 Broad St.* ☎ *206/905-2100. www.spaceneedle.com. Observation deck tickets: $26 adults, $24 seniors, $17 ages 4–13. Mon–Thurs. 10am–9pm; Fri–Sat 9:30am–10:30pm; Sun 9:30am–9:30pm.*

❷ ★★★ kids Pike Place Market Main Arcade. The heart and soul of Seattle, Pike Place is home to those famous flying fish, which you'll spot right behind Rachel the Pig. With just one day, you won't have time to go Down Under, but there's plenty to overwhelm the senses on the Market's top floor. Street musicians turn junk into instruments, farmers hawk a spectacular assortment of locally grown produce—which you can taste at many of Seattle's finest restaurants—and local artists display an

Travel Tip

Seattle's really is fun to walk—but sometimes your feet need a break! To get downtown from Seattle Center—home of the Space Needle (see bullet ❶ above)—hop on the monorail ($2.25 one-way for adults, $1 for seniors and ages 5–12) for the short ride to West-lake Center. From there, take a metro bus ($2.50 adult peak one-zone fare, 75¢ seniors, $1.25 ages 6–18,) anywhere in the downtown, Pioneer Square, Pike Place Market, and waterfront neighborhoods. You can catch a bus on the street, or in the bus tunnel, conveniently located underneath Westlake Center.

Pike Place Market is much more than a farmer's market and well worth exploring.

eclectic array of talents, from kazoo-making to wood-carving. The Market is a great place to sample some tasty wares and shop for high-quality souvenirs. My weakness is for the lavish bouquets of flowers, fresh from the fields in nearby lush valleys. They cost half what you'd pay at a grocery store for a much smaller spray. ⏱ *1 hr. Pike Place & Pike St.* ☎ *206/682-7453. www.pikeplacemarket.org. Mon–Sat 10am–6pm; Sun 11am–5pm.*

③ Daily Dozen Doughnuts. Around the corner from the Main Arcade, in the Economy Building, follow your nose to this heavenly kiosk. Don't let the line discourage you! These light confections, fresh from the fryer, are nothing like their heavier cousins you've encountered at some doughnut shops. Might as well buy two dozen while you're at it! *93 Pike St.* ☎ *206/467-7769.*

④ ★★ kids Seattle Waterfront. From Pike Place Market, take the elevator downhill and cross the street to Seattle's sparkling Elliott Bay, where you can amble from pier to pier. The waterfront is always lively, and the smell is a pleasant mix of saltwater and

fresh fish and chips, available at stands along the way. If you have little ones, a stop at Pier 57's Bay Pavilion with its antique carousel and game room offer a fun break. The waterfront's newest attraction, the **Seattle Great Wheel** (☎ 206/623-8607; www.seattlegreatwheel.com; $13 adults, $8.50 ages 4–11), is a 175-foot-tall observation wheel, with 42 fully enclosed "gondolas." But the harbor is not all about play; it's a real working waterfront, and one of the busiest in the nation. To get a good look at all the action, stop by Waterfront Park, which stretches between Piers 57 and 61, and peer through the free telescopes

The Lunar Orbiter dessert, complete with dry ice "steam," at SkyCity Restaurant.

out at the barges, tugboats, and ferryboats coming and going on the bay. ⓘ *1 hr.*

❺ **Occidental Park and Pedestrian Walkway.** From the waterfront, walk or take bus 99 to Jackson Street and Occidental Avenue. The bricked walkway occupies 1 block; the park claims the block to the north. In this area you'll find a sampling of Seattle's avant-garde art galleries, Victorian-Romanesque buildings constructed hurriedly during the Gold Rush, and **Glasshouse Studio,** 311 Occidental Ave. S. (☎ 206/682-9939), where you can watch skilled glassblowers at work. Several totem poles tower over visitors, and the Fallen Firefighter's Memorial pays tribute to those who have lost their lives battling Seattle's fires. ⓘ *1 hr. Occidental Ave. & Jackson St.*

❻ ★★★ **Seattle Art Museum.** SAM's eclectic global collections include Northwest Native American, Pan Asian, African, European, and American modern art. The museum also hosts first-rate traveling shows and special exhibits, and offers lots of activities for kids in conjunction with the displays. Despite its world-class reputation, SAM has a friendly feel, with a passionate staff that treats visitors as honored guests.

The Seattle Aquarium offers a view into life in Puget Sound.

SAM's permanent collections are on display at no charge the first Thursday of every month; free to seniors the first Friday. ⓘ *2 hr. 1300 1st Ave.* ☎ *206/654-3100. www.seattle artmuseum.org. Admission $20 adults, $18 seniors over 62, $13 students & kids 13–17, free for kids 12 & under. Wed & Fri–Sun 10am–5pm; Thurs 10am–9pm.*

❼ ★★ **kids** **Seattle Aquarium.** This is a sealife-lover's dream come true. The aquarium's pride and joy, a 40-foot-by-20-foot viewing window, gives visitors a glimpse of the intriguing creatures that swim in Puget Sound. Divers interact with fish in the tank several times a day, while volunteers explain what's going on. The aquarium is perched on a pier overhanging the sound, so many of these animals are also swimming under your feet. Don't miss the giant Pacific octopus—the largest in the world. ⓘ *2 hr. 1483 Alaskan Way on Pier 59.* ☎ *206/386-4300. www.seattle aquarium.org. Admission $22 adults, $20 seniors, $15 ages 4–13. Daily 9:30am–6pm (last entrance at 5pm).*

Good Deal

One of the best deals in town is CityPass (☎ 888/330-5008; www.citypass.com); with it, you can visit five popular Seattle destinations for half price. Better yet, you don't have to wait in line. The passes include the Space Needle, Seattle Aquarium, Pacific Science Center, Experience Music Project, a seat on an Argosy Cruises harbor tour of Elliott Bay, and the option of either the Museum of Flight or Woodland Park Zoo. A CityPass costs $64 for adults and $44 for kids ages 4–12. You can buy them at any of the included attractions, or order them ahead from the website.

The Best **in Two Days**

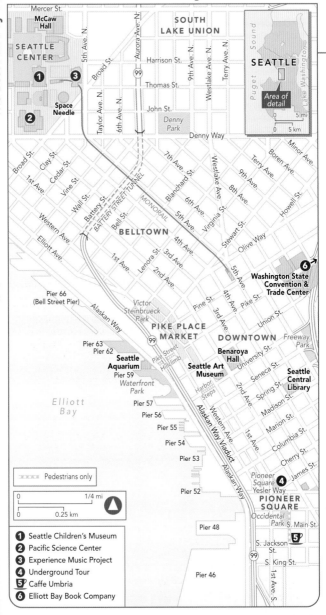

1 Seattle Children's Museum
2 Pacific Science Center
3 Experience Music Project
4 Underground Tour
5 Caffe Umbria
6 Elliott Bay Book Company

With just 1 day in Seattle you can visit only some of Seattle highlights; with a second day you can go back and spend some quality time at **Seattle Center,** the city's favorite hangout, and also visit two other stops that offer the quintessential Seattle experience. START: **Monorail or bus 3, 4, 8, 16 or 30 to Seattle Center.**

1 ★ kids Seattle Children's Museum. Inside the Center House, near the Space Needle at Seattle Center, you'll see the children's museum below, visible through a railed opening in the floor. The bright colors and enchanted forest are irresistible to kids, so hop on the glass elevator and ride down to the museum. On the fourth Wednesday of each month, the Family Fun Series offers an activity for the whole family, including a snack and a take-home project. *Note:* If you don't have kids in tow, give this museum a pass and start your day at the Pacific Science Museum (below). ⏱ *1 hr. 305 Harrison St.* ☎ *206/441-1768. www.thechildrensmuseum.org. $20 adults, $15 ages 2–17, free under age 1. Mon–Fri 10am–5pm (closed Tues Oct–Feb & major holidays).*

The dinosaurs that prowl the Pacific Science Center are fun for kids and adults alike.

2 ★★ kids Pacific Science Center. *Do touch!* is the rule at this museum at Seattle Center. There's plenty here to interest all ages, but this is mainly a youth-focused museum. Kids love the animatronic dinosaurs, the butterfly garden, and the Body Works area, where they can put their own physical abilities to the test. There are buttons to press, levers to pull, animals to touch, a playground for tiny tots, and special exhibits ranging from bubbles to snakes. You can gaze at the stars in the planetarium, and watch exciting laser shows (Thurs–Sun nights, plus Sat–Sun afternoons) set to music by the Beatles, Michael Jackson, Led Zeppelin, and more. The IMAX theaters show movies for varying ages. ⏱ *2 hr. 200 2nd Ave. N.* ☎ *206/443-2001. www.pacsci.org. Admission $18 adults, $16 seniors, $13 ages 6–15, $10 ages 3–5. IMAX: $9–$15 adults, $8–$14 seniors, $7–$12 ages 6–15, $6–$10 ages 3–5; discounts available for combination passes. Mon–Fri 10am–5pm (closed Tues Oct–Feb); Sat–Sun 10am–6pm.*

3 ★ Experience Music Project. Microsoft billionaire Paul Allen's monument to home-grown Seattle rock legend Jimi Hendrix features lots of interactive exhibits on music ranging from soul to rock to hip-hop. You can record your own CD in the Jam Studio, using guitars, drums, keyboard, and voice. With this technology, you don't need an instrument—or even talent. The two main exhibits, devoted to Jimi Hendrix and Nirvana, contain personal artifacts,

Be sure to explore the remains of old Seattle, which lie a full story beneath the modern city, on the Underground Tour.

pioneer town, a full story lower than the rebuilt city. (It seems there was a little problem with sewage coming back in with the tides.) You'll get the fascinating lowdown (literally) on the era's get-rich-quick schemers, gold-crazy prospectors, and colorful women who listed their occupation as "seamstress," though they seldom produced a stitch. Some of the content is mature, but it should go right over the heads of the little ones. In any case, they'll be more fascinated by the stories of the rats that once roamed the streets. The guides are witty, and they know their stuff. ⏱ *90 min. 608 1st Ave.* ☎ *206/682-4646. www.undergroundtour.com. $17 adults, $14 seniors & ages 13–17, $9 ages 7–12. Tours offer daily, on the hour (Apr–Sept 10am–7pm, Oct–Mar 10am–6pm; check the website for Christmas holiday hrs; no tours Thanksgiving & Christmas day).*

Music lovers and fans of modern architecture will both find something to love at the Experience Music Project.

memorabilia, and documentary footage. Within EMP, the Science Fiction and Horror Museum is worth a look, too. The museum is housed in a Frank Gehry–designed building meant to look, from above, like one of Hendrix's guitars. From the street, it looks more like an undulating blob of metal. ⏱ *90 min. 325 5th Ave. N. (at Seattle Center).* ☎ *206/770-2700. www. empsfm.org. Admission $20 adults, $17 seniors, $14 ages 5–17 (discount if purchased online). Late May–early Sept daily 10am–6pm; early Sept–late May 10am–5pm.*

④ ★★★ **Underground Tour.** The historic Pioneer Building at 1st and Yesler now houses the popular Underground Tour, which takes you beneath sidewalks of Seattle to view the remnants of the original

Whether you indulge in gelato or a latte, Caffè Umbria is a haven for weary walkers.

5 ★ The Emerald City is not exactly known for balmy weather, but that's never kept a Seattleite from indulging in a frozen treat— like the sinfully creamy gelato at **Caffè Umbria.** My favorites are cappuccino and pistachio. Sit at the window bar and gaze out at the passersby, or grab an outside table on a sunny day. The panini sandwiches and croissants are fresh and delicious. *320 Occidental Ave. S. 206/624-5847. www.caffeumbria. com. Mon–Fri 6am–6pm; Sat 7am–6pm; Sun 8am–5pm.*

6 ★★★ **Elliott Bay Book Company.** In its "new" location— a 20,000-square-foot historic 1917 building on quirky Capitol Hill— Elliott Bay still feels like Seattle's comfy living room. An old Ford truck service center, the space has fir floors and massive ceiling beams. Seattleites love to while away the hours here, perusing more than 150,000 books. Your challenge: not to bring home more than you can fit in your carry-on! ⏱ *1 hr. 1521 10th Ave. 206/624-6600. www.elliottbaybook.com. Mon–Thurs 10am–1pm; Fri–Sat 10am–11pm; Sun 11am–9pm.*

Get in from the rain at the Elliott Bay Book Company, housed in an historic 1917 building on Capitol Hill.

Seattle Makes Music

The Kingsmen, Jimi Hendrix, Heart, Queensrÿche, Pearl Jam, Nirvana, Alice in Chains, Death Cab for Cutie, Modest Mouse—Seattle seems to spawn great music. Since the 1950s, the Emerald City has been famous for its garage bands that end up going big-time. The "Louis Louis" phenomenon began when the Wailers from Tacoma (just south of Seattle) recorded the song in 1960 and it became a radio hit. (A couple of years later, two Northwest bands from a bit further south—Portland, Oregon—recorded the same song: The Kingsmen and Paul Revere and the Raiders.) In the 1990s, Seattle's Kurt Cobain and his band Nirvana kicked off the grunge era that made Seattle arguably the hippest place on the planet. The tradition lives on in Seattle's contemporary rockers, like Modest Mouse.

The Best in Three Days

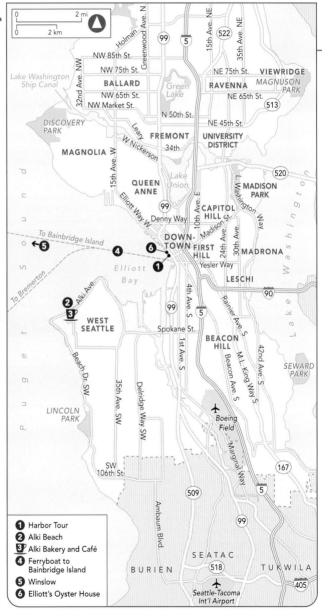

0 2 mi
0 2 km

Holman

Greenwood Ave. N

15th Ave. NE

522

35th Ave. NE

99

5

NW 85th St.

NW 75th St.

NE 75th St.

VIEWRIDGE

BALLARD

Green Lake

RAVENNA

MAGNUSON PARK

Lake Washington Ship Canal

NW 65th St.

NW Market St.

NE 65th St.

513

32nd Ave. NW

N 50th St.

NE 45th St.

DISCOVERY PARK

Leary

W. Nickerson

FREMONT

34th

UNIVERSITY DISTRICT

MAGNOLIA

15th Ave. W

QUEEN ANNE

Lake Union

520

MADISON PARK

L. Washington Way

Elliott Way W

99

Denny Way

10th Ave. E

CAPITOL HILL

Madison St.

24th Ave. E

30th Ave. E

MADRONA

To Bainbridge Island

⑤

④

⑥

DOWN-TOWN

FIRST HILL

Yesler Way

Elliott Bay

①

LESCHI

To Bremerton

Alki Ave.

4th Ave. S

Rainier Ave. S

90

②

③

99

1st Ave. S

Spokane St.

5

M.L. King Way S

42nd Ave. S

SEWARD PARK

Beach Dr. SW

WEST SEATTLE

BEACON HILL

Beacon Ave. S

35th Ave. SW

Delridge Way SW

Boeing Field

LINCOLN PARK

SW 106th St.

509

Marginal Way

167

5

Ambaum Blvd.

99

405

SEATAC

518

TUKWILA

BURIEN

Seattle-Tacoma Int'l Airport

① Harbor Tour
② Alki Beach
③ Alki Bakery and Café
④ Ferryboat to Bainbridge Island
⑤ Winslow
⑥ Elliott's Oyster House

To fully appreciate Seattle, you need to get out on the water. After all, nearly half the city is surrounded by the stuff! Plenty of fun awaits, whether you want to row, paddle, or sit back and relax while someone else navigates the lakes, canals and bays. START: **Bus 99, 16, 66 to Seattle Waterfront, Pier 55.**

❶ ★★ Harbor Tour. This lively, informative tour of Seattle's working harbor, offered by Argosy Cruises, lasts just an hour—perfect to keep the kids enthralled as the boat cruises past dry docks, tugboats, and one of the world's largest shipping terminal—offering great views of Seattle's distinctive downtown skyline. The popular tour has been drawing crowds since 1949 and leaves at 1:30pm every day (with additional tours depending on the day and season; check the website). If an hour isn't long enough, choose from a variety of dinner and pleasure cruises. ⏱ *1 hr.* ☎ *888/623-1445. www.argosy cruises.com. Cruises depart from Pier 55, Seattle Waterfront. Prices $24 adults, $21 seniors, $12 ages 5–12.*

❷ ★★★ Alki Beach. This is the best beach in Seattle—though technically, it's in West Seattle, where the settlers first arrived. The mood is festive, the view of Elliott Bay and the Seattle skyline breathtaking, and the water is always—even in the summertime—very chilly. That doesn't keep the locals from taking a dip, even in the cooler months when a wetsuit is needed. From spring through fall, you can zip across Elliott Bay from the Seattle Waterfront on the water taxi. In the wintertime, you'll need to drive over the West Seattle Bridge and take the Harbor Avenue/Avalon Way exit, then turn right onto Harbor Avenue and bear left at Alki Avenue. This wide, sandy beach has a great promenade for

The Alki Beach Promenade gives walkers and bikers a gorgeous view of the Seattle skyline.

walkers, joggers, and roller-bladers, and you can rent bikes or go-carts at shops across from the beach. Cafes and shops line the street across from the water. ⏲ 2½ hr.

3 Alki Bakery and Cafe. If all that salt air makes you hungry, head across the street to Alki for pastries and coffee or something more substantial—sandwiches, pastas, or seafood. Enjoy your snack outside, with the panoramic ocean and mountain view thrown in for free! *2738 Alki Ave. SW.* ☎ *206/935-1352. www.alkibakery.com. $*

4 ★★ Ferryboat to Bainbridge Island. Washington State runs the largest ferry system in the country, and this line is very popular with commuters. You could plug in your laptop and check e-mail for free, but don't. Instead, grab a cup of coffee and a raspberry scone at the onboard cafe, and go out on deck and enjoy the 35-minute ride. If you walk onto the ferry, arrive 15 minutes early; if you drive your car on (not recommended), arrive at least 20 to 30 minutes ahead of time. Drive-on wait times can be much longer during rush hours. *Catch the ferryboat at the Seattle Ferry Terminal at Pier 52.* ☎ *206/464-6400. www.wsdot.wa.gov/ferries.*

Fares $7.85 for adults, $3.90 for seniors & children 6–18, $11 for car & driver; check schedules for departure times).

5 ★★ Walk through Winslow. Once you're on the island, follow the crowds walking into the charming town of Winslow, where you can roam the art galleries, taste some wine, and do some shopping on Winslow Way. A great place to see the work of hundreds of area artists—both new and seasoned—is the non-profit Bainbridge Arts and Crafts gallery at 151 Winslow Way E. (☎ 206/842-3132; Mon–Sat 10am–6pm, Sun 11am–5pm). For a good cup of java, turn left (toward the water) at Madison Avenue South, then right onto Parfitt Way Southeast, and stroll over to Pegasus Coffee House and Gallery (131 Parfitt Way SW; ☎ 206/842-6725), a picturesque, ivy-covered brick shop on the waterfront that roasts its own tasty beans. ⏲ *3 hr.*

6 ★★ kids Elliott's Oyster House. Back in Seattle, this is a great place to stop for fresh local seafood. Or head for the raw bar if you just need an oyster fix. It's the perfect place to wrap up a day on the water. *1201 Alaskan Way, Pier 56.* ☎ *206/623-4340. www.elliotts oysterhouse.com. $$. See p 125.* ●

Riding the ferry is half the fun of a trip to Bainbridge Island.

Seattle Heritage

1 Museum of Flight

2 Klondike Gold Rush
National Historical
Park

3 Wing Luke
Asian Museum

4 Museum of History
& Industry (MOHAI)

5 Burke Museum of
History and Culture

6 Nordic Heritage
Museum

7 Larsen's Danish Bakery

8 Tillicum Village

Previous page: A detail from Pioneer Square's giant totem pole.

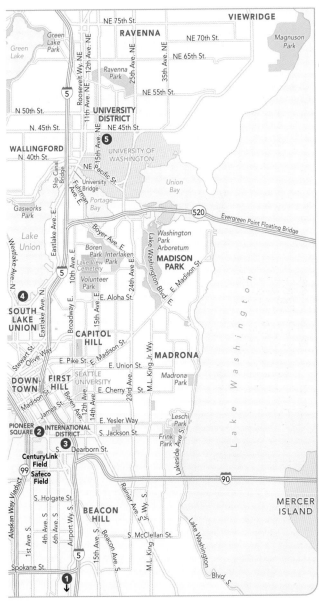

NE 75th St.

VIEWRIDGE

RAVENNA

NE 70th St.

Green Lake Park

Green Lake

NE 65th St.

Ravenna Park

Magnuson Park

25th Ave. NE

35th Ave. NE

NE 55th St.

N 50th St.

UNIVERSITY DISTRICT

Roosevelt Wy. NE

11th Ave. NE

12th Ave. NE

N. 45th St.

NE 45th St.

5

WALLINGFORD

15th Ave. NE

N. 40th St.

UNIVERSITY OF WASHINGTON

Ship Canal Bridge

NE Pacific St.

University Bridge

Furhmann Ave. E.

Union Bay

Gasworks Park

Portage Bay

520

Evergreen Point Floating Bridge

Lake Union

Eastlake Ave. E.

Boyer Ave. E.

Boren Park

Washington Park Arboretum

MADISON PARK

Westlake Ave. N.

5

10th Ave. E.

Interlaken Park

Lake View Cemetery

Lake Washington Blvd. E.

E. Madison St.

4

SOUTH LAKE UNION

Eastlake Ave. N.

Broadway E.

Volunteer Park

15th Ave. E.

24th Ave E.

E. Aloha St.

L a k e   W a s h i n g t o n

CAPITOL HILL

E. Madison St.

MADRONA

Stewart St.

Olive Way

E. Pike St.

E. Union St.

DOWN-TOWN

FIRST HILL

SEATTLE UNIVERSITY

Madrona Park

Madison St.

Boren Ave.

E. Cherry St.

23rd Ave.

M.L. King Jr. Wy.

James St.

12th Ave.

14th Ave.

E. Yesler Way

Leschi Park

PIONEER SQUARE

2

INTERNATIONAL DISTRICT

S. Jackson St.

Frink Park

3

S. Dearborn St.

Lakeside Ave. S.

CenturyLink Field

99

Safeco Field

S. Holgate St.

Rainier Ave. S.

90

MERCER ISLAND

Alaskan Way Viaduct

1st Ave. S.

4th Ave. S.

6th Ave. S.

Airport Wy. S.

15th Ave. S.

Beacon Ave. S.

BEACON HILL

S. McClellan St.

M.L. King

Lake Washington

5

Spokane St.

Blvd. S.

1
↓

When it comes to historic roots, Seattle may not compare to a city like Boston, but the Emerald City has such a colorful past, kids and adults alike get caught up in the fun. This tour will take you on an exploration from the days before the arrival of Europeans to the birth of the aerospace industry that helped modern Seattle take flight. START: **Bus 124, 154, 173 to the Museum of Flight.**

❶ ★★★ kids Museum of Flight. The focus here is the contemporary era—relatively speaking, that is, since the history of aviation goes back pretty far in Seattle. This top-flight museum will amaze anyone intrigued by the human species' dream of escaping the bonds of earth. The historic Red Barn (Boeing's first manufacturing building), houses exhibits on early aviation, including the mail bag carried by William E. Boeing and Eddie Hubbard on the first international U.S. Air Mail flight from Vancouver, B.C., to Seattle in 1919. The exhibit ends with the Boeing 707, which ushered in the jet age. The cavernous Great Gallery features dozens of historic aircraft, many of them suspended from the ceiling as though in flight. Visitors can climb into the cockpit of a real Blackbird, the fastest jet ever made. The Personal Courage Wing tells the

stories of fighter aviators in World Wars I and II. And at the Airpark, you can view legendary aircraft including the Concorde and the first jet Air Force One. The simulator exhibit lets you try virtual flight and hang-gliding. The museum's Space Gallery displays NASA and Russian spacecraft (and mock-ups). ⏱ *90 min. 9404 E. Marginal Way S.* ☎ *206/764-5720. www.museumof flight.org. $19 adults, $16 seniors, $11 ages 5–17, free 4 & under. Free 5–9pm 1st Thurs of every month. Daily 10am–5pm.*

❷ ★ kids Klondike Gold Rush National Historical Park. You're bound to catch Gold Fever as you listen to the tales of Yukon-bound prospectors and their families who passed through Seattle, and view personal items they left along the way. This is not only a museum but a national park. Kids can earn honest-to-gosh Junior Ranger

The aviation industry played a major role in Seattle's social and economic development.

At the interactive Klondike Gold Rush International Historical Park, you'll learn everything you ever wanted to know about the Gold Rush.

badges by filling in an activity book based on information gleaned from the two floors of exhibits. This keeps them conveniently busy while the grown-ups enjoy the displays. Films on the Gold Rush and Seattle's role in the mania are shown frequently. In the summer, you can watch gold-panning demonstrations twice a day or take a walking tour of Pioneer Square, led by a park ranger. 🕐 *1 hr. 319 2nd Avenue S.* ☎ *206/220-4240. www.nps. gov/klse. Free admission. Daily 9am–5pm (Oct–May from 10am).*

❸ ★★ Wing Luke Asian Museum. The Wing Luke celebrates the many Asian cultures that have emigrated to the Pacific Northwest. Its main exhibit, "Honoring Our Journey," tells the 150-year-old story of Asians and Pacific Islanders settling in Washington. Temporary exhibits have included refugees' personal stories and one called "Camp Harmony D-4-44," which re-created a livestock stall converted into a family holding cell, barbed wire and all, for Japanese Americans being sent to internment camps in 1942. The museum is housed in the former home of the historic Freeman Hotel, where many early Asian immigrants lived while working in the canneries and lumber mills. 🕐 *1 hr. 719 S. King St. (South King*

Explore the influence of Asian immigrants to Seattle at the Wing Luke Asian Museum.

St. & 8th Ave. South). ☎ *206/623-5124. www.wingluke.org. $13 adults, $9.95 seniors & students, $8.95 ages 5–12. Price includes tour of historic building/former hotel. Tues–Sun 10am–5pm, 1st Thurs of month & 3rd Sat of month 10am–8pm.*

❹ ★★ **Museum of History & Industry (MOHAI).** It may not have the most exciting name, but there is nothing dull about this museum. It's a great way to learn about Northwest history through riveting, often hands-on exhibits and historic photos. You can amble along the "sidewalks" of pre-fire Seattle, which would soon be reduced to ashes by the Great Fire of 1889. Every aspect of Seattle's scientific and industrial history is covered, right up to the arrival of Microsoft. In 2013, MOHAI moved to the historic Naval Reserve Building on the shores of Lake Union. 🕓 *1 hr. 820 Terry Ave. N.* ☎ *206/324-1126. www.mohai.org. $14 adults, $12 seniors, free ages 14 & under. Also, free first Thurs of the month. Daily 10am–5pm, Thurs until 8pm.*

Learn about Seattle's past, including the Great Fire that destroyed much of the city, at the Museum of History & Industry (MOHAI).

❺ ★★ kids **Burke Museum of Natural History and Culture.** I love this museum on the tree-lined campus of the University of Washington because it's doable in a couple of hours, and it's all about Washington State: from 40 million-year-old fossils to an extensive Native American arts collection. Dino Times, with its dinosaur skeletons and walk-through volcano, is enormously fun, and the cultural showcases are engaging and unique. 🕓 *1 hr. 17th Ave. NE & NE 45th St.* ☎ *206/543-5590. www.burkemuseum.org. $9.50 adults, $7.50 seniors, $6 students & youth, free under 5. Daily 10am–5pm. Free & open until 8pm 1st Thurs of month.*

❻ ★ **Nordic Heritage Museum.** This unassuming two-story museum is the only one in the country that celebrates the history of the five Nordic countries, many of whose descendants call the Pacific Northwest home. My favorite exhibit brings to life the arrival of early Scandinavian immigrants, via Ellis Island, to the land of their dreams. You can feel the excitement, and then the chaos of their new adventure. Each country—Denmark, Finland, Iceland, Norway, and Sweden—has a room at the museum to tell its story and show off its art and culture. Lots of kids' programs are offered, as well as classes in Nordic folk arts. 🕓 *1 hr. 3014 NW 67th St.* ☎ *206/789-5707. www.nordicmuseum.org. $8 adults,*

Seattle Takes Shape

In 1852, a windy, rain-drenched winter prompted Seattle's founders to move from Alki Point (now in West Seattle), where they had landed the previous year, to the more sheltered eastern shore of Elliott Bay. The reason for the zany layout of the town they created—now the Pioneer Square neighborhood—was the lack of agreement among the city fathers (and possibly the chronic drunkenness of at least one) about which direction the roads should go. Perhaps not surprisingly, squabbling over roads became a Seattle tradition. Thirty-five years later, Seattle struck it rich when gold was discovered in the Yukon. Would-be prospectors stocked up on supplies before they headed out to the gold fields; on the way back, those who had struck it rich dropped a large percentage of their profits here. After the fire in 1889, Seattle's businessmen, frantic at missing out on profits, scrambled to rebuild their city. They built fast, but they built to last.

$7 seniors & students, $6 children over 5. Tues–Sat 10am–4pm, Sun noon–4pm.

7 ★ Larsen's Danish Bakery. After your visit to the Nordic Heritage Museum enjoy some homemade Danish pastries with a cup of coffee at this long-established bakery. Here's your chance to sample a real Danish kringle or smorkaka. *8000 24th Ave NW. www.larsens bakery.com. $*

8 ★★★ kids Tillicum Village. Rewind to pre-European times in the Northwest. The local Indian tribes may have lived to regret their initial hospitality to the white settlers who landed at Alki Point and who, many years later, drove the Native Americans onto second-rate reservation land. But at Tillicum Village, the hospitality is in full force as a number of local tribes cooperatively present a salmon bake in the longhouse, then perform traditional dances illustrating creation stories. Skilled tribal artists carve masks and other items, many of which can be purchased. The setting is deeply forested Blake Island, believed to be an ancient campground of the Duwamish and Suquamish tribes, and the likely birthplace of Chief Seattle. There's a playground for children, and you'll likely spot a few deer. Now a state park, it can be reached only by boat. ⏱ *4 hr.* ☎ *206/933-8600. www.tillicum village.com. Argosy Cruises offers rides to & from Tillicum Village, leaving from Pier 55 on the Seattle waterfront. Price with the cruise: $79 adults, $72 seniors, $30 ages 5–12; free age 4 & under; dates & times vary by month.*

Seattle for Art Lovers

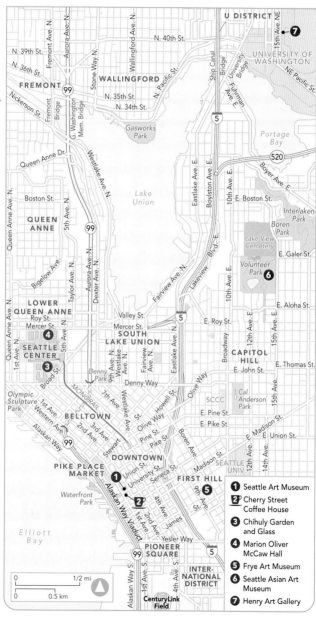

U DISTRICT NE
UNIVERSITY OF WASHINGTON
N. 40th St.
N. 39th St.
N. 36th St.
FREMONT
WALLINGFORD
N. 35th St.
N. 34th St.
Gasworks Park
Portage Bay
QUEEN ANNE
Lake Union
Boston St.
Interlaken Park
Boren Park
Lake View Cemetery
E. Galer St.
Volunteer Park
LOWER QUEEN ANNE
Roy St.
Mercer St.
E. Aloha St.
SEATTLE CENTER
SOUTH LAKE UNION
E. Roy St.
Mercer St.
CAPITOL HILL
E. Thomas St.
E. John St.
Denny Park
Denny Way
Olympic Sculpture Park
BELLTOWN
SCCC
Cal Anderson Park
E. Pine St.
E. Pike St.
SEATTLE UNIV.
DOWNTOWN
PIKE PLACE MARKET
Union St.
FIRST HILL
Waterfront Park
Elliott Bay
PIONEER SQUARE
Yesler Way
INTERNATIONAL DISTRICT
CenturyLink Field

0 — 1/2 mi
0 — 0.5 km

1. Seattle Art Museum
2. Cherry Street Coffee House
3. Chihuly Garden and Glass
4. Marion Oliver McCaw Hall
5. Frye Art Museum
6. Seattle Asian Art Museum
7. Henry Art Gallery

The Emerald City has always supported the arts with its extra cash, whether from gold, aerospace, or dotcom mania. The Pacific Northwest is known for its public art, particularly sculptures, and for its Venetian-influenced glass. Renowned home-grown glass artist Dale Chihuly launched an American glass-art movement in the late 1960s that is still going strong in Seattle.

START: **Bus 212, 216, 217, 255, 256 to Seattle Art Museum.**

The "Hammering Man" looms over the Seattle Art Museum.

❶ ★★★ Seattle Art Museum.

You'll know you're there when you see the hardworking "Hammering Man," a 48-foot tribute to the working classes that shaped Seattle's character. Appropriately, the arm of the animated outdoor sculpture, designed by Jonathan Borofsky, gets a rest every year on Labor Day. Entrance to the first two floors of this beautiful museum, expanded in 2007, is free of charge, and includes the Brotman Forum, which features changing exhibits and Cai Guo-Qiang's fanciful sculpture of nine cars falling across the space. Traveling exhibits and art from around the world fill the rest of the museum. ⏱ *2 hr. 1300 1st Ave.* ☎ *206/654-3100. www.seattleartmuseum.org.*

Admission $20 adults, $18 seniors 62 & over, $13 students & children 13–17, free children 12 & under. Wed–Sun 10am–5pm; Thurs 10am–9pm. See p 11.

❷ ★ Cherry Street Coffee House.

While you're in an arty mood, stop for a snack at this chic cafe, which showcases the works of local artists. The coffee is great, and so are the soups and sandwiches. If you're a carnivore, try their famous BLT; if not, you'll love the homemade veggie burgers. *1212 1st Ave.* ☎ *206/264-9372. $*

❸ ★★★ Chihuly Garden and Glass.

Not many artists are given a museum in their lifetime, but world-famous Seattle glass artist Dale Chihuly has one devoted entirely to his work right next to the Space Needle. Chihuly's work is so intensely colorful and inventive it

The magnificent Chihuly Garden and Glass includes galleries, a 100-ft-long sculpture in a light-filled glass house, and a magical glass garden.

Olympic Sculpture Park

You won't have to be cooped up indoors to enjoy this relative newcomer to Seattle's art scene. Run by the Seattle Art Museum, the **Olympic Sculpture Park** (2901 Western Ave.; www.seattleart museum.org) is a unique outdoor sculpture park that features very large permanent and traveling exhibits over 9 acres. Added bonus: It's all right on the waterfront and has a great on-site cafe. From "Father and Son," a double fountain by Louise Bourgeois that captures a sometimes problematic relationship, to "Eagle" by Alexander Calder, an abstract work on wings of fancy, the creations are both fun and thought-provoking. Admission is free, and the park is open daily from 30 minutes before sunrise to 30 minutes after sunset. Free hour-long tours are available through the **Seattle Art Museum** (☎ 206/654-3100) at varying times throughout the year.

seems to transcend the limits of glass. The museum presents a chronological portrait of his life and work, and ends in a garden with fabulous glass plants. ⏱ *45 min. 305 Harrison St.* ☎ *206/743-4940. www.chihulygardenandglass.com. $19 adults, $17 seniors, $12 ages 4–12. Sun–Thurs 11am–7pm, Fri–Sat 11am–8pm.*

④ ★ Marion Oliver McCaw Hall. Seattle has seen a burgeoning

Kids are welcome to climb on the stone camels outside the Seattle Asian Art Museum.

of art houses and expansions since the '90s, and this was one of the most notable. Home to the Seattle Opera and the Pacific Northwest Ballet, this remodeled performance hall—resplendent with color and drama—has drawn rave reviews for its acoustic excellence and stunning art exhibits. Outside, a contemporary fountain blends in seamlessly with the walkway; at night, colored lights create swirls of color. If you're in town over the holidays, the PNB's "Nutcracker"—complete with Maurice Sendak costumes and sets—is not to be missed. ⏱ *15 min. 321 Mercer St.* ☎ *206/ 389-7676. www. seattleopera.org. Ticket prices for performances vary.*

⑤ ★★ Frye Art Museum. Charles and Emma Frye, German immigrants who made their fortune in gold-mad Seattle, left their immense collection of then-contemporary art to the city to be displayed in one location. Thus was born the Frye. Its collected representational works—portraits, still lifes, landscapes—are by 19th- and 20th-century French, German, and American painters. But in recent

years, the museum has re-invented itself, adding modern and abstract art to the collection. These new works are often intriguingly juxtaposed with paintings that once hung in the Fryes' living room or meat house. ⏱ *1 hr. 704 Terry Ave.* ☎ *206/622-9250. www.fryemuseum. org. As mandated by Charles Frye, admission is free. Tues–Sun 11am–5pm; Thurs until 7pm.*

⑥ ★ kids Seattle Asian Art Museum. Set in the middle of lovely **Volunteer Park** (p 67) and operated by the Seattle Art Museum, SAAM features a noteworthy collection of historic and contemporary art from a variety of Asian cultures. If you love Eastern art—or want to learn more about it—this is the perfect venue. Most of the exhibits won't appeal greatly to younger kids, but they love playing in the child-size Japanese house. Shoes off first, of course! Kids also love climbing on the life-size camel statues that kneel on either side of the outside entrance. Don't miss (it would be hard to) Isamu Noguchi's captivating "Black Sun" outside the museum. A photo of the Space Needle taken through the sculpture's open center makes a great souvenir. ⏱ *1 hr. 1400 E. Prospect St.* ☎ *206/654-3100. www. seattleartmuseum.org. $7 adults, $5*

Statues of dancers adorn the lobby of Marion Oliver McCaw Hall.

seniors, students & ages 13–17, free 12 & under, Wed–Sun 10am–5pm; Thurs until 9pm, free first Thurs (& first Sat to families) of each month.

⑦ ★★ Henry Art Gallery. Old world meets new at the Henry, where you can find works by masters such as Rembrandt, but also avant-garde photography and sculpture. The Henry's solid reputation has soared since its mega-expansion in 1997. One of its most popular permanent exhibits is James Turrell's riveting "Skyspace," which turns light—both natural and artificial—into ever-changing art. ⏱ *1 hr. University of Washington campus, 15th Ave. NE & NE 41st St.* ☎ *206/543-2280. www.henryart.org. Wed–Sun 11am–4pm; Thurs–Fri until 9pm. $10 adults, $6 seniors, free for students & ages 13 & under.*

The Olympic Sculpture Park is operated by the Seattle Art Museum.

Seattle Film & Theater

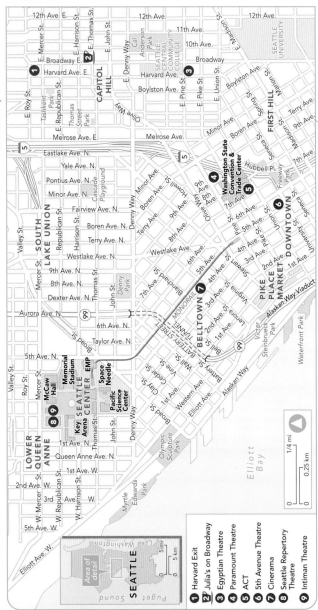

1 Harvard Exit
2 Julia's on Broadway
3 Egyptian Theatre
4 Paramount Theatre
5 ACT
6 5th Avenue Theatre
7 Cinerama
8 Seattle Repertory Theatre
9 Intiman Theatre

Seattleites spend those long-awaited summer days out-doors, but come fall, it's time to head for the theater. So perhaps the gray winters have played a role in making this an important film and theater town. The month-long Seattle International Film Festival (☎ 206/324-9996; www.seattlefilm.org), held in May at several venues throughout the city, is the largest film festival in the country and has launched a number of world premieres. The city also boasts several magnificent theaters built in the Roaring Twenties or earlier, as vaudeville houses, playhouses, movie palaces, or clubs. START: **Bus 9 or 49 to E. Roy St. & Harvard Ave.**

❶ ★ **Harvard Exit.** Tucked away in an unassuming brick building on a side street in the artsy Capitol Hill neighborhood, this art theater specializes in independent and foreign-language films. Built in 1925 as a club-house for The Woman's Century Club, it was converted in the '60s to a movie theater. In addition to the cozy fireplace, grand piano, and comfy chairs, its huge lobby houses a 1919 movie projector used for silent films. Parking can be tricky, so leave yourself plenty of time if you come for a show. ⏱ 15 min. 807 E. Roy at Harvard. ☎ 206/781-5755. www.landmark theatres.com/Market/Seattle/HarvardExitTheatre.htm. Free admission to see the lobby.

A detail from the Egyptian Theatre's elaborate lobby art.

❷ **Julia's on Broadway.** The spotlight is on Broadway at this light-hearted themed restaurant, complete with show-monikered cocktails. It's the perfect spot to grab a bite during a theater tour. I love their "afternoon breakfast"—try the Huevos Rancheros. The emphasis is on fun—and fresh, healthy ingredients. 300 Broadway E. ☎ 206/860-1818. $

❸ **Egyptian Theatre.** Though built in 1915, this former Masonic Temple didn't adopt its Egyptian theme until the '80s, when it became home to the Seattle International Film Festival. As of press time, this wonderful old theater was in the process of being sold, much to the chagrin of film- and theater-lovers, and there was no word on its eventual fate. You can still stop or drive by to have a look at its facade. Hopefully it won't be refitted as a store. ⏱ 15 min. 805 E Pine St. ☎ 206/781-5755.

❹ ★★★ **Paramount Theatre.** My one complaint about this opulent theater: I often find myself transfixed by the ceiling instead of the stage. Not that the shows aren't compelling. The Broadway series, silent movies, comedy shows, and diverse range of concerts are first-rate. It's just that the French Renaissance architecture is so lavish, and the intricate ceiling so intriguing, that the architecture *almost* steals the show. Built in 1928 as Seattle's most spectacular theater, the Paramount treated

A detail from the 5th Avenue Theatre's elaborate ceiling.

guests to stage shows and silent films, shown to the accompaniment of a custom-made Wurlitzer organ. Not a bit of its former splendor has been lost, a fact often noted by affluent Seattle brides, who make their entrances down the grand staircase in the lobby. At wedding receptions, the theater's sloped seating area converts to a flat hardwood floor for tables and dancing. 🕐 *15 min. 911 Pine St.* ☎ *206/467-5510. www.stgpresents.org. Free admission to the lobby.*

⑤ ★ ACT (A Contemporary Theatre). The focus at this nationally recognized theater is on presenting contemporary and new plays, a number of which have gone on to New York. However, one of its most popular performances is the classic "Christmas Carol." The audience sits in a semicircle around the central stage. The beautiful 1924 terra-cotta building became home to the ACT in 1973. The theater doesn't have a parking lot, but ample parking is available across the street, in the Convention Center Garage. 🕐 *15 min. 700 Union St.* ☎ *206/292-7676. www.acttheatre.org.*

⑥ ★★★ 5th Avenue Theatre. The 5th was one of the first vaudeville houses built with an Asian design in the 1920s, when all things Eastern were in vogue. Architect Robert Reamer intended the magnificent interior to look like three Imperial Chinese masterpieces: the Forbidden City, the Temple of Heaven, and the Summer Palace. The theater has undergone two transformations since its vaudeville days: first, to a movie palace; then, after a major renovation in the '80s, to a playhouse. Its stage has been graced by an array of personalities including Katharine Hepburn, Robert Goulet, and Carol Channing. The 5th hosts more than 100 live performances each year, including touring Broadway musicals and Broadway-bound shows. Nearby parking garages offer evening discounts. 🕐 *15 min. 1308 5th Ave.* ☎ *206/625-1900. www.5thavenue.org.*

7 ★ Cinerama. If you recall the old wraparound cineramic films, you're in for a treat at the historic Seattle Cinerama Theatre, one of only three venues in the world that can show the classic three-panel Cinerama films. Once sentenced to demolition, Cinerama was saved in 1999 by former Microsoft co-founder Paul Allen. And, as you might expect, the renovation was done in high-tech fashion, with a 90-foot-long louvered screen and cutting-edge acoustics. There's also a smaller screen for contemporary films. The theater also underwent a major renovation that brought better digital sound and a 3-D experience. ⏲ *15 min. 2100 4th Ave. ☎ 206/441-3080. www.cinerama. com.*

ACT features mostly modern works.

8 Seattle Repertory Theatre. This Tony Award–winning regional venue has two stages, both housed in a graceful curved building in the northwest corner of Seattle Center. The focus here is on serious art theater. ⏲ *15 min. 155 Mercer St. ☎ 206/443-2222. www.seattlerep. org.*

9 Intiman Theatre. Specializing in international drama—both classics and contemporary plays—this intimate Tony-winning regional theater, sandwiched between the Seattle Repertory Theatre and the Seattle opera's McCaw Hall, has launched world premieres. ⏲ *15 min. 201 Mercer St. ☎ 206/269-1900. www.intiman.org.*

The Paramount Theatre is not to be missed.

Seattle for Kids

1 Seattle Aquarium
2 Seattle Children's Theatre
3 Seattle Center House Food Court
4 Seattle Children's Museum
5 Pacific Science Center
6 Seattle Center Skatepark
7 Center for Wooden Boats
8 Northwest Puppet Center
9 Woodland Park Zoo
10 Green Lake Park

Though Seattle is heavy on young professionals with relatively few kids, it is an unusually child-friendly town. Glaring shopkeepers and condescending waiters are rare. Kids love the natural beauty of Puget Sound, the mountains, and parks; and there is a wealth of activities to keep youngsters busy any time of the year. START: **Bus 99 to Pier 59.**

Experience the beauty of underwater life at the Seattle Aquarium.

❶ ★★ kids Seattle Aquarium. A perennial favorite, the aquarium offers stories for tots, crafts for older kids, and animal feedings and presentations. Most special programs are included with admission. At the tidepool exhibit, kids love to get their hands on anemones and sea stars. ⏱ *2 hr. 1483 Alaskan Way on Pier 59.* ☎ *206/386-4300. www. seattleaquarium.org. Admission $22 adults, $15 ages 4–13. Daily 9:30am–5pm (exhibits close at 6pm). See p 11.*

❷ ★★★ kids Seattle Children's Theatre. It's hard to say who's having more fun, the kids or their parents. The sets are clever, the costumes ingenious, and the acting first rate. The season runs September through June. You can get a healthy snack at intermission, but hurry or you'll spend the whole time waiting in line—in which case you'll miss out on the gift area, stocked with books and clever items that relate to the show.

Even adults will be entertained by the inventive performances at the Seattle Children's Theatre.

Afterward, the characters chat with kids and sign autographs. *201 Thomas St. at Seattle Center.* ☎ *206/441-3322. www.sct.org. Ticket prices vary.*

3 **kids** **Seattle Center Armory Food Court.** You'll find lots of quick and tasty options here, from Thai noodles to fish and chips. There are plenty of treats as well, from warm, sugar-dusted beignets to homemade taffy. The perfect "grown-up" outing for kids is dinner at the food court, followed by a play at the Seattle Children's Theatre. *305 Harrison St.* ☎ *206/684-7200. $*

4 ★ **kids** **Seattle Children's Museum.** Most of the special exhibits here are geared toward the 6-and-under crowd, but children up to 10 will enjoy the hands-on science section and Imagination Studio, where they create art projects. Make that an early stop, in case paint needs to dry, then pick up the finished product on your way out. In the Lil' Green Thumbs outdoor exhibit, kids learn about growing flowers and veggies and plant their own seed to take home. ⏱ *90 min. 305 Harrison St.* ☎ *206/441-1768. www.thechildrens museum.org. See p 13.*

5 ★★ **kids** **Pacific Science Center.** Older kids will love the interactive exhibits, such as Adventures in 3Dimensions, which shows how 3-D technology involves our brains to create special effects. Younger one go for the crawl-and-climb area, which includes a tree-house and a table-height "stream" for water play. At the Insect Village, kids of all ages thrill and chill to the giant robotic insects and live animal displays. ⏱ *90 min. 200 2nd Ave. N.* ☎ *206/443-2001. www.pacsci.org. Admission $18 adults, $16 seniors,*

$13 ages 6–15, $10 ages 3–5. IMAX: $9–$14 adults, $8–$12 seniors, $7–$11 ages 6–15, $6–$9 ages 3–5; discounts available for combination passes. Mon, Wed–Fri 10am–5pm; Sat–Sun 10am–6pm. See p 13.

6 ★ **kids** **Seattle Center Skatepark.** Let the kids loose at this 10,000-square-foot, cutting-edge skateboard park. Known to local skateboarders as Sea Sk8, it features a fully skateable vertical glass wall. ⏱ *1 hr. 2nd Ave. N. & Thomas St.* ☎ *206/684-7200. www.seattlecenter. com/skatepark. Free admission. Daily during daylight hours.*

7 **kids** **Tugboat Story Time at the Center for Wooden Boats.** Stories about the sea are even more entertaining when told on the deck of a boat like the historic tug *Arthur Foss.* These maritime tales are geared for ages 2 to 5. ⏱ *1 hour. 1010 Valley St.* ☎ *206/382-2628. www.cwb.org. Free admission. 11am second & fourth Thurs.*

8 ★★ **kids** **Northwest Puppet Center.** The Carter Family Marionettes, a local multi-generational

Little ones will be thrilled to be let loose in the interactive Seattle Children's Museum.

Children's Museum

The Northwest Puppet Center.

family of puppeteers, present high-quality performances geared toward children of various ages. The artistry is remarkable, and the genial Carters bring in puppeteers from around the world, and the stories are often based on books or folk tales. After the show, puppets are often brought out on stage for children to come up and touch. *9123 15th Ave. NE.* ☎ *206/523-2579. www.nw puppet.org. Tickets: $11 adults, $9 seniors, $8.50 children. Public shows are on weekend afternoons.*

⑨ ★★★ kids Woodland Park Zoo. Woodland Park has won awards for several exhibits, including the primate area and the African Savanna. The newest exhibits are the Humboldt penguin habitat, where an underwater viewing area gives guests a close-up view of frolicking penguins from Peru, and the fun-loving meerkats area. At the Zoomazium, an indoor play area, kids 8 and under can explore nature, listen to stories and burn off a little energy. Special programs are offered for toddlers in the

morning and school-age kids in the afternoon. The zoo also has a beautiful 1918 carousel; rides cost $2. ⏱ *2 hr. 750 N. 50th St.* ☎ *206/684-4800. www.zoo.org. Admission May–Sept: $19 ages 13–64, $12 ages 3–12; Oct–Apr: $13 ages 13–64, $8.75 ages 3–12. May–Sept daily 9:30am–6pm; Oct–Apr: daily 9:30am–4pm.*

⑩ kids Green Lake Park. Seattle's favorite place to walk, the 2.8-mile path around lovely Green Lake draws moms with strollers, joggers, dog-walkers, bicyclists, and nature-lovers. An **indoor warm-water pool** (☎ 206/684-4961; $4.85 ages 18-64, $3.25 ages 1–17 and 65+, free under 1) offers family, public and lap swimming. Tots can splash away in a large outdoor wading pool, open daily 11am–8pm from mid-June to Labor Day. This is a great playground for younger kids, because it's divided into separate areas for toddlers and their rowdier older siblings. ⏱ *1 hr. 7201 E Green Lake Dr. N.* ☎ *206/684-4075. www.seattle.gov/parks. The park is open 24 hr.*

The Woodland Park Zoo is famous for its tigers, among other things.

Caffeinated Seattle

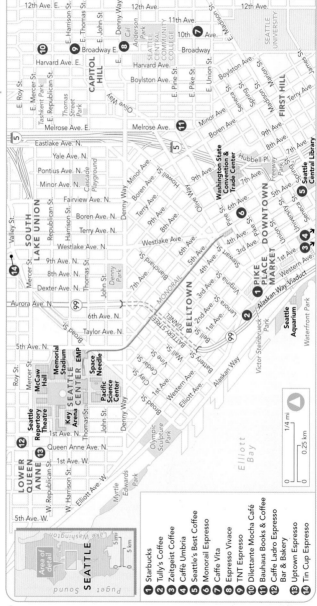

1 Starbucks
2 Tully's Coffee
3 Zeitgeist Coffee
4 Caffe Umbria
5 Seattle's Best Coffee
6 Monorail Espresso
7 Caffe Vita
8 Espresso Vivace
9 TNT Espresso
10 Dilettante Mocha Café
11 Bauhaus Books & Coffee
12 Caffe Ladro Espresso Bar & Bakery
13 Uptown Espresso
14 Tin Cup Espresso

Even inveterate tea-drinkers like myself can't help but get caught up in the coffee frenzy that permeates Seattle. Pumpkin-spice lattes, peppermint mochas, white chocolate lattes with raspberry, caramel macchiatos—who could resist their favorite flavors blended tastefully with the drug that keeps Seattleites going through the drizzle? Purists may opt for espresso or Americanos. If you just don't like coffee, try a chai tea latte. There's no coffee in it, just creamy, delightfully spiced tea that makes the world seem warm and cozy. In the summer, order your favorite drink served over ice. Don't worry about being picky; the person in line ahead of you is likely to demand a double short half-caff extra-hot soy no-foam latte. Watch the barista's face; he or she won't blink an eye.

START: **Bus 10, 99, 113, 121 or 122 to Pike Place Market.**

❶ ★ Starbucks. You must begin, of course, where Seattle's coffee culture itself really began back in 1971. The very first Starbucks, at Pike Place Market, still features the chain's original mascot, the topless mermaid with a double fish tail, which has been toned down over the years in other locations. Many coffee-lovers gripe that Starbucks stores are ubiquitous; but I think their flavored drinks are hard to beat, and consistently good from store to store. *The original: 1912 Pike Pl.* ☎ 206/448-8762.

❷ ★ Kids Tully's Coffee. With shops in several Western states—including a number in Seattle—

Zeitgeist offers an urbane oasis from busy city life.

Love them or hate them, this is the site where the Starbucks phenomenon began.

Tully's still roasts its coffee painstakingly, in small batches in antique roasters. The stores are friendly and welcoming, the drinks and baked goods terrific, and they usually have tables where kids can read and draw while the grown-ups sit by the fireplace and chat. My favorite is the one near Pike Place Market (2001 Western Ave. # 110A; ☎ 206/443-1915). *The original: 1401 4th Ave.* ☎ 206/625-0600.

❸ ★★ Zeitgeist Coffee. This spacious, hip European-style coffeehouse serves up film screenings and rotating works by up-and-coming artists along with its popular Italian beans, illy caffè. *See p 52.*

4 ★ Caffe Umbria. The Bizzarri family has been roasting beans since Emanuele's grandfather Ornello opened his first shop in Perugia, Italy. Five blends are available, including fair-trade beans. Umbria's Italian-style coffee is served by many demanding establishments, including the Bellagio Hotel and Resort in Las Vegas. You can enjoy a heavenly extra-foamy cappuccino right here in Pioneer Square. *See p 15.*

5 ★ Seattle's Best Coffee. An early player on the local coffee scene, Seattle's Best Coffee was bought out by Starbucks a few years ago. But SBCs are still allowed to serve their own coffee blends. The chain got its name many years ago, after winning a contest for the best cuppa joe in town. *Downtown: 1100 4th Ave.* ☎ *206/623-0104; Pike Place Market: 1530 Post Alley.* ☎ *206/467-7700.*

6 ★ Monorail Espresso. Back in 1980, even before Starbucks began selling coffee drinks at its original store, Chuck Beek came up with the idea of running a little espresso cart in Seattle. He

Uptown Espresso's signature Velvet Foam.

peddled his wares underneath the monorail track. Fifteen years later, with a greatly expanded coffee menu, he opened a permanent shop a few blocks away. It's a great spot to drink in a little history with your double latte. *520 Pike St. (at 5th).* ☎ *206/625-0449.*

7 ★ Caffe Vita. This roastery also claims many devotees who swear by its beans and blends from around the world. Vita forms relationships with coffee growers in Africa, Indonesia, and the Americas,

Is this really Seattle's best? After this tour, you decide.

and offers a wide variety of tastes. Locations include Capitol Hill: *1005 E. Pike St.* ☎ *206/709-4440. Queen Anne: 813 5th Ave. N.* ☎ *206/285-9662.*

⑧ ★★ Espresso Vivace. David Schomer's slow-roasting process is designed to produce a sweet caramel flavor, and the roasting is stopped early to keep the oils in and prevent a burned flavor. For many coffee aficionados, this is as good as it gets. *Capitol Hill cafe location: 532 Broadway Ave. E.* ☎ *206/860-2722. Capitol Hill Stand: 321 Broadway Ave. E.*

⑨ ★ TNT Espresso. This small, friendly Capitol Hill stand serves Zoka coffee, which is roasted in Seattle using beans from around the globe, including an organic chocolaty fair-trade blend of beans from Java and Yemen. Zoka's Paladino blend is sweet and nutty, and is a favorite of many baristas at competitions. *324 Broadway Ave E.* ☎ *206/323-9151.*

⑩ ★★ Dilettante Mocha Café. Silky-smooth, top-quality chocolate makes for sinfully rich mochas, and the presentation is style. The chocolate melts in pots right beside the espresso machine. *Locations include 538 Broadway E.* ☎ *206/329-6463. See p 88.*

⑪ ★ Bauhaus Books & Coffee. This hip spot in a very diverse neighborhood is stacked with books, which makes it seem very cozy. The people-watching can't be beat, either inside or at the outdoor tables. Nor can the dramatic views of the Space Needle. Best of all? It's open every night till 1am. *414 E. Pine St.* ☎ *206/625-1600.*

⑫ ★ Caffe Ladro Espresso Bar & Bakery. Serving only organic, fair-trade, shade-grown coffee, Caffe Ladro has about a dozen locations around metro Seattle. The urban-hip shops serve delicious quiche and baked goods. Try a Medici latte with orange peel. *600 Queen Anne Ave. N.* ☎ *206/282-1549. Downtown: 801 Pine St.* ☎ *206/405-1950.*

⑬ ★ Uptown Espresso. This is a serious coffeeshop, with rough wood tables occupied by quietly chatting friends and furiously typing computer-users. The coffee and baked goods are excellent. Lattes come topped with a layer of Uptown's heavenly Velvet Foam. *525 Queen Anne Ave N.* ☎ *206/285-3757. Belltown: 2504 4th Ave.* ☎ *206/441-1084.*

⑭ ★ Tin Cup Espresso. You might think a town known for its showers would boast lots of covered drive-throughs for its favorite beverage. Not so. This is the only one, and fortunately the drinks, made with Caffe Appassionato beans, are great. I love to start the day sipping a Rush cafe—flavored with vanilla and cinnamon. *900 Broad St.* ☎ *206/464-7296.*

The drinks at Espresso Vivace look like works of art.

Architecture & Design

1. Safeco Field
2. CenturyLink Field
3. Union Station
4. King Street Station
5. Pioneer Building
6. Pioneer Square Pergola
7. Smith Tower
8. Arctic Building
9. Specialty's Café & Bakery
10. Seattle Central Public Library
11. Seattle Art Museum
12. Banana Republic
13. Experience Music Project
14. Space Needle

Although a city this young may not have the widest range of architectural styles, there are many historic gems to be found; and Seattleites have put a great deal of cash into preserving their colorful past. Most of the renovations have been undertaken with care, and it is delightful to see the modern uses to which these old buildings have been put, with all due respect paid to their history. But architecture here is also moving forward. The city's rapid growth and penchant for adventure has attracted world-renowned architects, who have designed a number of cutting-edge buildings. START: **Bus 106, 123, 124, 131 or 132 to Safeco Field.**

A tour of CenturyLink Field gives a behind-the-scenes look at the stadium.

❶ ★ kids Safeco Field. The Seattle Mariners' stadium, erected after the team demanded a new facility to replace the not-so-old but leaky Kingdome, was built amid even more controversy than usual in Seattle. But it has won the hearts of Seattleites, partly because it keeps the rain off but lets the fresh air in. It has one of the few retractable stadium coverings in the country, and the only one that doesn't fully enclose the field. On a perfect sunny day when the roof is open, baseball doesn't get better than this. If you can't make a game, take the hour-long tour—you'll get to see off-limits areas such as the private suites and press box, if they're not in use. Even if you're not a sports fan, you'll enjoy the views of the city and sound, and the baseball-inspired art on display by

Northwest artists. ⏱ *1 hr. 1250 1st Ave. S.* ☎ *206/346-4001. www. mariners.mlb.com. Ticket prices for games vary. Tour: $9 adults, $8 seniors, $7 ages 3–12, free under 3.*

Check out a baseball game at the ultra-modern Safeco Field.

A totem pole guards the entry to the Pioneer Building.

② ★ CenturyLink Field. The Mariners weren't the only sports team to demand a new stadium. The Seahawks also insisted on moving out of the ill-fated Kingdome. So it was destroyed in a fantastic implosion and replaced by Century-Link Field. Its graceful double-arched roof, studded with blue lights that glow as you fly into the city or drive along I-5, has become a treasured part of the city's skyline. The roof also overhangs most of the bleachers, keeping about 70% of the fans dry. The field is open-air, and so is the north end, which allows drop-dead views of downtown. If you want to taste the luxury suite experience—and walk right onto the field—take a tour. They're offered all year long. ① *90 min. 800 Occidental Ave. S. ☎ 206/381-7555. www.centurylinkfield.com. Tours: $7 adults, $5 seniors & ages 4–12; Sept. 1–May 30, Fri–Sat 12:30 & 2:30pm; June 1–Aug 31, daily 12:30 & 2:30pm.*

③ ★ Union Station. Opened in 1911, this was a transcontinental train station for 60 years. Sadly, the vast Beaux Arts building was then abandoned and sat around deteriorating until Microsoft billionaire Paul Allen came to the rescue in the 1990s. It landed a National Preservation Award in 2000, and now it serves as the headquarters for Sound Transit, a regional commuter train. Its spectacular hall, which features a beautifully lighted barrel-vaulted ceiling, is rented out for weddings and other grand occasions, and it's easy to see why. In the daytime, natural light pours in through an enormous semi-circular window. The elegant architecture is worth an admiring look. ① *15 min. 401 S. Jackson St. ☎ 206/682-7275. Free admission.*

④ King Street Station. This bustling Amtrak and Sound Transit commuter station was built in 1906 for the Great Northern Railway and Northern Pacific Railway. An extensive restoration, completed in 2013, returned it to its former glory. Its elaborate high ceilings were uncovered—hidden since the 1960s by drab suspended tiles. The entry hall, dubbed the Compass Room because of marble-tiled directional points on the floor, has also been refurbished, as has the station's clock tower, once the tallest structure in Seattle. And its clock is once again keeping time. ① *15 min. 303 S. Jackson St. ☎ 206/382-4125. Free admission.*

⑤ Pioneer Building. This elegant, Romanesque-style structure, hurriedly built right after the Great Fire, was named the "finest building west of Chicago" by the American Institute of Architects when it was completed in 1892. The Underground Tour (see p 14) offers a fascinating look at the building and at Seattle's colorful history, if you have the time (tours last 90 min.). ① *15 min. 1st Ave. & Yesler Way. Underground Tour, 610 1st Ave., #200. ☎ 206/682-4646. www.undergroundtour.com. $17* *adults, $9 children 7–12. Tours offered daily, throughout the day. See p 51.*

⑥ ★ Pioneer Square Pergola. You wouldn't know it today, but Seattle's eye-catching iron-and-glass pergola gained its fame for what once lay beneath: elegant public restrooms made of marble and bronze, widely considered the most luxurious in the world in 1910. People would enter the restrooms on stairways leading from the pergola. It was a project in keeping with Seattle's traditional egalitarian ethics. The "comfort stations" have long since been closed, and the graceful Victorian pergola itself was crushed by a veering truck in 2001. Fortunately, it was restored using as much of the original materials as possible. ⏱ *15 min. 1st Ave. & Yesler Way.*

⑦ Smith Tower. The tallest building west of the Mississippi when it was built in 1914, this 42-story neoclassical office building is a grand old lady, worth a visit if only for a ride in its 1914 brass-caged elevators. They're the last manually operated ones on the West Coast. The elaborate Chinese Room, with its carved blackwood furniture, is on the 35th floor, as is the observation deck. The panoramic view is spectacular. ⏱ *30 min. 506 2nd Ave.* ☎ *206/622-4004. www.smithtower.com. Observation deck admission $7.50 adults, $5 kids 6–12, free 5 & under. Daily 10am–5pm. (Check first to make sure no private events are scheduled.)*

⑧ Arctic Building. Fondly dubbed the "Walrus Building," this eight-story art deco structure was once an exclusive club for the relatively few gold-miners who struck it rich in the Yukon. In homage to the land where the riches were made, the building featured Alaskan marble hallways and a row of sculpted walrus heads around the third floor of the colorful terracotta exterior. Members could do everything from sip tea to go bowling here. A few years ago, investors transformed it into a charming hotel, the Arctic Club Hotel Seattle, featuring period décor. ⏱ *15 min. 700 3rd Ave.* ☎ *206/340-0340. Free admission to the lobby. See p 157.*

After being crushed by a truck in 2001, the Pioneer Square Pergola is back to its former glory.

Say hello to the walruses that adorn the Arctic Building.

9 **Specialty's Café & Bakery.** Grab a hearty sandwich or a healthy Cobb salad, followed by a delicious, fresh-from-the-oven peanut butter cookie. For the bargain-minded, the day-old baked goods are a good value. *1023 3rd Ave.* ☎ *206/264-0882. $*

10 ★★★ kids **Seattle Central Public Library.** The most talked-about design in Seattle—since the Experience Music Project museum, anyway—is the $165 million central public library, an avant-garde showpiece by Dutch architect Rem Koolhaas. This is not your third-grade teacher's library. Tourists from around the world have been coming specifically to see this building since its 2004 opening. Outside, its odd, asymmetrical glass and steel angles jut powerfully over the sidewalk. Inside, patrons walk up a spiraling ramp that gradually leads to the top floor. Elevators and electric-hued escalators are another option. On your way up, stunning views of the surrounding downtown buildings can be seen through the net-like steel structure. ① *30 min. 1000 4th Ave.* ☎ *206/386-4636. www.spl. org. Free admission. Mon–Thurs 10am–8pm, Fri–Sat 10am–6pm, Sun noon–6pm.*

11 ★★★ **Seattle Art Museum.** This museum with its postmodern facade was designed by Pritzker Prize–winner Robert Venturi. It moved to this location after spending its first 60 years in that art-deco building in Volunteer Park that now houses the Seattle Asian Art Museum (see p 29). Fifteen years later, the museum was again bursting at the seams, and a large expansion was undertaken. The outside of the building—the upper 12 floors of which are office space—already looks dated, but the blending of old and new is impressive. The "wow" factor was reserved for the lovely interior, where exhibit spaces have doubled, prompting donations of 1,000 new

Wooden carvings overlook Smith Tower's old-fashioned elevators.

The Seattle Public Library.

pieces of art. ⏱ *1 hr.* ☎ *206/654-3100. www.seattleartmuseum.org. Admission $20 adults, $18 seniors over 62, $13 students & kids 13–17, free for kids 12 & under. 1300 1st Ave. Wed–Sun 10am–5pm, Thurs until 9pm. See p 11.*

⓬ **Banana Republic.** Yes, it's a chain store, but it's set in a stunning building that once housed the old Coliseum Theatre, built in 1916 by renowned Seattle architect B. Marcus Priteca for wealthy local property owner Joseph Gottstein. The Coliseum was one of the first elegant movie palaces built for showing silent films. Priteca also designed the Pantages theaters, including California's famous one at Hollywood & Vine. After the boom in suburban theaters in the '70s, the Coliseum stood empty until its reinvention as a clothing store. The original grandeur is preserved, and the white terracotta exterior is striking. ⏱ *15 min. 500 Pike St.* ☎ *206/622-2303.*

⓭ ★ **Experience Music Project.** Without question, this is the oddest structure in Seattle, built by eccentric Microsoft co-founder Paul Allen, a huge fan of the late local guitar legend Jimi Hendrix. At ground level the museum looks, well, rather like amorphous blobs of colorful sheet metal, but from the air, designer Frank Gehry's building is supposed to resemble one of Hendrix's famed smashed guitars. The inside, also architecturally engaging, showcases the history of rock 'n' roll, including its roots in soul, jazz, and other genres. Your ticket will also get you into the

Heads Up!

One of the best ways to sample the city's architecture is to take one of the many popular walking tours offered by the Seattle Architecture Foundation. Most tours last about 2 hours and showcase a wide variety of styles and locations, from the Seattle waterfront to the art deco district to the Craftsman bungalows north of the city. There are even tours for families, "Eye Spy Seattle" geared at adults and kids ages 5–10, and the Family Tour for grown-ups with kids ages 8–14. Check the website (www.seattlearchitecture.org) for dates and times. Most tours cost $15 in advance or $25 for same-day tickets, $10 for children 5–12 (Family Tour only).

The Experience Music Project is one of Seattle's most fascinating buildings.

Science Fiction Museum and Hall of Fame (see p 13), under the same roof. ① 1 hr. 325 5th Ave. N. (at Seattle Center). ☎ 206/770-2700. www.epmmuseum.org. Admission $20 adults, $17 seniors/ages 5–17. Late May–early Sept daily 10am– 7pm; early Sept–late May 10am–5pm.

The Space Needle defines the Seattle skyline.

⑭ ★★★ Kids **Space Needle.** In typical Seattle style, there was much disagreement over what the centerpiece for the 1962 World's Fair should look like and where it should go. The futuristic design morphed considerably from the original "Needle" sketched out on a paper placemat by a hotel chain president. By the time architect John Graham (designer of Seattle's Northgate, the first shopping mall in the world) and his team came up with something everyone agreed on, the fair was only 1½ years away. Finding a site was even trickier, and was finally accomplished with just 13 months to go. Construction went at breakneck speed, and the last elevator car arrived the day before the fair opened. The Space Needle went on to become the world-recognized symbol for its city, and a decade ago got a snazzy $20 million facelift. ① 1 hr. 400 Broad St. ☎ 206/905-2100. Observation deck tickets: $26 adults, $24 seniors, $17 ages 4–13. Mon–Thurs. 10am–9pm; Fri–Sat 9:30am–10:30pm; Sun 9:30 am–9:30pm. See p 9. ●

Pioneer Square

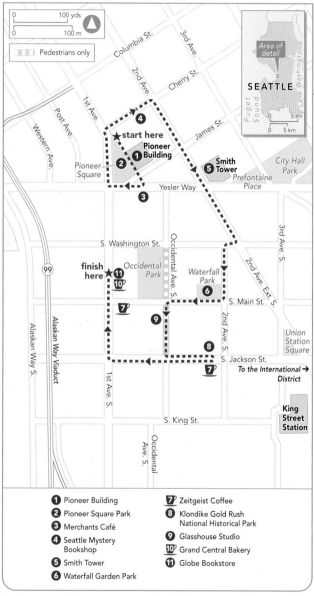

0 ——— 100 yds
0 ——— 100 m

Pedestrians only

Columbia St.

3rd Ave.

Cherry St.

2nd Ave.

1st Ave.

Post Ave.

Western Ave.

James St.

SEATTLE

Puget Sound

Lake Washington

Area of detail

0 ——— 5 mi
0 ——— 5 km

★ start here

Pioneer Building ❶

Pioneer Square ❷

Smith Tower ❺

City Hall Park

Prefontaine Place

❸ Yesler Way

S. Washington St.

Occidental Ave. S.

3rd Ave. S.

99

finish here ★ ⓫
🔟

Occidental Park

Waterfall Park ❻

2nd Ave. S.

2nd Ave. Ext. S.

S. Main St.

Union Station Square

☕ ❼

❾

❽

☕ ❼

S. Jackson St.

To the International → District

Alaskan Way Viaduct

Alaskan Way S.

1st Ave. S.

King Street Station

S. King St.

Occidental Ave. S.

❶ Pioneer Building
❷ Pioneer Square Park
❸ Merchants Café
❹ Seattle Mystery Bookshop
❺ Smith Tower
❻ Waterfall Garden Park

☕ Zeitgeist Coffee
❽ Klondike Gold Rush National Historical Park
❾ Glasshouse Studio
🔟 Grand Central Bakery
⓫ Globe Bookstore

Previous page: Traditional entrance to Seattle's Chinatown.

For a taste of Seattle's quirky past, wander the oddly angled streets of Pioneer Square, where some of the city's finest art galleries intermingle with the shops and restaurants. The charming Victorian brick and stone buildings were slapped up after the Great Fire of 1889 by local fat cats, eager to get back to selling supplies—and services of every kind—to prospectors en route to the Yukon. At night the district's clubs still spring to life. START: **Bus 10, 11, 16, 66 or 99 to Pioneer Square.**

❶ ★★ Pioneer Building. Begin your tour at the very spot where pioneer Henry Yesler built his sawmill in the 1850s, then rebuilt after the Great Fire. He hired famed architect Elmer Fisher—who designed more than 50 post-fire structures—to create the stylish building. Go inside and check out Doc Maynard's Pub and the entertaining Underground Tour, which gives you the insider scoop on Seattle's colorful past. This is one of my favorite ways to amuse visitors. Some younger kids may find it boring, as much of the spiel will (thankfully) be over their heads. ⏱ *90 min. 1st Avenue & Yesler Way. Underground Tour, 608 1st Ave. (☎ 206/682-4646. www.undergroundtour.com. $17 adults, $14 seniors & students, $9 children 7–12; offered daily, throughout the day.*

❷ ★ Pioneer Square Park. The pergola (see p 45), Seattle's most beloved hunk of iron, graces the south end of this triangular park—really more of a courtyard—directly in front of the Pioneer Building. It's popular with tourists, but also with vagrants looking for a bench to while away the day. Another rebuilt item in the park is a 60-foot Tlingit totem pole, a replacement for one stolen from an Alaskan village in 1938 by a group of prominent Seattle citizens. When the pole burned years later,

the city hired the descendants of the original Native American carvers to produce its replacement. ⏱ *15 min. 1st Avenue & Yesler Way.*

❸ Merchants Cafe. Step back in time at the oldest watering hole in Seattle. Back in the day, prospectors would quaff a brew at the saloon, then head upstairs to the brothel, now converted into apartments. So much gold was dropped here by prospectors on the weekends, it came to be known as the Sunday Bank. Today, you can enjoy lunch, dinner, or a beer in the remodeled restaurant. ⏱ *15 min. 109 Yesler Way.* ☎ *206/935-7625. Sun–Fri 11am–midnight, Sat 11am–2am.*

❹ Seattle Mystery Bookshop. Whodunit aficionados can spend hours tracking down mystery books, both collectable and current, at this terrific little shop. There are frequent author signings, and if you miss one you like, check with JB—he keeps a large number of autographed volumes on hand. ⏱ *15 min. 117 Cherry St.* ☎ *206/587-5737. www.seattlemystery.com. Mon–Sat 10am–5pm, Sun noon–5pm.*

Seattle Mystery Bookshop is the perfect place to while away a few hours.

5 ★ **Smith Tower.** Ride the antique caged elevators up to the 35th floor observation deck for a fabulous view of downtown Seattle and Mt. Rainier, though the building is now dwarfed by more modern 'scrapers. ⏲ *30 min. 506 2nd Ave.* ☎ *206/622-4004. www.smith tower.com. Observation deck admission $7.50 adults, $5 kids 6–12, free under 6. Daily 10am–5pm (Check first to make sure no private events are scheduled). See p 45.*

6 ★★ **Waterfall Garden Park.** This little-known oasis is my favorite place to hang out with a latte. You'll know you're there by the crash of water tumbling 22 feet down a wall of boulders, drowning out the urban bustle. The two-level gem of a park was built in honor of United Parcel Service employees. At lunchtime, office workers sit among its trees and flowers to escape the concrete. ⏲ *15 min. 219 2nd Ave. S.*

7 **Zeitgeist Coffee.** Drop by for a muffuletta and espresso, then enjoy people-watching or discussing world events. If the conversation turns contentious, a world globe and a monster-size dictionary are on hand to help resolve matters. *171 S. Jackson St.* ☎ *206/583-0497. $*

8 ★ **kids Klondike Gold Rush National Historical Park.** In 1897 and 1898, 120,000 fortune-hunters stampeded north to Canada's Yukon Territory, where gold had recently passed through Seattle, and the impact on the city was enormous. This park tells the story of the Klondike Gold Rush with great attention to detail (e.g., 1 in 10 of those headed for the gold fields were women). ⏲ *1 hr. 319 2nd Ave. S.* ☎ *206/220-4240. www. nps.gov/klse. Free admission. Daily 9am–5pm. See p 22.*

9 ★★★ **kids Glasshouse Studio.** Seattle is home to some of the world's finest glass artists. (Dale Chihuly, famed for his outrageously colorful, fanciful works, has his own museum [p 27] near the Space Needle.) Here, you can watch artists at work in Seattle's oldest glass-blowing studio as they shape glowing globs of color into amazing things of beauty. You can buy their vases, chandeliers, jewelry, and more in the adjacent shop. ⏲ *30 min. 311*

Waterfall Garden Park is one of Seattle's best-kept secrets.

Watch artisans at work at the Glasshouse Studio.

Occidental Ave. S. ☎ 206/682-9939. www.glasshouse-studio.com. Mon–Sat 10am–5pm, Sun 11am–4pm.

10 Grand Central Bakery. You'll smell it before you see it. Some of the best pastries, sandwiches, and soups in town come from this gem of a bakery, which you can enter from Occidental Park or the Grand Central Arcade on 1st Avenue. Start with a basil egg sandwich, followed by a sweet-tooth-pleasing chocolate croissant, then take home a Como Loaf, one of Seattle's original artisan loaves. *214 1st Ave. S. ☎ 206/622-3644. $*

11 ★ Globe Bookstore. From Beowulf to Harry Potter, you'll likely find what you're looking for in this wonderful, musty bookshop. The focus is on used and collectable books, but you'll find new titles as well. The cookbook and children's sections are especially impressive. The owner really knows his stuff, and the prices are right. He tracked down a cookbook I'd been hunting for years—and charged me less than half the price I'd seen on eBay. *30 min. 218 1st Ave. S. ☎ 206/682-6882. Daily 10am–6pm.*

First Thursday Gallery Walk

The country's first art walk, this monthly event is great fun, and a terrific way to catch all the latest exhibits. Best of all, it's free. First Thursday showcases the Pioneer Square area's eclectic array of galleries. The best new artists and exhibits are featured, and the art ranges from paintings to sculptures to blown glass. It all starts at Main Street and Occidental, in Occidental Park, where vendors hawk their art and street musicians entertain. Skip that big dinner before you come, because some of the galleries serve wine and cheese. The walk runs noon–8pm the first Thursday of every month (www.firstthursdayseattle.com).

Pike Place Market

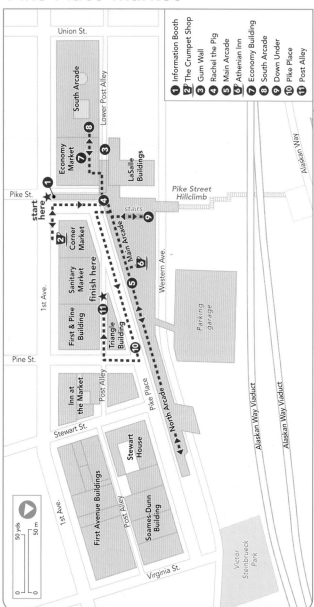

Union St.

South Arcade

Lower Post Alley

Economy Market

LaSalle Buildings

Pike St.

start here

Pike Street Hillclimb

Corner Market

stairs

Sanitary Market

finish here

First & Pine Building

Main Arcade

1st Ave.

Triangle Building

Pine St.

Inn at the Market

Post Alley

North Arcade

Stewart St.

Stewart House

Western Ave.

Parking garage

First Avenue Buildings

Post Alley

Soames-Dunn Building

Pike Place

Alaskan Way

Alaskan Way Viaduct

Alaskan Way Viaduct

Virginia St.

Victor Steinbrueck Park

50 yds
50 m

1. Information Booth
2. The Crumpet Shop
3. Gum Wall
4. Rachel the Pig
5. Main Arcade
6. Athenian Inn
7. Economy Building
8. South Arcade
9. Down Under
10. Pike Place
11. Post Alley

Buzzing with tourists, savvy locals, and finicky restaurateurs, Pike Place Market is the heart and soul of Seattle. Kids love the street performers and the "flying" fish; adults are mesmerized by the mind-boggling variety of shops, food, and entertainment. You can find just about anything you want here, from salted herring to $4,000-a-pound Piemontese truffles to handmade mandolins. It's a wonderful place to spend a day—or two. Plus, it's the only neighborhood in town where jaywalking won't get you a ticket! START: Bus 10, 99, 113, 121 or 122 to Pike Place Market.

❶ **Information Booth.** Make this your first stop—not just to pick up a market newspaper and map, but to arm yourself with coupons for tours, including the popular Argosy Cruises of the harbor and Seattle's lakes and locks, and discounts on current theatrical shows in town. (Also check www.goldstar. com and click on "Seattle" at the bottom of the page for deals on tickets.) *Pike St. & 1st Ave.* ☎ *206/ 228-7291. www.pikeplacemarket.org.*

❷ ★ **The Crumpet Shop.** Start your day off here at this British-flavored spot. As a tea fanatic in a java town, I especially appreciate the variety of tasty global teas served daily, with free refills. Of course, there are also the mouth-watering crumpets, baked fresh daily. Crumpet purists can get one with just marmalade, but I love them with smoked salmon, cream cheese, and cucumber. Come early and you can watch the bakers at work. *1503 1st Ave.* ☎ *206/682-1598. $*

❸ **kids Gum Wall.** If you're not too easily grossed out, take a detour down the ramp from the Information Booth before you tackle the Market proper. Hang a left and be careful not to lean against this wall! It is covered in several inches' worth of chewed gum. After several years of futile efforts to clean it off, the city

Pike Place Market's Gum Wall.

dubbed it a tourist attraction. *1530 Post Alley.*

❹ **kids Rachel the Pig.** Seattle's beloved bronze porker stands just under the famous neon "Public Market Center" sign and clock. I like to drop a few coins in the piggybank to help support the Market Foundation's charities. The civic-minded folks who saved the Market in the 1970s decided the revival should include social services, such as low-income apartments for seniors. *Rachel* has quite a cult following. *Pike Place & Pike Street.*

❺ ★★ **kids Main Arcade.** Get ready for sensory overload! The most tender asparagus, freshest

Go ahead, climb up on Rachel for a photo.

daffodils, richest sockeye salmon and most unusual Northwest crafts can be found here. Start right behind Rachel the Pig and elbow your way through the North

Arcade. Everything sold here is required to be grown, caught or created locally. From the world-famous fish throwers at **Pike Place Fish Market** to the tulip-growers from Snoqualmie Valley, the North Arcade is alive with scents, sounds, and colors. Salad greens with edible flowers? Chocolate pasta? Pepper jelly? You'll find them all here. Try the tasty free samples at **Sosio's Fruit & Produce,** and stop for a complimentary cup of specially blended MarketSpice Tea at **MarketSpice,** which has been here since 1911. Head to the back of the shop and look for the carafe. On the north end of the Main Arcade, you'll find the handmade-craft booths, where you can buy anything from clay ocarinas to watercolor paintings of umbrellas. ○ 90

Spirit of the Market

Tales abound of ghosts and ghouls wandering among the old narrow halls, stairwells, dusty corners, nooks and crannies of Pike Place Market, looking for closure—or at least their old haunts. So many ghosts have been reported by workers and visitors to the Market that a few even have names—like Jacob, supposedly a horse groom in real life, back in the days when the Market had stables. Now, he's fabled to haunt the Down Under, where he reportedly mixes up the bead colors at the Bead Zone shop. Jacob favors red beads. Then there's Frank, who supposedly introduces himself to guests at the Alibi Room nightclub before fading away. And more than one ghost has been reported hanging around Kell's Irish Pub on Post Alley, the former site of a mortuary. The Market's colorful history includes brothels, orphans who worked for pennies, a deadly flu epidemic, and the old mortuary. It all adds up to fertile ground for spirits. Even if you don't believe in them, you'll enjoy taking a 75-minute Market **Ghost Tour** (1499 Post Alley; ☎ 206/805-0195; www.seattleghost.com). Tours start at 5 and 7pm Thursday through Sunday, but check the website, because more times and dates may be added due to demand. Reservations are required via phone or website. The 5pm tour is more family-friendly, particularly for those with younger kids. Tickets cost $17; free for accompanying children 9 and under.

Food Market is a favorite spot for Seattleites to buy wine, cheeses, and olive oil. It also has a terrific deli. What I like best is being able to pick the brains of the knowledgeable staff. On your way to the Economy Atrium, you'll pass by the nut, crepe, and doughnut kiosks. Then stop and play at **The Great Wind-Up,** which specializes in—you guessed it—wind-up toys. Usually, the try-out table is monopolized by adults with big, goofy grins on their faces. ⏱ *30 min.*

8 South Arcade. The Economy Building opens onto a newer row of shops and restaurants, including **Pike Pub & Brewery,** one of the area's many excellent micro-breweries. **Northwest Tribal Art** is a great place to find colorful masks, totem poles, soapstone figurines, and silver jewelry crafted by local Native Americans. ⏱ *30 min.*

Be sure to dodge the flying fish as you head through the fish market.

min. Mon–Sat 10am–6pm; Sun 11am–5pm. (Fine-dining restaurants stay open later.)

6 The Athenian Inn. Tucked off the Main Arcade, this is a favorite hangout of longtime Seattleites—and the tourists who remember it from "Sleepless in Seattle." You can get all-day breakfast here, or seafood straight from the Market. The Athenian, which recently celebrated its centennial, is a dark, homey kind of place with a long bar. Sit upstairs for the best views of Puget Sound. *1517 Pike Place.* ☎ *206/624-7166. www.athenianinn. com. $$*

7 Economy Building. On the corner of this building, beside the Information Booth, is **First And Pike News ★,** where the shelves groan under the weight of newspapers from around the world and magazines of every ilk. You're likely to find your hometown paper here. **DeLaurenti Specialty**

One of the many street performers at the market.

Pike Place Market features farm fresh fruit and veggies from all over the Northwest.

9 ★ Down Under. Pike Place Market is perched on the top of a hillside, with a labyrinth of eclectic stores sprawling beneath the Main Arcade. It's worth venturing down the staircase to explore them. The shops are jammed with gems, books, ethnic clothing, and jewelry, and there's even an old-fashioned barbershop. Craft stores sell unusual items, including **Afghani Crafts** women's clothing; **Hands of the World,** featuring folk art mainly from developing nations; and **Polish Pottery Place,** where beautifully detailed items are made by a handful of families who've been at it for generations. ⏱ *30 min.*

10 ★★ Pike Place. Once you've jostled your way through the market and out into the fresh air (or drizzle), you're far from done. A brick street runs between the Main Arcade and several facing blocks, and brims with shops, food stands, restaurants, and yet more produce. The "Big Ass Grapes" at the corner shop are appropriately named. This area is just as lively as the inside Market, with street performers entertaining the crowds. Someone could well be tickling the ivories of a full-size piano on a street corner. The ethnic food stands are great places to grab a snack. Try the steamed-pork humbow and red bean sesame balls at **Mee Sum Pastries.** Or, for more substantial fare, **Piroshky Piroshky** serves an array of delicious savory and sweet pastries. I usually order the potato and mushroom, with a marzipan piroshky for dessert. The original **Starbucks** is right in the mix, for a

Dining at the Market

You won't go hungry at Pike Place Market, where dining options range from booths selling sausage, noodles, or pastries to first-rate restaurants like **Place Pigalle** (p 130), perched over the water and serving mussels to die for. For a cheap lunch, pick up sandwiches in the market, then head toward the water from Rachel the Pig, where there's a tucked-away indoor sitting area with the same panoramic view of the sound that you'll get in the high-end restaurants.

Tour the Market

There's no happier place in Seattle than the Market, where every turn brings a kaleidoscope of produce, crafts, garrulous vendors, and shoppers from around the world. On the hour-long **Market Heritage Tour** (www.publicmarkettours.com; $15 for adults, $13 for seniors/ages 13–17, $10 for children 12 and under), you can pick up some great insider tips on shopping the market, while learning the history on how it came to be in 1907, and how it almost came not to be in the 1970s. (Fortunately, Seattleites decided they couldn't bear to see their market turned into parking garages and office buildings.) The tour runs Friday through Sunday at 2pm, rain or shine, and meets at the corner of Western Avenue and Virginia Street. But if you're more into sampling some of the best the market has to offer, **Seattle Food Tours** (☎ 206/725-4483; www.seattlefoodtours.com) offers a daily 2½-hour walk. Delectable edibles might include smoked salmon, homemade gelato, to-die-for clam chowder, and locally grown fruit.

latte to wash it all down (see p 39). 🕐 30 min.

⓫ **Post Alley.** Hike east up the hill a block and you'll find yourself on a winding little street where the din is lower but the shops and cafes still delightful. **Perennial Tearoom** (1910 Post Alley; ☎ 206/448-4054) is a lovely place to stop for a spot of tea; then pick out a few varieties from the wall of teas to enjoy at

Stop by First and Pike News and see what they have in stock.

Post Alley is the perfect spot to escape the hubbub of Pike Place Market.

later. The shop stocks teas and teapots from around the world. A block farther south on Post, you can find classy souvenirs—no kidding—at **Made in Washington.** 🕐 30 min.

Downtown

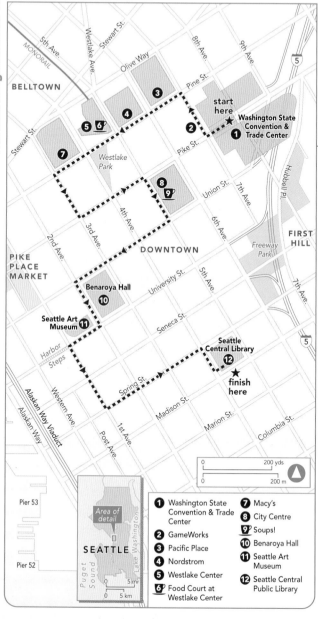

1 Washington State Convention & Trade Center
2 GameWorks
3 Pacific Place
4 Nordstrom
5 Westlake Center
6 Food Court at Westlake Center
7 Macy's
8 City Centre
9 Soups!
10 Benaroya Hall
11 Seattle Art Museum
12 Seattle Central Public Library

Seattle's downtown core is a world-class destination, bustling with shoppers and gawkers from all over the globe. Once declining, this neighborhood was livened up more than a decade ago by the dotcom millionaires. That came right on the heels of the grunge rock era, which had already focused the world's attention on the Emerald City. Downtown tenants include Nordstrom, the world-famous department store that started here as a humble shoe store in 1901; the world's first GameWorks, dreamed up in part by Steven Spielberg; and Pacific Place mall, boasting high-end retailers such as Tiffany. Today, Seattle's downtown is vibrant, colorful, and one of the most walkable in the country. START: **Bus 306, 312, 10, 11, 14 to the Washington State Convention & Trade Center.**

❶ Washington State Convention & Trade Center. Space was an issue when Seattle's convention center was built in 1988, and it was solved with a unique freeway-straddling design. Look up if you're driving on I-5 and you'll see the center's greenery draping along the overpass. Just a few years later, when the city's economy began to skyrocket, it became clear that the convention center needed yet more elbow room. The problem? There was nowhere to expand, except across Pike Street. So that's just where the other half went in 2001, connected to the original building by an enormous glass skybridge. Enter on the south side of Pike Avenue, and ride up the multiple escalators to check out the ever-changing local art exhibits. If it's raining, you can hang out in the underground concourse, which starts at the convention center, winds under the Seattle Hilton and past shops, cafes, and historical exhibits, and comes out at 5th Avenue Theatre and the Rainier Square Shopping Center. ⏱ *15 min. 800 Convention Place.* ☎ *206/447-5000. www.wscc.com. Daily 6am–10pm.*

❷ 🅺🅸🅳🆂 GameWorks. This 30,000-square-foot virtual-entertainment center is a bit too loud for my ears, but for kids (including many of

the grown-up variety) it's a paradise of futuristic fun and games. Stay all day if you like: There's a cafe, sports bar, and pool room upstairs. But if you're over 30, bring earplugs. On Thursday, play from 7 to 10pm for $10. ⏱ *15 min. 1511 7th Ave.* ☎ *206/521-0952. www.gameworks.com/locations/seattle. Mon–Thurs 11am–midnight, Fri 11am–1am, Sat 10am–1am, Sun 10am–midnight.*

❸ ★ Pacific Place. You can gaze at all four floors of this upscale, contemporary mall as you wind

Get your one-stop shopping done at Pacific Place.

The nationwide Nordstrom chain got its start in Seattle.

several restaurants to choose from, including **Il Fornaio,** which serves fresh Italian fare in three locations, depending on your budget and time constraints: an atrium kiosk, a cafe, and a full-service restaurant. No matter where I'm going downtown, I always park at Pacific Place. It's centrally located, owned by the city, and one of the best deals in a town where parking is at a premium. At night, there's a special 4-hour rate of $6. ⏱ *1 hr. 6th Ave. & Pine St.* ☎ *206/405-2655. www. pacificplaceseattle.com. Mon–Sat 10am–8pm, Sun 11am–7pm.*

❹ ★★ **Nordstrom.** The Nordstroms, one of Seattle's oldest families, moved their flagship store in 1998 from its cramped quarters to an empty 1918 building that was the former home of the iconic Frederick & Nelson department store. Nordstrom has come a long way since Swedish immigrant John Nordstrom opened his first shoe store in 1901, using Gold Rush money he brought back from Alaska. My favorite story about the chain's legendary customer service is about a businessman who called the store from the airport, in a panic because he didn't have a tie for a business meeting. A salesperson was

your way up the escalator up to the 11-screen theater. The shops along the way are a who's who of retail: Barneys New York, Eddie Bauer, Williams-Sonoma, Barnes & Noble, Cartier, J. Crew, Tiffany & Co., Restoration Hardware. If you find yourself at Pacific Place at lunch or dinner time, you'll find

Shop Savvy

Shopping at Pacific Place can be a full-day experience. But if you'd rather skip the national chain stores and focus on the local highlights, stop by **Twist ★★★**, a Northwest boutique that's as colorful as it is fun. The glassware and home decor items will lure you in; the unusual jewelry by artists around the world will keep you browsing. Then there's **Top Ten Toys,** where you won't find Barbies, but you will find quality old-fashioned toys and mind-challenging games. And don't miss the chic **Sixth Avenue Wine Seller,** where owner Beverly Shimada pours wines from around the world for $5 a glass during happy hour, from 3 to 6pm weekdays. You can also grab a bite from the yummy menu of shareable plates.

Dotcom Delirium

Seattle has always been a boom-or-bust town, starting with the Gold Rush, and continuing much later with a series of massive hirings and devastating layoffs by Boeing. Then in the 1990s, strange things began happening in the once aviation-dependent economy. First, grunge rock grabbed the limelight for Seattle. Then a little company named Microsoft, started by hometown boys Bill Gates and Paul Allen, mushroomed into a billion-dollar-a-year-plus business by 1990, helping to spawn an entire industry of dotcom start-ups. By the late '90s, Seattle's economy was flying high from the glorious infusion of dotcom dollars. World-class restaurants, theater, and other cultural activities sprang up or expanded, eager to fill the after-hour entertainment needs of the newly moneyed. Though the dotcom bubble burst in Seattle, and throughout the country, just a couple of years later, Seattle's now-diversified economy quickly revived. While Seattle has struggled during the recent economic downturn, its downtown remains vibrant and its night scene lively.

dispatched to the airport with a selection of ties. Considering Seattle's tangled traffic, I wouldn't count on the ties arriving in time these days, but the store's service is still hard to beat. And, though today's Nordstrom is a full-service department store, the shoes ★★★ are still exquisite. But before I try on a pair, I usually walk a block south to check out Nordstrom Rack (400 Pine St.), where you can save up to 75% on clothing and shoes. ⏱ *30 min. 500 Pine St.* ☎ *206/628-2111. Mon–Sat 9:30am–9pm, Sun 11am–7pm.*

❺ ★★ **Westlake Center.** This is a chic mall, but with a comfy Seattle feel. I especially love browsing in the Northwest-based shops, such as the flagship RYU sports-apparel store from Portland; Fireworks, an incredibly fun store crammed with playful art; and **Made in Washington ★★★**, which sells souvenirs your friends will actually like. Seattle's mile-long monorail, built for the 1962 World's Fair, runs between Seattle Center and the top floor of

Westlake Center. If your kids can't take any more shopping, treat them to a quick ride for a break. ⏱ *1 hr. 400 Pine St.* ☎ *206/467-1600. www. westlakecenter.com. Mon–Sat 10am–8pm, Sun 11am–6pm.*

❻ ★ **kids Food court at Westlake.** This is a food court like none other I've seen. There's something to please every palate, from quesadillas to sushi, all amazingly fresh and tasty. It's easy on the family budget, and wiggle worms have plenty of room to stretch when they're done eating. A few highlights: Bobachine bubble tea & baguettes, Bombay Wala, Salena Mexicana, Noodle Zone, Sarku-Japanese Sushi, Mediterranean Avenue, and Emerald City Smoothie. *400 Pine St. $*

❼ ★ **Macy's.** The famous New York–based department store is housed in the former Bon Marche department store, which for over

Head to the escalators to check out the bronze plates on display in Macy's.

100 years catered to Seattle's working class. Look closely and you'll find traces of the old Bon. Check beside the escalators for the intricate 1929 bronze panels depicting industries of the Northwest, from fisheries to technology. And check the sales racks for good clothing buys. ⏱ *15 min. 1601 3rd Ave.* ☎ *206/506-6000. www.macys.com.*

8 City Centre. This mixed-use building is a prestigious downtown office address, but it also houses some great little shops, including American Eagle Outfitters, Aldo (leather goods), Grace Diamonds, and Facèrè (antique and art jewelry). You can grab a veggie sub at Jimmy John's, a wrap at Sandella's Flat Bread Café, or some sushi rolls (veggie options available) at Sushi Kudasai. On the top retail floor, you'll find an excellent full-service restaurant (Palomino—with both a cafe and fine-dining room). But what I like best about City Centre is its dazzling glass collection by the famed Pilchuck Glass School. Kids go nuts for the life-size glass dinosaur skeleton. ⏱ *15 min. 1420 5th Ave.* ☎ *206/624-8800. Store hours vary. Most open at 10am Mon–Sat & noon Sun & close daily between 5pm & 9pm (Palomino stays open later).*

9 Soups! A bowl of soup is just the thing for a drizzly Seattle day. I can never decide between the chicken basil chili and the lobster bisque. Usually I ask for a sample of one, and buy a bowl of the other. This is just a small stand on the first floor of City Centre, but the taste is big, and there's plenty of room to sit and enjoy your soup. *1420 5th Ave. $*

The schockingly chartreuse escalators at the Seattle Central Public Library.

Cai Guo-Qiang's massive work greets visitors to the Seattle Art Museum.

⑩ ★★★ Benaroya Hall. Home to the Seattle Symphony, Benaroya is a modernist dream. I highly recommend catching a concert here, but even if you're not in the mood, the hall is worth a peek. Check out the colossal glass chandeliers by world-famous Seattle glass artist Dale Chihuly. ⏱ *30 min. 200 University St. ☎ 206/215-4800. www.seattlesymphony.org. Ticket prices vary; free admission to see the chandeliers. See p 148.*

⑪ ★★★ Seattle Art Museum. Seattleites take their art seriously, and SAM is a reflection of that. The museum is home to an outstanding array of works from all over the world, but be sure to check out the Northwest Native American collection, which is one of the finest you'll find anywhere. ⏱ *90 min. ☎ 206/654-3100. www.seattleartmuseum.org. Admission $20 adults, $18 seniors over 62, $13 students & kids 13–17, free for kids 12 & under. 1300 1st Ave. Hours: Wed–Sun 10am–5pm, Thurs 10am–9pm. See p 11.*

⑫ ★★★ kids Seattle Central Public Library. It's hard to say which is more fun, admiring the building or browsing its well-stocked shelves. One thing is for sure: You'll have to drag the kids out of the children's section. Of course you can get a latte! *1000 4th Ave. ☎ 206/386-4636. www.spl.org. Free admission. Mon–Thurs 10am–8pm, Fri–Sat 10am–6pm, Sun noon–6pm. See p 46.*

Kids go nuts for the life-size glass dinosaur skeleton at City Centre.

Capitol Hill

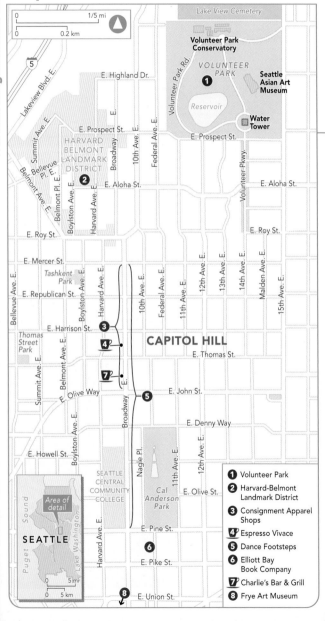

0 — 1/5 mi
0 — 0.2 km

Lake View Cemetery

Volunteer Park Conservatory

VOLUNTEER PARK

Seattle Asian Art Museum

E. Highland Dr.

Reservoir

Water Tower

E. Prospect St.

E. Prospect St.

HARVARD BELMONT LANDMARK DISTRICT

E. Aloha St.

E. Aloha St.

E. Roy St.

E. Roy St.

E. Mercer St.

Tashkent Park

E. Republican St.

E. Harrison St.

CAPITOL HILL

E. Thomas St.

Thomas Street Park

E. Olive Way

E. John St.

E. Denny Way

E. Howell St.

E. Olive St.

SEATTLE CENTRAL COMMUNITY COLLEGE

Cal Anderson Park

E. Pine St.

E. Pike St.

SEATTLE

Area of detail

Sound

Puget Sound

Lake Washington

0 — 5 mi
0 — 5 km

E. Union St.

Lakeview Blvd. E.

Summit Ave. E.

Belmont Ave. E.

Bellevue Pl. E.

Belmont Pl. E.

Boylston Ave. E.

Harvard Ave. E.

Broadway

10th Ave. E.

Federal Ave. E.

Volunteer Park Rd.

Volunteer Pkwy.

11th Ave. E.

12th Ave. E.

13th Ave. E.

14th Ave. E.

Malden Ave. E.

15th Ave. E.

Bellevue Ave. E.

Summit Ave. E.

Nagle Pl.

Harvard Ave. E.

1 Volunteer Park
2 Harvard-Belmont Landmark District
3 Consignment Apparel Shops
4 Espresso Vivace
5 Dance Footsteps
6 Elliott Bay Book Company
7 Charlie's Bar & Grill
8 Frye Art Museum

Remnants of the grunge era live on in this eclectic neighborhood, which is also the center of gay life in Seattle. In addition to jet-black attire and gratuitous piercings, expect to see the occasional neon-blue Mohawk, cross-dressing shoppers, and panhandlers who may at times be a bit unsteady on their feet. The housing is also diverse, with seedy apartments sharing blocks with spectacular mansions. Likewise, the shops along Broadway range from retro-consignment to ultra-trendy fashion. It's safe to bring young children here, but there's not much of interest for them, except for Volunteer Park—far removed from the Broadway street scene.

START: **Bus 10 to Volunteer Park.**

❶ ★★ kids Volunteer Park. Flush with Gold Rush money, Seattle hired the Olmsted family (of New York City's Central Park fame) in 1903 to design an elaborate series of parks, including this one. There's lots of room to run and many trails to explore in this urban oasis. If you climb the 106 indoor steps to the top of the Water Tower at the south end of the park, you'll be rewarded with one of the best views in town. But if you're out of breath by the time you climb the two flights to the entrance, don't even bother! Just west of the tower is the **Seattle Asian Art Museum** (p 29). Farther west is the Volunteer Park Conservatory, bursting with colorful exotic plants, including a large orchid collection. You'd

An exotic bloom at Volunteer Park Conservatory.

hardly be surprised if a parrot landed on your shoulder. ⏱ *1 hr. 1400 E. Galer St.* ☎ *206/684-4743. www.seattle.gov/parks. Free*

The greenhouse at Volunteer Park.

admission. Conservatory Tues–Sun 10am–4pm.

② Harvard-Belmont Landmark District. Seattle has more than its share of millionaires—both dotcom and otherwise—and quite a few live in this tree-shaded neighborhood, ensconced in graceful, sprawling mansions built in the early 20th century. The best walk is along the northern end of Broadway, between East Highland and East Roy. You can also drive, but walking affords better peeking through the hedges. ⏱ *30 min. Bounded roughly by Harvard Ave., Broadway, Bellevue Place & Boylston.*

③ Consignment Apparel Shops. With two colleges nearby (Seattle University and Seattle Central Community College), previously worn—and retro—clothing is highly sought after. There aren't as many vintage apparel shops as there once were along Broadway, but the ones that remain are excellent. **Crossroads Trading Co.** (325 Broadway Ave. E.; ☎ 206/328-5867) focuses on contemporary styles. Some items are new, but the only way to tell is by their blue tags. This is not the cheapest consignment shop in town, but the

Pick up some funky footwear at Metro Clothing in Capitol Hill.

Take a moment to add a little dance to your day.

merchandise is top-flight. There's also a men's section. At **Metro Clothing Co.** (231 Broadway Ave. E.; ☎ 206/726-7978) only the hip—or wannabes—need enter this delightfully eccentric shop. ⏱ *1 hr. Broadway Ave. E.*

④ ★★ Espresso Vivace. This is a no-frills stand, but the coffee drinks are sublime, right down to the Rosetta pattern the barista "draws" in the foam. Sidewalk seating is available. My favorite: the rich, creamy caffe caramel. *321 Broadway Ave. E. $*

⑤ Dance Footsteps. One of the most unusual displays of public art you'll find is embedded in the sidewalks along Broadway. Dancers' Series: Steps consists of bronze shoeprints of dancers performing various steps. There are eight sets along the avenue, from the tango to the foxtrot, and a couple of steps that artist Jack Mackie made up just for fun. Go ahead and try them out! No need to feel self-conscious: It takes a lot to turn heads

Bigfoot

The most popular legend in the Northwest, without a doubt, is that of Sasquatch, more fondly dubbed Bigfoot. Believers swear that Sasquatches roam the forests and mountains of the Pacific Northwest. Reports of an enormous hairy beast in the region have been circulating since the early 1800s. Some, but not all, of the stories have been proven fraudulent. In 1969, a man in northern Washington reported finding Sasquatch footprints in a ghost town called Bossburg. Bigfoot hunters rushed to the scene and found additional tracks nearby—more than 1,000 in all. One of them was measured at more than 17 inches long. At least one British anthropologist was impressed with the find. Sasquatch-spotters often report an awful, skunklike smell just before they see the beast or its tracks. But with no scientifically confirmed hard proof, the mystery—and perhaps the ape-man—lives on.

on Capitol Hill. ⏱ *15 min. Along Broadway.*

6 **Charlie's Bar & Grill.** This cozy spot has been serving up comfort food for about as long as Microsoft has been around. Even a hefty hunger will be tamed by the Monte Cristo sandwich, but if you're in the mood for something lighter, Charlie's is famous for its pepper pot soup. *217 Broadway E.* ☎ *206/323-2535. broadwaycharlies. com. $*

7 ★★★ kids **Elliott Bay Book Company.** Seattleites love their books, and this is the city's favorite bookstore. In its new location—a 20,000-square-foot historic 1917 building on quirky Capitol Hill—Elliott Bay still feels like Seattle's comfy living room. Peruse the shelves at your leisure in this old Ford truck service center with its fir floors and massive ceiling beams.

Your challenge: not to bring home more than you can fit in your carry-on! ⏱ *30 min. 1521 10th Ave.* ☎ *206/624-6600. www.elliottbay book.com. Mon–Thurs 10am–10pm; Fri–Sat 10am–11pm; Sun 11am–9pm.*

8 ★★ **Frye Art Museum.** A gift to the city by a prominent pioneer family that earned a fortune in the meat-packing business and used their money to buy modern art of the late-19th and early-20th centuries, the Frye is a lovely surprise of a museum. In addition to the Frye family's impressive personal art collection, which still hangs in the house they lived in, you'll see new acquisitions and intriguing installations of contemporary art. It's located on First Hill, a few minutes' walk from Capitol Hill, but well worth the brief detour to see the collection and enjoy the old Seattle neighborhood around it. ⏱ *1 hr. 704 Terry Ave. See p. 28,* **5**.

Chinatown/International District

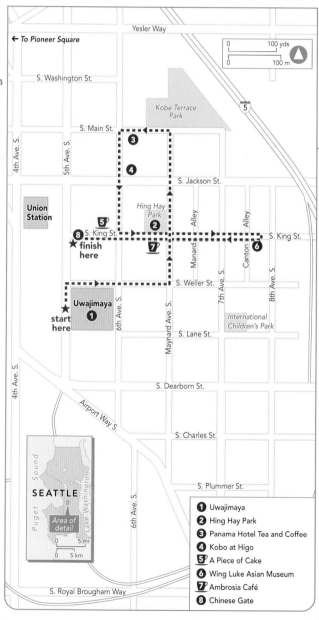

Yesler Way

← To Pioneer Square

S. Washington St.

S. Main St.

Kobe Terrace Park

5

4th Ave. S.

5th Ave. S.

S. Jackson St.

3

4

Union Station

Hing Hay Park

5

S. King St.

8 S. King St.

★ finish here

7

2

Manard

Alley

Canton

Alley

S. King St.

6

S. Weller St.

7th Ave. S.

8th Ave. S.

6th Ave. S.

Maynard Ave. S.

start here

★

Uwajimaya

1

International Children's Park

S. Lane St.

4th Ave. S.

S. Dearborn St.

Airport Way S

S. Charles St.

6th Ave. S.

S. Plummer St.

Sound

SEATTLE

Puget

Lake Washington

Area of detail

0   5 mi

0   5 km

S. Royal Brougham Way

1 Uwajimaya
2 Hing Hay Park
3 Panama Hotel Tea and Coffee
4 Kobo at Higo
5 A Piece of Cake
6 Wing Luke Asian Museum
7 Ambrosia Café
8 Chinese Gate

0   100 yds
0   100 m

Although not as large as San Francisco's Chinatown, this Asian neighborhood is lively—and about as diverse as they come, with a flood of Southeast Asian immigrants joining the mix in recent years. Its name has morphed from Chinatown to International District to the current compromise. When I feel like globe-trotting but can't spare the time, I'll spend an afternoon here, strolling past shops with whole barbecued ducks hanging in the window, riotously colorful vegetable markets spilling out into the streets, window displays of exotic herbs and medicines, and pastry shops hawking some of the tastiest wares in town. It's all about the smells, the colors, and the single-minded shoppers tracking down bargains. START: **Bus 3 or 4 to 5th Avenue & James Street.**

❶ ★★ **kids** **Uwajimaya.** Yes, it's a grocery store, but this is also a bona fide tourist destination. Built by a Japanese patriarch whose family was interned during World War II, this enormous supermarket—now run by his children—is stocked with exotic Asian produce, meats, baked goods, and other products. You can check its website for recipes from eight Asian countries, then do some shopping! There is also an Asian bookstore, gift shop, and a large dine-in area that gives an entirely new meaning to the term "food court." It's easy to lose track of time in here. ⏱ *1 hr.* 600

5th Ave. S. ☎ *206/624-6248. www.uwajimaya.com. Mon–Sat 8am–10pm, Sun 9am–9pm.*

❷ **kids** **Hing Hay Park.** This small but unusual park is situated on a red-bricked square. The colorful pagoda, crafted in Taipei, Taiwan, is the genuine article, as is the spectacular dragon artwork. If you have time, settle in at one of the chess tables for a leisurely game. The city is in the process of doubling the size of the park, a popular gathering spot that often hosts the Lunar New Year Lion Dances in February. ⏱ *15 min. 423 Maynard Ave. S. (King St. & Maynard).*

Hing Hay Park reflects the influence of Chinese culture on the neighborhood.

At the Panama Hotel, trunks left behind by Japanese families sent to internment camps are a reminder of a painful past.

❸ ★ Historic Panama Hotel Bed & Breakfast Tea & Coffee House.

You can sip Italian Lavazza coffee or choose from a global tea menu at this elegant shop in the historic Panama Hotel, which housed Japanese workingmen in the early 20th century. When owner Jan Johnson bought the hotel, she discovered trunks full of personal items left behind and never reclaimed by Japanese families sent off to internment camps. You can view one of these trunks through a glass window in the tea shop's wooden floor. Many other items are on display as a history lesson and a reminder of a regrettable moment in time. ① *30 min. 607 S. Main St.* ☎ *206/515-4000. www. panamahotelseattle.com.*

❹ ★ Kobo at Higo.

History stands still at this shop, housed in the former Higo Variety Store, a Japanese five-and-dime that stood in this spot for 75 years. The Murakami family had to board it up while they were sent to an internment camp, but reopened when they returned. Sadly, Mr. Murakami died very shortly afterward, but his widow and children kept the shop going until 2003, when the youngest daughter retired. Happily, the new owners, John Bisbee and Binko Chiong-Bisbee, have preserved much of the past, including pre-war merchandise and family mementos. Be sure to check out the display wall devoted to the old Higo. But the new shop, a Japanese and Northwest fine-art and craft gallery, features stylish new treasures. ① *30 min. 604 S. Jackson St.* ☎ *206/381-3000. www.koboseattle.com. Mon–Sat 11am–6pm, Sun noon–5pm.*

❺ ★★ A Piece of Cake.

This is my favorite bakery in Seattle. The cakes are feather-light, the frosting flavorful but not too sweet, and the fillings creative. My favorite, in season, is the melon ball–filled cake. Yum! The cakes here are works of art, perfect for a very special occasion. Other times, I order a cup of tea and a pineapple bun. ① *30 min. 514 S. King St.* ☎ *206/623-8284. $*

❻ ★★ kids Wing Luke Asian Museum.

This Smithsonian Institution–affiliated museum, one of the best of its kind in the nation, is a great community resource in the midst of a diverse neighborhood. Its library, which is open to the public during museum hours, includes a wealth

The desserts at A Piece of Cake taste as good as they look.

Kobo at Higo is more than a shop—it offers a glimpse into the area's past.

of oral and video histories, photos, and books about the experiences of Asian-Pacific Americans in the Northwest. ⏱ *1 hr. 719 S. King St. (S. King St. & 8th Ave. S.) .* ☎ *206/623-5124. www.wingluke. org. $13 adults, $9.95 seniors & students, $8.95 ages 5–12. Price includes tour of historic building/former hotel. Tues–Sun 10am–5pm, 1st Thurs of month & 2nd Sat of month 10am–8pm. See p 23.*

7 Ambrosia Cafe. This was the first shop in the International District to specialize in pearl tea, a craze that started in Taiwan. Now available all over town—more often called "bubble tea"—the icy drink consists of brewed tea mixed with sweetened milk and syrups, poured into a tall cup filled with gumball-size tapioca balls. You drink it through a straw wide enough to suck up the "bubbles." It's an odd sensation the first time or two, but then you get hooked. Try the mango and green tea flavors. *619 S. King St.* ☎ *206/623-9028. $*

8 Chinese Gate. After a half-century of grassroots efforts, Seattle's Chinatown has its own traditional entrance gate, just like other major cities with large Chinese populations, such as San Francisco and Los Angeles. The eye-catching, 45-foot archway was unveiled in 2008. The $500,000 gate, according to tradition, should bring luck and strength. It also greets visitors and makes it easier to spot the district. There are hopes of building a second gate on the other end of the neighborhood. *S. King St., just east of 5th Ave. S.*

Bathhouse Tour

When early Japanese immigrants came to the United States, they built hundreds of community bathhouses, just like they had at home. The bathhouses, or *sentos*, were culturally important places to socialize, relax in the hot waters, and clean off after a hard day's work. Only one remains intact in its original location—the marble bath in the basement of the **Historic Panama Hotel Bed & Breakfast** (see above). The bath officially closed in 1950, but is still open for historic tours. To schedule one, call the **Panama Hotel** at ☎ 206/223-9242.

Wallingford

7th Ave. NE

finish here

4th Ave. NE

Latona Ave. NE

Thackery Pl. NE

2nd Ave. NE

1st Ave. NE

1st Ave. NE

Eastern Ave. N.

Sunnyside Ave. N.

Corliss Ave. N.

Bagley Ave. N.

Meridian Ave. N.

Burke Ave. N.

Wallingford Ave. N.

Wallingford Playfield

Densmore Ave. N.

Woodlawn Ave. N.

Ashworth Ave. N.

Interlake Ave. N.

Interlake Ave. N.

Stone Way N.

Midvale Ave. N.

start here

N. 45th St.

N. 46th St.

N. 45th St.

N. 44th St.

N. 43rd St.

N. 42nd St.

N. 41st St.

N. 40th St.

NE 45th St.

NE 43rd St.

NE 42nd St.

NE 40th St.

NE Pacific St.

Area of detail

SEATTLE

Puget Sound

Lake Washington

5 mi

5 km

200 yds

200 m

1 Archie McPhee
2 Alphabet Soup
3 Molly Moon's Ice Cream
4 Bottleworks
5 Fuel Coffee
6 Bad Woman Yarn
7 The Sock Monster
8 Wallingford Playfield
9 Guild 45th
10 The Erotic Bakery
11 Irwin's Neighborhood Bakery and Café
12 Wine World & Spirits

One of Seattle's most charming residential neighborhoods, Wallingford is lined with trees, sidewalks and lovingly restored Craftsman bungalows. Some of the city's finest ethnic restaurants—and a few of its most eclectic shops—can be found in Wallingford's lively business district. There are parks galore for the kids to romp in, and a great little 1920s-era art deco movie house—it's an ideal spot to catch a blockbuster or, especially, an Indie film. If you're here in early July, check the neighborhood website (www.wallingford.org) for the date of the annual Seafair Kiddies Parade & Fair. It's a day full of pirates, clowns and general merrymaking for all ages. START: Bus 16 or 44 to Stone Way North & N. 45th Street.

❶ ★★ kids Archie McPhee.
From rubber chickens to avenging narwhals to underpants for your hands—if it's weird, wacky, and fun, you'll find it. For a quarter-century, Seattleites have flocked to Archie McPhee for sensory overload—or just a giggle. And yes, there really was an Archie McPhee, a fun-loving guy. ⏱ 30 min. 1300 N. 45th St. ☎ 206/297-0240. www.archie mcpheeseattle.com. Mon–Sat 10am–7pm, Sun 11am–6pm.

❷ ★ kids Alphabet Soup. This
is a magical place for kids, well-stocked with new, used, and

If it's wacky, you'll find it at Archie McPhee.

vintage children's books—and even a small used section for Mom and Dad. The picture books are wonderful, and the prices are low enough that you'll leave with an armful. ⏱ 15 min. 1406 N. 45th St. ☎ 206/547-4555. Wed–Fri 11am–8pm, Sat 10am–8pm, Sun noon–6pm.

❸ ★★ kids Molly Moon's Ice Cream.
Sure, you can find an ice cream shop just about anywhere. But you can only find Molly Moon's in two locations on the planet, and this is one of them. The ingredients are locally made, but the flavors are celestial. Try the maple bacon, blood orange sorbet, or balsamic strawberry. Of course, you could order vanilla, but why? ⏱ 15 min. 1622 N. 45th St. ☎ 206/547-5105. Daily noon–11pm.

❹ Bottleworks.
With 16 beers on tap and hundreds of bottled varieties from around the world, this neighborhood bottle shop, the oldest in Seattle, is a destination for beer-lovers from all over. ⏱ 15 min. 1710 N. 45th St. ☎ 206/632-1057. www.bottleworks.com. Sun–Wed 11am–8pm, Thurs 11am–9pm, Fri–Sat 11am–11pm.

❺ Fuel Coffee.
Friendly baristas and comfy chairs make this a great spot for refueling. You might need the caffeine to keep you moving

Try the maple bacon at Molly Moon's Ice Cream, where the ingredients are local and the flavors are out of this world.

post–Molly Moon's. And if you need to catch up on email, you'll find lighted tables in the back, and free Wi-Fi. ⏱ *15 min. 1705 N. 45th S.* ☎ *206/634-2700.* $

⑥ Bad Woman Yarn. Tucked into the Wallingford Center—a historic schoolhouse-turned-shopping-destination—is this gem of a shop, overflowing with colorful, fluffy balls and a staff that will help you find the right yarn to bring a perfect pattern to life. If you have an open afternoon or evening, join the locals for a free knitting group or sign up for a class ($17 and up). Check the schedule on the website. ⏱ *15 min. 1815 N. 45th St.* ☎ *206/547-5384. www.badwoman yarn.com. Mon–Fri 10am–8pm, Sat 10am–6pm, Sun 11am–5pm.*

⑦ ★ The Sock Monster. Tootsie fashion for everyone (women, men, kids), in every conceivable color, pattern, and style, is what this playful neighborhood sock shop offers. The selection is staggering. ⏱ *15 min. 1909 N. 45th St.* ☎ *206/724-0123. www.thesock monster.com. Mon–Fri 11am–7pm, Sat 11am–8pm, Sun noon–6pm.*

⑧ kids Wallingford Playfield. After a morning of shopping, the kids will be ready to burn off some energy, and Wallingford Playfield is the perfect spot. Here you'll find lots of equipment for climbing, a water play area for splashing—and a huge grassy area. ⏱ *30 min. 4219 Wallingford Ave. N.* ☎ *206/684-4075. www.seattle.gov/parks. Daily 4am–11:30pm.*

⑨ Guild 45th. This art deco–style theater has screens in two separate buildings. The first one opened in 1919; the second in the 1980s. The Guild specializes in screening edgy and foreign films. *2115 N. 45th St.* ☎ *206/781-5755. www.landmark theatres.com/Market/Seattle/ Guild45thTheatre.htm.*

⑩ The Erotic Bakery. Oh, my! These baked goods—cookies and cakes with suggestive decorations—are for adults only. They're in demand for bachelor and bachelorette parties, and the staff is happy to ship for you. ⏱ *15 min. 2323 N. 45th St.* ☎ *206/545-6969. www.theeroticbakery.com. Mon–Sat 10am–7pm.*

Gasworks Park

Seattle's favorite place to go fly a kite, this former gas-manufac-turing-plant-turned-park also boasts one of the most spectacular views in town. If you don't happen to have a kite, stop at the **Gasworks Park Kite Shop** (3420 Stone Way; ☎ 206/633-4780; www.gasworksparkkiteshop.com), where you'll find an assortment ranging from box to stunt kites to windsocks. Take along a blanket and throw a picnic at the top of the hill, overlooking Lake Union, the Space Needle and—on a clear day—Mount Rainier. It doesn't get better than this. Years ago, the city—making lemonade out of the proverbial lemon—turned the abandoned boiler house into a picnic shelter and the old compressor building into a play area where kids can explore the now brightly painted machinery. From the parking lot, you can also access the popular Burke-Gilman Trail, a 12½-mile route following the old path of the Burlington-Northern Railroad. Walkers, joggers, cyclists and skaters share the fresh air.

11 Irwin's Neighborhood Bakery and Cafe. Right about now, a homemade pizza, soup, or chicken pot pie should hit the spot. Real men—and women—will love the quiche Diablo, chock-full of hot peppers. Go ahead, finish up with a slice of pie. *2123 N. 40th St.* ☎ *206/675-1484.* $

12 Wine World & Spirits. The latest addition to Wallingford's shopping menu is this 23,000-square-foot superstore, the largest wine shop in the Northwest. It's packed with gleaming bottles from around the world—including at least 500 wines from Washington State, whose wineries have made a major global splash in recent years. Step up to the elegant tasting bar for daily wine samplings (Mon–Fri 6–8pm, Sat–Sun 2–5pm) from up to

10 wineries. ⏲ *30 min. 400 NE 45th St.* ☎ *206/402-6086. wineworldspirits.com. Mon–Sat 10am–9pm, Sun 11am–7pm.*

Flying a kite at Gasworks Park.

Fremont

1. Fremont Troll
2. Statue of Lenin
3. Royal Grinders
4. Fremont Rocket
5. PCC Natural Markets
6. *Waiting for the Interurban* Statue

The self-proclaimed center of the universe (with a sign to prove it), this funky north-end neighborhood has a quirkiness that several years of gentrification have failed to destroy. Tech firms Adobe Systems and Getty have built their headquarters here, and high-end condos followed. Though some of the cottage-industry art studios have given way to higher-rent tenants, this is still an artsy kind of place. One of my favorite things about Fremont is the eccentric public art scattered about the neighborhood. When I'm not in the mood for the urban pace of shopping downtown, I head for friendly, relaxed Fremont. START: **Under the north end of the Aurora Avenue Bridge, at N. 36th St.**

1 ★★ kids Fremont Troll. If you drive over the Aurora Avenue Bridge, better hope your car doesn't suffer the same fate as the Volkswagen Bug plucked off the road by the nasty-tempered troll lurking below. At least, that's how the story goes. The 18-foot-high troll, which reflects the

neighborhood's Scandinavian roots, is much friendlier if you visit him in person. You can climb on him all you want, and he's okay with family pictures, too. Back in 1989, when the Fremont Arts Council held a nationwide search for a piece of public art to go under the bridge, Fremont residents overwhelming

Yes, that rocket was once property of the U.S. Army.

voted for the troll—and the VW held in his clutches. ⏱ *15 min. N. 36th St., under the Aurora Avenue Bridge, also known as the George Washington Memorial Bridge.*

② ★ **Statue of Lenin.** We're talking Vladimir. The sculpture of the former Russian revolutionary ended up in Fremont on a fluke, and here it has stayed, despite controversy. It was

Stop by and say hi to Vladimir Lenin.

brought back from Slovakia by a Seattle-area bronze artist who was considering selling it for scrap when he met with an untimely death. His family had the statue moved near a brass foundry in Fremont, and no one has figured out what to do with it since. Now it's become a part of this eccentric neighborhood where hardly anything seems out of place. If you're here during a holiday season, expect to see Lenin decked out in appropriate garb. ⏱ *15 min. 36th & Evanston Ave. N.*

③ **Royal Grinders.** Tucked behind Lenin's statue is a great little spot where you can cool off with a tasty gelato. The challenge is choosing from the eclectic menu of flavors—a couple of dozen, ranging from lavender to cappuccino chip. Feeling droopy? Try one "drowned" in espresso. If you're hungry, the freshly made, toasted subs come piled high with veggies and meats. *3526 Fremont Place N.* ☎ *206/545-7560.* $

Commuters everywhere can relate to Waiting for the Interurban.

④ ★ Fremont Rocket. It's an odd twist of fate that the statue of Lenin ended up just down the block from a 55-foot for-real Cold War-era rocket, taken from an Army surplus store, mounted on a building in Fremont and—voila!—turned into art. Stop by in the evening to see the rocket's onboard lights ablaze. ○ *15 min. 35th & Evanston Ave. N.*

⑤ PCC Natural Markets. Fruits and veggies have never been so much fun, and these are bursting with flavor, much of it from local farms. PCC is an organic store with a produce section that's so irresistible, I'll go out of my way to shop here. Kids get free fruit, so be sure to ask. This is a full-service grocery store, and all the cosmetic and fragrance products are cruelty-free. It's technically a co-op, but non-members can shop here, too. I can never pass by the bakery, which features such unusual items as Paris balsamic pear tarts—a personal favorite—and vegan carrot cake. *600 N. 34th.* ☎ *206/632-6811.*

⑥ ★ Waiting for the Interurban. Six passengers and a dog wait endlessly for their train in this cast-aluminum sculpture memorializing the era of the electric rail line. It also memorializes a squabble between the sculptor and Fremont political leader Armen Stepanian: unless you look closely, you might mistake the riders for real people, as they are often dressed seasonally. ○ *15 min. South side of N. 34th St.* ●

Shopping Best Bets

Best Art Jewelry
★★★ Twist, *600 Pine St. (p 92)*

Best Bookstore (New Books)
★★★ Elliott Bay Book Company, *1521 10th Ave. (p 88)*

Best Bookstore (Used)
★★ Twice Sold Tales, *1833 Harvard Ave. (p 88)*

Best Gifts
★★★ Millstream, *112 1st. Ave. S. (p 92)*

Best Glass
★★★ Glasshouse Studio, *311 Occidental Ave. S. (p 93)*

Best Hand-Crafted Wood Furniture
★★ Northwest Fine Woodworking, *101 S. Jackson St. (p 91)*

Best Pirates' Booty
Pirates Plunder Gift Shop, *1301 Alaskan Way, Pier 57 (p 92)*

Best Place to Find an Out-of-Town Newspaper
★ First and Pike News, *93 Pike St. (p 88)*

Best Rugs
★ Palace Rug Gallery, *323 1st Ave. S. (p 96)*

Best Fashion Bargains
★★★ Nordstrom Rack, *400 Pine St. (p 89)*

Best Place to Find a Manly Skirt
★ Utilikilts, *620 1st Ave. (p 90)*

Best Shoes
★★★ Nordstrom, *500 Pine St. (p 89)*

Best Souvenirs
★★ Made in Washington, *400 Pine St. (p 92)*

Best Place to Buy a Gown for the Opera
★★ Mario's, *1513 6th Ave. (p 90)*

Best Toys
★★ Magic Mouse Toys, *603 1st Ave. (p 96)*

Glass as works of art at Glasshouse Studios. Previous page: Scarves and fabrics at Simo Silk.

Downtown Shopping

Barnes & Noble **5**
City Centre **13**
Driscoll Robbins
  Fine Carpets **16**
Easy Street
  Records & CDs **3**
Eddie Bauer **6**
E.E. Robbins **4**

Facèré **13**
Fireworks **8**
Jeffrey Moose
  Gallery **14**
LUSH **8**
Macy's **9**
Mario's **11**
Niketown **12**

Nordstrom **7**
Nordstrom Rack **8**
Pacific Place **6**
Pelindaba Lavender
  Gallery **13**
Pirates Plunder **15**
Seattle Glassblowing
  Studio **2**

See's Candies **10**
Silver Platters **1**
Twist **6**
Watson Kennedy
  Fine Home **17**
Westlake Center **8**
Young Flowers **18**

Pioneer Square Shopping

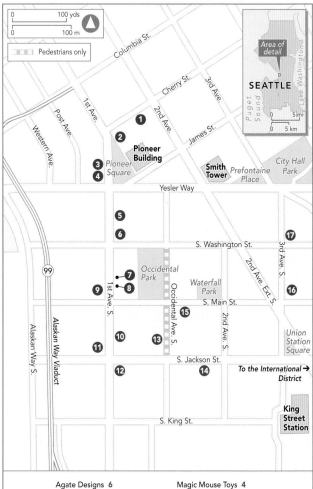

Agate Designs 6

Akanyi African & Tribal Art Gallery 15

The Clog Factory 9

Cutty Sark Nautical Antiques 10

Flanagan & Lane Antiques 14

Foster/White 16

G. Gibson Gallery 17

Glasshouse Studio 13

Globe Bookstore 8

Magic Mouse Toys 4

Millstream 5

Noble Horse Gallery 7

Northwest Fine Woodworking 12

Palace Rug Gallery 11

Ragazzi's Flying Shuttle 3

Seattle Mystery Bookshop 1

Utilikilts 2

Pike Place Market Shopping

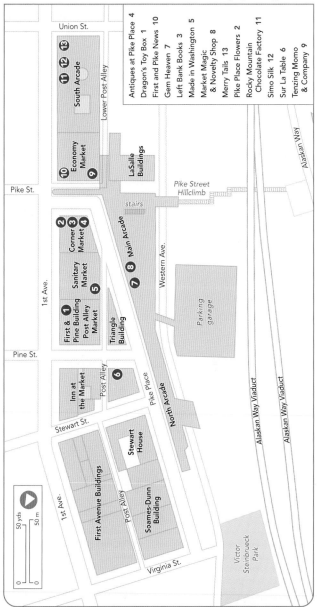

Antiques at Pike Place 4
Dragon's Toy Box 1
First and Pike News 10
Gem Heaven 7
Left Bank Books 3
Made in Washington 5
Market Magic
& Novelty Shop 8
Merry Tails 13
Pike Place Flowers 2
Rocky Mountain
Chocolate Factory 11
Simo Silk 12
Sur La Table 6
Tenzing Momo
& Company 9

Union St.

South Arcade

Lower Post Alley

Economy Market

LaSalle Buildings

Pike St.

Pike Street Hillclimb

stairs

Corner Market

Sanitary Market

Main Arcade

Western Ave.

First & Pine Building

Post Alley Market

Triangle Building

1st Ave.

Pine St.

Inn at the Market

Post Alley

Pike Place

North Arcade

Stewart St.

Stewart House

Parking garage

Alaskan Way

First Avenue Buildings

Post Alley

Soames-Dunn Building

1st Ave.

Virginia St.

Victor Steinbrueck Park

Alaskan Way Viaduct

Alaskan Way Viaduct

50 yds
50 m

Capitol Hill Shopping

Crossroads Trading Co. **3**
Dilettante Mocha Café **2**
Elliott Bay Book Company **9**
Kobo Shop and Gallery **1**
Metro Clothing Co. **5**

Mud Bay Granary **4**
Panache **6**
Trendy Wendy **7**
Twice Sold Tales **8**
Wall of Sound **10**

Seattle **Shopping A to Z**

Antiques

Antiques at Pike Place PIKE PLACE MARKET This is a wonderful shop to poke around in, and you'll likely find something you can't live without, whether it's a Mickey Mantle baseball card, a toy from your past, or a gorgeous estate ring. *92 Stewart St.* ☎ *206/441-9643. www.antiquesatpike place.com. AE, DISC, MC, V. Bus: 10, 99. Map p. 85.*

Cutty Sark Nautical Antiques
PIONEER SQUARE Nautical antiques—from compasses to ship's wheels—are sold here, making it the perfect place to grab gifts for all the old salts on your list. *320 1st Ave. S.* ☎ *206/262-1265. www.cutty antiques.com. AE, DISC, MC, V. Bus: 85, 99. Map p 84.*

Flanagan & Lane Antiques features fine china and glassware, among other items.

★ Flanagan & Lane Antiques PIONEER SQUARE The French furniture is exquisite; so are the Chinese fans and dishes. Don't miss the interesting assortment of antique clocks. *165 S. Jackson St.* ☎ *206/682-0098. www.flanagan-laneantiques.com. AE, DISC, MC, V. Bus: 13, 85, 99. Map p 84.*

Art
Akanyi African & Tribal Art Gallery PIONEER SQUARE African and tribal art are showcased at this unique shop, which features a large collection of musical instruments, masks, and furniture from all over the continent. *155 S Main St.* ☎ *206/381-3133. AE, DISC, MC, V. Bus: 1, 2, 4, 13, 43, 49, 85, 99. Map p 84.*

G. Gibson Gallery PIONEER SQUARE The focus here is on fine art photography, but you'll also find contemporary sculptures and paintings by locally and internationally important artists. *300 S. Washington St.* ☎ *206/587-4033. www.ggibsongallery. com. MC, V. Bus: 1, 2, 4, 13, 43, 49. Map p 84.*

★★ Jeffrey Moose Gallery DOWNTOWN This eclectic shop specializes in indigenous art, including Australian aboriginal works and Native-American masks and carvings. *1333 5th Ave., Ste. 511.* ☎ *206/467-6951. www.jeffrey moosegallery.com. AE, MC, V. Bus: 85, 106, 150, 255, 545, 577. Map p 83.*

Books & Magazines
★★★ Barnes & Noble DOWNTOWN B&N is the largest bookstore

Jeffrey Moose Gallery specializes in indigenous art.

in downtown Seattle, and it remains a great place to browse for new titles and every other title still in print and to attend author signings and events. Another big, browsable B&N is located in Bellevue at 626 106th Ave. NE (☎ 425/451-8463). *600 Pine St.* ☎ *206/264-0156. www. bn.com. AE, DISC, MC, V. Bus: 10, 11, 14. Map p 83.*

★★★ kids **Elliott Bay Book Company** CAPITOL HILL Seattle's premier bookstore is a must for any bibliophile. *1521 10th Ave.* ☎ *206/ 624-6600. www.elliottbaybook.com. AE, DISC, MC, V. Bus: 10, 11, 43, 49, 60, 84. Map p 86.*

★ **First and Pike News** PIKE PLACE MARKET With more than 1,000 magazine titles and over 200 newspapers from around the world, this is Seattle best place to go to read all about it. *93 Pike St.* ☎ *206/ 624-0140. AE, DISC, MC, V. Bus: 10, 99, 113, 121 or 122. Map p 85.*

★ **Globe Bookstore** PIONEER SQUARE Be forewarned: It's easy to spend more time than you planned in this terrific little bookshop, packed with new and used mysteries, history books, children's books, and cookbooks. *218 1st Ave. S.* ☎ *206/682-6882. AE, DISC, MC, V. Bus: 16, 66, 86, 99. Map p 84.*

★ **Left Bank Books** PIKE PLACE MARKET Since 1973, this employee-owned collective has reflected Seattle's labor-movement roots. Its collections include an anarchy section, LGBT literature, short stories, an amazing collection of magazines, and lots of clever, left-leaning T-shirts. *92 Pike St.* ☎ *206/622-0195. www.leftbank books.com. AE, DISC, MC, V. Bus: 10, 99, 113, 121 or 122. Map p. 85.*

★ **Seattle Mystery Bookshop** PIONEER SQUARE Skullduggery reigns supreme here. Word of

Mystery buffs will want to set aside plenty of time for the Seattle Mystery Bookshop.

warning to mystery-lovers: This will not be a quick stop for you. And good luck stumping the well-informed staff. *117 Cherry St.* ☎ *206/587-5737. www.seattle mystery.com. MC, V. Bus: 16, 66, 99, 554, 594. Map p 84.*

★★ **Twice Sold Tales** CAPITOL HILL You'd be hard-pressed to find a deeper inventory of used books. Plan on plenty of time to browse. And if you're a cat-lover, make time to play with the kitties that roam the shop as well. *Locations include 1833 Harvard Ave. (*☎ *206/324-2421) & 4501 University Way NE (*☎ *206/545-4226). www.twicesold tales.info. MC, V. Bus: 8, 43, 49, 60. Map p 86.*

Candy
★★ **Dilettante Mocha Café** CAPITOL HILL Don't pass up the hand-dipped truffles, made with recipes passed down from the owners' great uncle, who prepared them for the Imperial Court of Austria. If you fall in love, you can join

their chocolate club and get treats delivered to your door every month. *Locations include 538 Broadway E.* ☎ *206/329-6463. www.dilettante.com. AE, MC, V. Bus: 49, 60. Map p 86.*

Rocky Mountain Chocolate Factory PIKE PLACE MARKET The colorful rows of apples dipped in rich chocolates and caramel, then rolled in a variety of toppings, are almost irresistible. And once you're inside, you may as well sample a piece of creamy homemade fudge. *1419 1st Ave.* ☎ *206/262-9581. www.rmcf.com. AE, DISC, MC, V. Bus: 10, 99, 113, 121 or 122. Map p 85.*

★★ See's Candies DOWNTOWN See's offers scrumptious gourmet candies at a good value. The company has been in business since 1921, but offers a variety of new tastes alongside its tried-and-true favorites. *Downtown location: 1518 4th Ave.* ☎ *206/682-7122. www.sees.com. AE, DISC, MC, V. Bus: 10, 11, 14, 43, 81. Map p 83.*

Department Stores
★★ Macy's DOWNTOWN High-end clothing, jewelry, housewares, and cosmetics are beautifully displayed in a historic Seattle building. Check out the sales racks. *1601 3rd Ave.* ☎ *206/506-6000. www.macys.com. AE, DISC, MC, V. Bus: 1, 11, 13, 14, 43. Map p 83.*

★★★ Nordstrom DOWNTOWN The shoes! Nordstrom got its start over a century ago as a humble Seattle shoe store and, while it's hardly humble anymore, it's still those fabulous shoes that lure me in. Of course, there's much, much more, and it's high quality, with high price tags to match. Watch for Nordstrom's legendary Half Yearly sales. *500 Pine St.* ☎ *206/628-2111. www.nordstrom.com. AE, DISC, MC, V. Bus: 10, 11, 14, 43, 83. Map p 83.*

Discount/Consignment Shopping
Crossroads Trading Co. CAPITOL HILL Not all the clothes here are used, but the only way to tell is by the tags, because everything looks new and hip. This is not the cheapest consignment shop, but you'll find great stuff here, especially since its new expansion doubled the fun. *325 Broadway Ave. E.* ☎ *206/328-5847. www.crossroadstrading.com. DISC, MC, V. Bus: 8, 43, 49, 60. Map p 86.*

★★★ Nordstrom Rack DOWNTOWN You'll have to do some hunting, but that's part of the fun. Among the racks of marked-down designer

Stock up on fabulous fashions at Trendy Wendy (p 90).

clothes, housewares, and—yes!—shoes, quite a few treasures are usually waiting to be discovered. *400 Pine St.* ☎ *206/448-8522. www.nordstrom.com. AE, DISC, MC, V. Bus: 10, 11, 14, 99, 554. Map p 83.*

Fashion

Eddie Bauer DOWNTOWN This Northwest-based company specializes, fittingly, in sportswear and outdoor gear. You can also find business casual attire and bedding. *600 Pine St., Ste. 230.* ☎ *206/622-2766. www.eddiebauer.com. AE, DISC, MC, V. Bus: 10, 11, 14, 43, 49. Map p 83.*

★★ Mario's DOWNTOWN For that perfect evening gown, if money is no object, you're sure to find a jaw-dropper here. The men's clothing is also exceptional. Everything is beautifully tailored, and the service equally impeccable. *1513 6th Ave.* ☎ *206/223-1461. www.marios.com. AE, DISC, MC, V. Bus: 10, 11, 14, 43, 49. Map p 83.*

The Metro Clothing Co. CAPITOL HILL This shop is for the painfully hip only (except at Halloween!), or just the curious. If you're looking for leather and lace, or thigh-high red boots, this is your destination. *231 Broadway E.* ☎ *206/726-7978. MC, V. Bus: 8, 9, 43, 49, 60. Map p 86.*

Panache CAPITOL HILL The name fits this quirky little shop perfectly. The clothing here is trendy but elegant, and there are plenty of options for accessorizing. They have misses' and junior sizes, plus a separate men's section. *225 Broadway E.* ☎ *206/726-3300. MC, V. Bus: 9, 49, 60. Map p 86.*

★ Ragazzi's Flying Shuttle PIONEER SQUARE The art is wearable at this shop, which offers hand-woven apparel and accessories, and a fun collection of original

Artisan woodworkers craft stunning furniture at Northwest Fine Woodworking.

contemporary jewelry. *607 1st Ave.* ☎ *206/343-9762. www.ragazzisflyingshuttle.com. AE, MC, V. Bus: 10, 11, 16, 66, 99. Map p 84.*

★ Simo Silk PIKE PLACE MARKET Named for the owner's sons, Simeon and Moses, this shop offers a large selection of buttery soft, mostly washable, silk shirts, scarves, jackets, and bedding from Asia. There's a second location in Pioneer Square. *1411 1st Ave., #108.* ☎ *206/521-8816. www.simosilk.com. AE, DISC, MC, V. Bus: 10, 99, 113, 121 or 122. Map p 85.*

Trendy Wendy CAPITOL HILL You'll get the red-carpet welcome here, literally. Very hip clothes and accessories. And there's even a plus-size section. *211 Broadway E.* ☎ *206/322-6642. AE, DISC, MC, V. Bus: 8, 9, 43, 49, 60. Map p 86.*

★ Utilikilts PIONEER SQUARE If the slogan "Free Your Balls and Free Yourself" appeals, you'll want to check out these liberating kilts for men. There are eight basic styles, all handmade; custom orders cost extra. *620 1st Ave.* ☎ *206/282-4226. www.utilikilts.com. AE, DISC, MC, V. Bus: 10, 11, 16, 66, 99. Map p 84.*

Flowers

★ **Pike Place Flowers** PIKE PLACE MARKET This charming little corner shop, near the entrance to Pike Place Market, has been the focus of many photos of the Market. The arrangements are unique. *1501 1st Ave.* ☎ *206/682-9797. www.pikeplaceflowers.com. AE, DISC, MC, V. Bus: 10, 99, 113, 121 or 122. Map p 85.*

★ **Young Flowers** DOWNTOWN If you're looking for something sophisticated and different, you can't do better than this little shop, small in size but very big in creativity. *1111 3rd Ave.* ☎ *206/628-3077. AE, MC, V. Bus: 11, 15, 18, 121, 122. Map p. 83.*

Furniture

★ **Northwest Fine Woodworking** PIONEER SQUARE The one-of-a-kind furniture and decor items you'll find at this 30-year-old cooperative are crafted by artisan woodworkers. They feature stunning blends of woods. The price tags are high, but the quality is superb. *101 S. Jackson.* ☎ *206/625-0542. www.nwfinewoodworking.com. AE, DISC, MC, V. Bus: 10, 11, 85, 99. Map p 84.*

Gems

★ **kids Agate Designs** PIONEER SQUARE A 300-pound amethyst geode might be a bit large for your house, but a pair of bookends or a small fountain might be just right. The items sold here are made from dazzling gems, minerals, and fossils. There's something for every budget, and the owner is happy to share his wealth of knowledge. *120 1st Ave S.* ☎ *206/621-3063. www.agatedesigns.com. AE, DISC, MC, V. Map p 84.*

kids Gem Heaven PIKE PLACE MARKET You'll feast your eyes on gorgeous gemstones, crystals, minerals, and jewelry at this great little shop "Down Under" in the Market. *1501 Pike Place #408.* ☎ *206/381-9302. www.gemheaven.net. AE, MC, V. Bus: 10, 99, 113, 121 or 122. Map p 85.*

Gifts

★★★ **kids Fireworks** DOWNTOWN There are two themes at Fireworks: whimsy and inspiration, and often a combination of the two. Check out the revolving shadow lanterns, handmade by Northwest artists. *400 Pine St.* ☎ *206/-682-6462. www.fireworksgallery.net. AE, DISC, MC, V. Bus: 10, 14, 41, 71, 72. Map p 83.*

Rock collectors rejoice! Even noncollectors will enjoy checking out Agate Designs' cool offerings.

Fireworks offers one-stop shopping for all of those items you don't really need but really, really want.

★ **Kobo Capitol Hill** CAPITOL HILL Beautiful and sophisticated Northwest and Asian products are the focus here: pottery, teas, unusual gifts, and travel items. *814 E. Roy St.* ☎ *206/726-0704. www.koboseattle.com. MC, V. Bus: 9, 49. Map p 86.*

★★ **Made in Washington** PIKE PLACE MARKET This is no tacky souvenir shop. Take something home to your friends from Made in Washington and it's guaranteed not to end up at their garage sale. *1530 Post Alley.* ☎ *206/467-0788. Downtown location: 400 Pine St.* ☎ *206/623-9753. www.madeinwashington.com. AE, DISC, MC, V. Bus: 10, 99, 113, 121 or 122. Map p 85.*

★ **Merry Tails** PIKE PLACE MARKET This is a great place to find a souvenir for Fido, or for any pet lover on your list. You'll find lots of breed-specific items and unusual gifts. *1409 1st Ave.* ☎ *206/623-4142. AE, DISC, MC, V. Bus: 12, 99, 125. Map p. 85.*

★★★ **Millstream** PIONEER SQUARE I always feel like I'm stepping into a mountain cabin when I enter this woodsy-themed shop. Inside you'll find the talents of many serious Pacific Northwest artists—jewelry crafted from British Columbia jade and wood carvings. Millstream is back in its original location after spending a decade at Westlake Center. *112 1st. Ave. S.* ☎ *206/233-9719. www.millstreamseattle.com. AE, DISC, MC, V. Bus: 10, 11, 16, 66, 99. Map p 84.*

★ **Noble Horse Gallery** PIONEER SQUARE True to its name, this unusual shop is filled with every horse item imaginable—and quite a few you'd never think of. You can buy equestrian-themed art, clothes, books and home decor, including horse-shaped shower hooks. And yes, you can buy a saddle here. *216 1st Ave. S.* ☎ *206/382-8566. www.noblehorsegallery.com. AE, DISC, MC, V. Bus: 10, 11, 16, 66, 99. Map p 84.*

kids **Pirates Plunder** WATERFRONT Here's where to go for everything pirate! Seriously, this shop specializes in pirate-related booty ranging from T-shirts to artwork. *1301 Alaskan Way.* ☎ *206/624-5673. www.piratesplunder.com. AE, DISC, MC, V. Bus: 10, 11, 12, 99, 113. Map p 83.*

★★★ **Twist** DOWNTOWN This exuberant Northwest store, located in Pacific Place shopping mall, features whimsical hand-carved

Millstream showcases the work of local talent.

Ahoy matey! A wooden pirate keeps an eye on Pirates Plunder.

furniture, avant-garde art jewelry, and beautiful glassware. *600 Pine St., Ste. 130.* ☎ *206/315-8080. www. twistonline.com. AE, DISC, MC, V. Bus: 10, 11, 14, 43, 49. Map p 83.*

Glass
★★★ Foster/White PIONEER SQUARE This gallery, housed in a century-old building, is more than glass; you'll also find contemporary paintings and sculptures by premier artists. But its claim to fame is representing world-famous glass artist Dale Chihuly. Check the website for upcoming exhibitions. *220 3rd Ave. S.* ☎ *206/622-2833. www.foster white.com. AE, MC, V. Bus: 1, 2, 13, 14. Map p 84.*

★★★ kids Glasshouse Studio PIONEER SQUARE In addition to being a working artists' studio, Glasshouse sells the wares of many local glass artists. The colors are exuberant, and you can buy everything from a simple vase to a huge chandelier shaped like an explosion of peppers. *311 Occidental Ave. S.* ☎ *206/682-9939. www.glasshouse-studio.com. AE, DISC, MC, V. Bus: 10, 85, 99. Map p 84.*

★★★ kids Seattle Glassblow-ing Studio DOWNTOWN The studio offers classes in glassblowing, and the gallery features elegant and fanciful work by a variety of artists. Be sure to check out the unique glass-art sinks. The studio is open to the public, so you can watch the artists at work. *2227 5th Ave.* ☎ *206/448-2181. www.seattle glassblowing.com. AE, DISC, MC, V. Bus: 56, 82, 202. Map p 83.*

Housewares
★ Sur La Table PIKE PLACE MARKET Everything at this store inspires even a mediocre cook like myself to go home and put on an apron. Better yet, pick one from the beautiful selection of kitchen and dining linens. My favorite section is the exotic oils and spices. *84 Pine St.* ☎ *206/448-2244. www.surla table.com. AE, DISC, MC, V. Bus: 99, 113, 121, 122. Map p 85.*

★ Watson Kennedy Fine Home DOWNTOWN You'll feel like you're shopping along the Left

One of the unique displays at Twist.

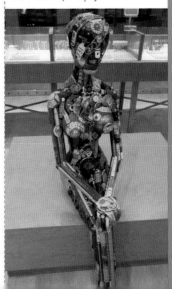

Bank in this charmingly eclectic store, stocked with French teas and soaps, antiques, housewares, and bath products. I once bought a decorative map of the Paris metro here. *1022 1st Ave.* ☎ *206/652-8350. www.watsonkennedy.com. AE, MC, V. Bus: 12, 16, 66, 99. Map p 83.*

Jewelry

★ **E.E. Robbins** DOWNTOWN Seattle's a romantic place, and if you to decide to pop the question while you're here, head to E.E. Robbins, where the owner is a third-generation diamond expert. The staff is friendly, never pushy, and they'll offer you a glass of wine while you shop. *2200 1st Ave.* ☎ *206/826-7464. www.eerobbins.com. AE, DISC, MC, V. Bus: 81, 99. Map p 83.*

★ **Facèré** DOWNTOWN This small store at City Centre is chock full of stylish, unique art jewelry by Northwest, national and international artists. You'll also find just the right antique or vintage piece to make your party dress sparkle. *1420 5th Ave. #108.* ☎ *206/624-6768. www.facerejewelryart.com. AE, MC, V. Bus: 306, 312, 522. Map p 83.*

Malls

City Centre DOWNTOWN Despite a limited number of stores, City Centre features some interesting clothing, leather goods, and jewelry shops; several excellent fast-food restaurants, and Palomino, a beautiful sit-down restaurant that happens to be among my favorite lunch spots. *1420 5th Ave.* ☎ *206/624-8800. Store hours vary. Most open at 10am Mon–Sat & noon Sun; & closed daily btw. 5 & 9pm (Palomino stays open later). Bus: 306, 312, 522. Map p. 83.*

★ **Pacific Place** DOWNTOWN This elegant upscale mall is a great place for shopping, if your budget allows, but I also love just browsing its many unusual and artsy shops. *6th Ave. & Pine St.* ☎ *206/405-2655. www.pacificplaceseattle.com. Bus: 10, 11, 14, 43, 49. Map p 83.*

★★ **Westlake Center** DOWNTOWN This is usually where I go when I actually want to buy something at a mall. You'll find lots of clothing and gift stores, with merchandise in just every price range. *400 Pine St.* ☎ *206/467-1600. www.westlakecenter.com. Link Light Rail Westlake Station or Bus: 41, 71, 72, 301, 316. Map p 83.*

Markets

★★★ **Ballard Sunday Market** BALLARD This year-round Sunday farmer's market in the picturesque heart of the old Ballard neighborhood sells organic produce, cheeses, meats, fish, baked goods, wine, and crafts. There are ethnic food stalls, and many of Ballard's most delightful shops are open as well. *Ballard Ave. NW, btw. NW 20th & 22nd Ave. www.ballardfarmersmarket.wordpress.com.*

Music/CDs

★★ **Easy Street Records and CDs** QUEEN ANNE This roomy store is a music-lover's nirvana, offering a vast inventory of CDs and vinyl, and even in-store concerts. Private listening stations are scattered throughout the store. *20 Mercer St.* ☎ *206/691-3279. www.easystreetonline.com. AE, DISC, MC, V. Bus: 1, 8, 13, 15, 18. Map p 83.*

★★ **Silver Platters** QUEEN ANNE Odds are you'll be able to find that obscure CD at this spacious independent music shop, whether you're into punk or jazz. The staff is very knowledgeable. They also have a great movie selection on DVD. Check online for in-store performances and signings. *701 5th Ave. N.* ☎ *206/283-3472.*

If you don't have time to visit the San Juan Islands, at least stock up on the area's finest lavender at Pelindaba Lavender Gallery.

www.silverplatters.com. MC, V. Bus: 3, 16, 82. Map p 83.

★★ **Wall of Sound** CAPITOL HILL This eclectic shop specializes in international, avant-garde, electronic, and experimental music, and you'll also find a great selection of mainstream CDs. Check the website for visiting artists and indie movie screenings. *315 E. Pine St.* ☎ *206/441-9880. www.wosound. com. AE, DISC, MC, V. Bus: 10, 11, 14, 43, 49. Map p 86.*

Perfume/Skincare/Herbal Products
LUSH DOWNTOWN Who would have thought soap could be so much fun? You can suds yourself in just about any scent your heart desires. If you like, pick a sparkly bar, with glitter that lasts as long as the soap. *400 Pine St., Ste. 100.* ☎ *206/624-5874. www.lush.com. AE, DISC, MC, V. Link Light Rail Westlake Station or Bus: 41, 71, 72, 301, 316. Map p 83.*

Pelindaba Lavender Gallery DOWNTOWN The home decor, personal care and culinary items in this beautiful little shop are made from flowers grown on the organic Pelindaba Lavender farm on San Juan Island, northwest of Seattle.

400 Pine St. ☎ *206/624-3236. www. pelindabalavender.com. AE, DISC, MC, V. Link Light Rail Westlake Station or Bus: 41, 71, 72, 301, 316. Map p 83.*

Tenzing Momo & Company PIKE PLACE MARKET This little shop will meet all your New Age needs: aromatherapy oils and books, incense, herbs, and tarot cards. *93 Pike St., Ste. 203.* ☎ *206/ 623-9837. www.tenzingmomo.com. AE, DISC, MC, V. Bus: 10, 99, 113, 121 or 122. Map p 85.*

Pets
Mud Bay Granary CAPITOL HILL The pet food is natural and healthy, and you'll find every accessory a wellheeled doggy—or feline—could dream of. *321 E. Pine St.* ☎ *206/322-6177. www.mudbay.us. AE, DISC, MC, V. Bus: 8, 43, 49 or 60. Map p 86.*

Rugs
★ **Driscoll Robbins Fine Carpets** DOWNTOWN Yes, there is a Driscoll Robbins, and he travels around the world in search of eye-catching hand-woven rugs—from traditional to contemporary designs—then displays them in an equally beautiful showroom. *Warning:* They are hard to resist. *1002*

Western Ave. ☎ 206/292-1115. www.driscollrobbins.com. AE, MC, V. Bus: 12, 16, 66. Map p 83.

★ **Palace Rug Gallery** PIONEER SQUARE Colorful wool and silk rugs from Afghanistan, Pakistan, and China are stacked high in this large space. They are all handmade, and some take up to 16 months to complete. If you're local, you can take several home and try them out. *323 1st Ave. S.* ☎ *206/382-7401. www. palacerug.com. AE, MC, V. Bus: 10, 85, 99. Map p 84.*

Shoes

★ **The Clog Factory** PIONEER SQUARE Talk about a niche! If you're in the market for clogs, this is your place. Even if you're not, you might change your mind. They've got high-quality clogs in all colors, shapes and sizes, Mary Janes to slippers. *217 1st Ave. S.* ☎ *206/682-2564. www. clogheaven.com. AE, DISC, MC, V. Bus: 10, 85, 99. Map p 84.*

kids Niketown DOWNTOWN You'll find all the latest Nike shoes here, and lots of tributes to the top athletes who endorse them. *1500 6th Ave.* ☎ *206/447-6453. AE, DISC, MC, V. Bus: 10, 11, 14, 81. Map p 83.*

Nordstrom DOWNTOWN No footwear listing is complete without the name that's synonymous with shoes in Seattle. *Map p 83.*

Guess what The Clog Factory specializes in?

Toys & Novelties

★ **kids Dragon's Toy Box** PIKE PLACE MARKET From bath toys to puppets to chemistry sets, the shelves here are filled with top-quality toys designed to stimulate the imagination. The very helpful owners are a mother-and-daughter team. *1525 1st Ave., Ste. 2A.* ☎ *206/652-2333. www.dragonstoy box.com. AE, DISC, MC, V. Bus: 10, 99, 113, 121 or 122. Map p 85.*

★★ **kids Izilla Toys** CAPITOL HILL You'll find a world of fun here—literally. The shop features quality games and unusual toys from places like Vienna and Germany, plus a unique selection of arts & crafts projects. There's something for every kid here, from a Sock Monkey Jack-in-the-Box to medieval castle blocks. *1429 12th Ave., Ste. D.* ☎ *206/322-8697. www.izillatoys.com. AE, DISC, MC, V. Bus: 2, 12.*

★★ **kids Magic Mouse Toys** PIONEER SQUARE Grown-ups have just as much trouble as kids in tearing themselves away from this wonderful, multi-level shop where the toys are built to last. Wander through rooms filled with learning-focused books, games and kits--there's an entire room dedicated to puzzles. And of course, everyone is encouraged to play. *603 1st Ave.* ☎ *206/682-8097. AE, DISC, MC, V. Bus: 10, 99, 157, 158. Map p 84.*

★★ **kids Market Magic & Novelty Shop** PIKE PLACE MARKET Making magic for 30 years, this store buried deep in the Market has been visited by a number of well-known magicians over the years. There's usually some sleight-of-hand in progress; just look for the row of gawking kids. *1501 Pike Place #427.* ☎ *206/624-4271. AE, DISC, MC, V. Bus: 10, 99, 113, 121 or 122. Map p 85.* ●

The Seattle **Waterfront**

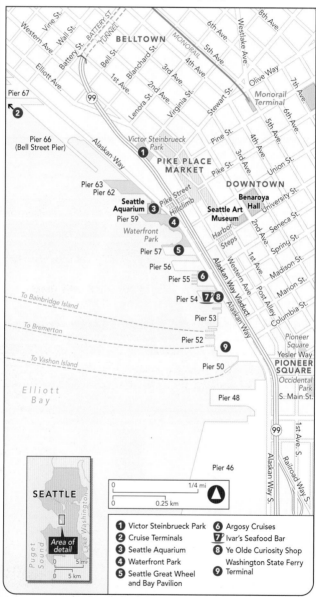

1. Victor Steinbrueck Park
2. Cruise Terminals
3. Seattle Aquarium
4. Waterfront Park
5. Seattle Great Wheel and Bay Pavilion
6. Argosy Cruises
7. Ivar's Seafood Bar
8. Ye Olde Curiosity Shop
9. Washington State Ferry Terminal

Previous page: Get a bird's-eye view above the Puget Sound on the city's newest landmark, the Seattle Great Wheel.

If there's one thing that rivals mountains in the hearts of Pacific Northwesterners, it's water. At the Seattle waterfront— on a clear day—you get both. The Olympics form a jaggedly endearing backdrop to sparkling Elliott Bay. Add a few gleaming white ferryboats crisscrossing their way over Puget Sound, and your souvenir snapshot is waiting. This is a lively place to spend the day— though noisy, because of traffic rushing along an elevated highway across from the waterfront. The city has plans to have it removed by 2016, replaced by a waterfront park that will transform the city. START: **Bus 99, 113, 121 or 122 to 1st Avenue, walk to Western Avenue.**

1 Victor Steinbrueck Park. Just north of Pike Place Market, this waterfront park is a great place for a picnic or people-watching. If the weather gods are with you, you'll be treated to a panorama of mountains—the Cascades (starring Mount Rainier) curving around to the east and the Olympics to the west. *2001 Western Ave. Daily 6am–10pm.*

2 Cruise Terminals. Seattle is a great hopping-off point for cruises to Alaska, and that's where most of the luxury cruise ships you'll see here are headed. Six major cruise lines come and go from Seattle. A second terminal, Smith Cove terminal, was added in 2009 at Pier 91 north of the old Bell Street terminal at Pier 66. Check the Port of Seattle's website for an up-to-date cruise schedule. *2225 Alaskan Way S., Pier 66; 2001 W. Garfield St., Pier 91.* ☎ *206/615-3900. www.port seattle.org/seaport/cruise.*

3 ★★ kids Seattle Aquarium. Be sure to grab a schedule of animal feeding times when you buy your tickets. It's not every day you'll get to see a gentle, giant octopus dine! Each mealtime "show," is accompanied by a short talk by a naturalist. *1483 Alaskan Way on Pier 59.* ☎ *206/386-4300. www.seattle aquarium.org. Admission: $22 adults, $15 ages 4–13. Daily 9:30am–5 pm. See p 11.*

4 Waterfront Park. Stretching between Piers 57 and 59, this concrete park is my favorite spot for watching all the action out in Elliott Bay. It's not a green oasis, but you can't beat the location. With the "Waterfront Fountain" sculpture splashing merrily in the background, you can peer at your leisure at the working boats, cruise ships, and the occasional seal. *1301 Alaskan Way.*

5 kids ★★ Seattle Great Wheel and Bay Pavilion.

A statue of Christopher Columbus graces Waterfront Park.

Rides on the vintage carousel at Bay Pavilion cost $1.50 per person.

Seattle's newest landmark, the Seattle Great Wheel, opened in 2012, takes visitors up 175 feet in enclosed pods for fabulous views of Puget Sound, the Olympic Mountains, and the city. Behind the wheel, Bay Pavilion is a good place to let the kids play arcade games or take a spin on the merry-go-round. *Pier 57, 1301 Alaskan Way. $13*

adults, $8.50 ages 4–11. Mon–Thurs 11am–10pm, Fri 11am–midnight, Sat 10am–midnight, Sun 10am–10pm.

6 ★★★ **Argosy Cruises.** In addition to its tours of Tillicum Village and Elliott Bay, Argosy offers brunch, lunch, and dinner cruises; a tour of lakes Washington and Union (including the famous Seattle houseboats); and a cruise through the Hiram M. Chittenden Locks. There are themed cruises, holiday cruises, musical cruises—you name it, they've got a cruise for it. ⏱ *1–2½ hr. Pier 55, Seattle Waterfront.* ☎ *206/622-8687. www.argosycruises.com. See p 105.*

7 ★ **Ivar's Seafood Bar.** The best bowl of clam chowder in Seattle, for my money, is right here at Ivar's, which has been dishing out local seafood since 1938. You can also get clams 'n chips, oysters 'n chips and a variety of other fresh, locally caught treats for munching as you wander the waterfront. Or take a break and relax at one of the outdoor tables set up beside the bar. *Pier 54, 1001 Alaskan Way.* ☎ *206/624-6852. $*

Stop into Ivar's and try the excellent clam chowder.

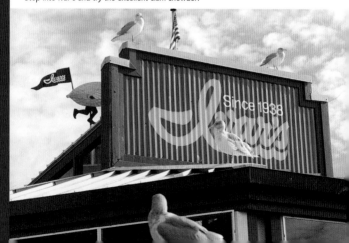

Seattle Celebrates Summer

When the winters are as long and gray as they are in Seattle, who can blame the locals for a little excess when summer shows up, with its picture-perfect days that stretch until 10 at night? Getting a jump on the season is the **Northwest Folklife Festival,** which is held at Seattle Center in May and showcases the region's cultures. In June, the **Seattle Pride Festival** celebrates the LGBT community. At **Bite of Seattle** in July, crowds elbow their way into Seattle Center to hear live bands and sample gourmet treats and wine from local restaurants. Summer is officially kicked off by the **Fourth of July** fireworks over Lake Union, one of the finest displays in the nation. **Seafair** is a month of parades, competitions, and hydroplane races celebrating pirates and all things aquatic. The mother of all festivals, **Bumbershoot,** marks the end of summer and the return of drizzle. Fine arts, crafts, acrobats, big-name bands, and general zaniness rule supreme at Seattle Center over the Labor Day weekend.

8 Ye Olde Curiosity Shop. A century-old Seattle landmark, this is as much quirky museum as it is souvenir shop. The owner's great-grandfather gathered oddities from around the world and hired local Native Americans to carve totem poles. Shrunken heads and mummies share the shelves with Seattle T-shirts and homemade fudge. *Pier 54, 1001 Alaskan Way.* ☎ *206/682-5844. www.yeoldecuriosityshop.com.*

9 Washington State Ferry Terminal. From here, you can glide your way to Bainbridge Island, Bremerton, or Vashon Island. There is passenger-only service to Vashon from this spot, and if you're headed to Bainbridge Island or Bremerton you can walk on or take your car. The latter is pricier, and the lines can be much longer. If you just want to walk on a ferry, go for a ride and poke around town, Bainbridge (35 min.) is your best option. If you'd like a long, leisurely ride, take the hour-long Bremerton run. And if you want to go exploring the Kitsap or Olympic peninsulas (the latter takes you through the rainforest to the northwestern edge of the state), drive onto the Bremerton ferry and leave from the western side of Puget Sound. *801 Alaskan Way, Pier 52. See p 18.*

Lake Union

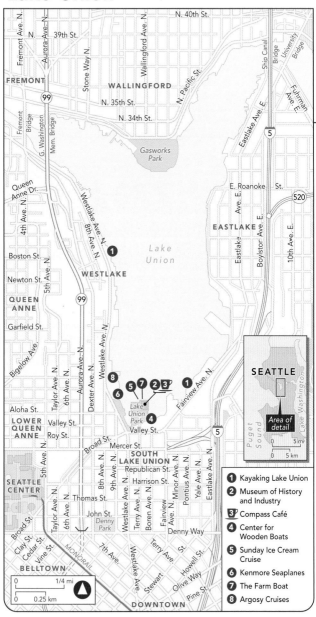

1 Kayaking Lake Union
2 Museum of History and Industry
3 Compass Café
4 Center for Wooden Boats
5 Sunday Ice Cream Cruise
6 Kenmore Seaplanes
7 The Farm Boat
8 Argosy Cruises

Despite its prime waterfront location, this neighborhood north of downtown has been some what underutilized by Seattleites. That's all changing now, as apartments, shops, and restaurants pop up along the shore, and the adjacent South Lake Union area undergoes a dramatic urban transformation. This is an entertaining and evolving neighborhood, where you'll see seaplanes gracefully taking off and landing, sailboats gliding dreamily along the lake, neighborhoods of houseboat-dwellers, and spanking-new towers and businesses. START: **South Lake Union Streetcar 98, or Bus 17, 70, 71, 72 or 73 to Lake Union.**

The Seattle Streetcar runs along Lake Union.

❶ ★★ Kayaking Lake Union. There's nothing quite like paddling a boat in the heart of a city, especially one as picturesque as Seattle. Seaplanes buzz overhead and splash down nearby as you explore the houseboat "neighborhoods" and soak in the dramatic view of the Space Needle and Seattle's distinctive skyline. If you want to pay for the extra rental time, you can paddle up to the dock at one of the waterfront restaurants and enjoy a scenic lunch. *Boats may be rented at Moss Bay (1001 Fairview Ave. N., #1900; ☎ 206/682-2031; kayak rentals June 1–Sept 15 $14/hr. single, $19/hr. double) or Northwest Outdoor Center (2100 Westlake Ave. N., Ste. 1; ☎ 206/281-9694; kayak rentals $14/hr. single, $15/hr. double,* or $22/hr. triple). Standup paddle boards are also available at Northwest Outdoor Center.

❷ ★★ kids Museum of History & Industry (MOHAI). This gem of a museum relocated to its present location in the refurbished Naval armory building in 2012. Exhibits provide a fascinating overview of Seattle's history, including major events, iconic personalities, and original artifacts. ⏱ *1 hr. 860 Terry Ave. N. ☎ 206/324-1126. www.seattlehistory.org. $7 adults, $5 seniors & ages 5–17. Daily 10am–5pm.*

❸ ★ Compass Cafe. Enjoy the fabulous view of Lake Union with fresh soups and sandwiches or an

The Center for Wooden Boats has an extensive collection of historic boats, both human- and wind-powered.

espresso at this bright cafe in the northwest corner of MOHAI. *860 Terry Ave. N.* 📞 *206/324-1126.* $

❹ ★ Center for Wooden Boats. This unusual spot is basically an outdoor museum, where you can walk along the dock and enjoy a fascinating collection of historic and replica human- and wind-powered boats. You can also rent a sailboat or rowboat and take sailing lessons; old salts love the maritime library. *1010 Valley St.* 📞 *206/382-2628. www.cwb.org. Center admission free. Rowboats & sailboats from $25/hr. Free sailboat ride 2pm Sun; arrive as early as 10am to sign up— these are popular events.*

❺ ★ Sunday Ice Cream Cruise. Capt. Larry (Kezner) is your congenial host for a 45-minute cruise of Lake Union on his charming ferry boat. The captain knows everything there is to know about Lake Union, its houseboat communities and environs—and provides a lively, entertaining narrative while passengers slurp chocolate ice cream floats. Other treats are also available. The boat—the *m/v Fremont*—leaves on the hour from 11am to 4pm year-round. *Valley St. & Terry Ave. N.* 📞 *206/713-8446, www.seattleferryservice.com. $11 adults, $10 seniors, $7 ages 5–13, $2 ages 4 & under.*

❻ ★ Seaplane Flights. What better way to see Seattle than from

Don't miss getting an up-close view of Lake Union's charming houseboats.

Mega-Makeover

South Lake Union is undergoing a major transformation, thanks in large part to Microsoft co-founder/real estate magnate Paul Allen's vision of the former warehouse and industrial area as a biotech hub and urban center. It's easy to get there via the new, bright red or green South Lake Union Streetcar, which runs between this neighborhood and downtown every 15 minutes. In addition to the biotechs, online bookseller Amazon.com has built a huge campus in South Lake Union, and the old Navy armory building has reopened as the new home of Seattle's much-loved Museum of History & Industry (MOHAI). Visitors can enjoy the wide variety of boating and other waterfront activities along South Lake Union. If you work up a hunger, grab a burger or taco—or dine at one of the stylish lakeside restaurants. Try **Daniels' Broiler** (809 Fairview Pl. N.), or watch the boats from the outdoor deck at **McCormick & Schmick's Harborside** (1200 Westlake Ave. N.).

the air, and what more fitting take-off and landing than the water? Seaplanes have been leaving from Lake Union since 1916, and Kenmore Air has been flying floatplanes in the Pacific Northwest for more than half a century. Its Lake Union facility is the busiest commercial seaplane terminal in the country. You can take the popular 20-minute City Explorer flightseeing excursion, or opt for a longer flight to a private beach and a gourmet catered picnic, a day trip to the San Juan Islands, or even a getaway to Victoria (don't forget your passport). *950 Westlake Ave. N.* ☎ *425/486-1257. www.kenmoreair.com. 20-min. City Explorer tour: $99 per person; prices vary for longer tours.*

❼ **The Farm Boat.** At this unique floating farmers' market at South Lake Union you can buy fresh-picked produce and local crafts on a classic 125-ft. wooden steamship called the Virginia, which is operated by a farmers' cooperative. The

Virginia stops at nearby island and coastal farms, gathering produce and goods as it makes its way to Lake Union for the market, held Thursdays 11am to 3pm, June through October. *Lake Union Park Wharf, 860 Terry Ave. N.* ☎ *206/355-0133.*

❽ ★★ **Argosy Cruises.** Year-round, Seattle's premier sightseeing cruise company offers a fun and informative 2-hour narrated cruise that begins on Lake Union and ventures into neighboring Lake Washington. Along the way you'll see the floating houseboat neighborhoods made famous in the movie "Sleepless in Seattle" and learn about the cultural and industrial history of the lakes. *Departs from AGC Marina. 1200 Westlake Ave.* ☎ *888/623-1445. www.argosycruises.com. Oct–May Sat–Sun 1:15pm; June–Sept daily 1:15pm (add'l cruises at 11am & 3:30pm depending on season; check website for details). $34 adults, $31 seniors, $17 ages 4–12. Parking $4.*

Hiram M. Chittenden Locks

1. Visitors Center
2. Carl S. English, Jr. Botanical Garden
3. Fish Ladder
4. Hiram J. Chittenden Locks
5. Lockspot Café

NW Market St.

BALLARD

32nd Ave. NW

NW 54th St.

Carl S. English, Jr. Botanical Garden

Lake Washington Ship Canal

Commodore Park

W. Commodore Way

MAGNOLIA

Area of detail

Puget Sound

SEATTLE

Lake Washington

0   5 mi
0   5 km

0   100 yds
0   100 m

Watching the boats navigate the locks is a fascinating enough way to spend an afternoon, but at Hiram M. Chittenden, there's much more: those amazing climbing fish, the painstakingly tended botanical gardens, and the best grassy hills in town for kids to roll down. (Do keep an eye out for goose droppings.) You'll find lots of prime picnic spots where you can munch as you watch the boats go by. START: **Bus 44 to Northwest 54th Street & 30th Ave. NW.**

1 Visitors Center. Stop here first for free brochures on the locks and garden, and watch the informational video shown every half-hour. Free hour-long guided tours of both the locks and the garden are offered March 1 through November 30 (call for tour times). *3015 NW 54th St.* 📞 *206/783-7059. May 1– Sept 30: Daily 10am–6pm; Oct 1– April 30: Thurs–Mon 10am–4pm.*

Come watch the salmon head upstream with little help from human technology at the Fish Ladder.

The Botanical Garden is one of Seattle's hidden gems.

② Carl S. English, Jr. Botanical Garden. Building and dredging the locks produced a vast amount of empty space. Botanist Carl S. English Jr. came to the rescue, transforming the grounds into a splendid English-style garden with plants from around the globe. This fragrant, blooming quilt is a little-known Seattle secret. *3015 NW 54th St. ☎ 206/783-7059. Daily 7am–9pm.*

③ ★ kids Fish Ladder. Salmon have got to be the most inspirational fish in the sea. They hatch in streams, swim out to the ocean, then years later manage to swim upstream, against the odds, back to their exact birthplace to start the cycle again. Here, they swim from the ocean into Puget Sound, leap up a 21-"step" ladder to get up to freshwater Lake Washington level, then head home. It takes a lot of energy for a salmon to swim and flop its way up the ladder, but persistence pays. At different times during the summer you might see sockeye, Chinook, Coho, and steelhead salmon. Watch them climbing the ladders outdoors, then head down to an underwater viewing room for a different perspective. Though it's open year-round, you won't find much but water from

October through May. Call ahead to see what's running. *3015 NW 54th St. ☎ 206/783-7059. Daily 7am–9pm.*

④ kids Hiram M. Chittenden Locks. I never tire of watching the boats of all shapes and sizes make their ascent from salty Puget Sound up into the fresh waters of Lake Washington. Some pretty magnificent boats come through here. If you're lucky, you might spot one of billionaire Paul Allen's mega-yachts. You might also spot a sea lion or harbor seal, hoping for a tasty salmon lunch. *3015 NW 54th St. ☎ 206/783-7059. Daily 7am–9pm.*

⑤ Lockspot Cafe. You can't miss this eatery at the entrance to the locks: Just look for the undersea mural, complete with mermaid and orca. Grab some fish 'n chips at the outside counter and have a picnic at the locks. You can also dine inside in a pub-like atmosphere, but if it's a nice day, opt for the picnic. *3005 NW 54th St. ☎ 206/789-4865. $*

The Lockspot Cafe is a perfect place for a seafood break.

Green Lake Park

1. Green Lake Path
2. Swimming Pools
3. Playground
4. Tennis Courts
5. Boating
6. 72nd Street Café
7. Bathhouse

Rain or shine, the locals grab their babies and dogs and head here for their daily dose of fresh air. The path, nearly 3 miles long, winds around a beautiful glacier-carved lake, ringed by spectacular trees and Northwest plants. Cars zoom past on busy State Road 99, but the highway is just far enough away from this green oasis that you barely notice. START: **Bus 16 or 316 to Woodlawn Avenue & NE 71st St., walk to East Green Lake Drive North.**

❶ ★★ **Green Lake Path.** This 2.8-mile trail around the lake has a crushed granite inner lane for walkers, joggers, and strollers; and an outer asphalt lane for bicyclists and skaters. The bird-watching is great! *7201 E. Green Lake Dr. N.*

❷ kids **Swimming Pools.** In addition to the outdoor wading pool and indoor heated pool, there is a beach on the lakefront with lifeguards and diving boards in the summertime. *Note:* Green Lake has frequent algae blooms when the weather turns warm, which means the lake will be closed to swimmers, so check for informational signs before you go for a dip. *See p 37,* ❿.

❸ ★ kids **Playground.** Parents and kids alike can take a break at this terrific play area, which offers some cool features not found in other parks. My daughter's favorite was always the sand pit with the sand-digging machine and canoe

Strolling along Green Lake Path affords excellent views of the surrounding area.

for imaginary trips. If the weather turns nasty, the park's nearby community center has an indoor playroom for the younger set. *E. Green Lake Way & Latona Ave. NE (near the main entrance).*

4 Tennis Courts. You'll find some just inside the main entrance, at 7201 E. Green Lake Dr. N., and also at W. Greenlake Way & Stone Ave. N. To reserve a court, call ☎ 206/684-4075. Fees to rent the tennis courts are $32 for singles and $40 for doubles, for a 1¼-hour reservation.

5 Boating. Take a canoe out on the lake—or a kayak or paddle boat. Or try out one of the new stand-up paddle boards. You can rent them north of the main entrance, from Green Lake Rentals, and launch from there or the boat launch on the southwest side of the lake. *7351 E. Green Lake Dr. N. ☎ 206/527-0171. Rentals start at $16/hour.*

6 72nd Street Café. Genial baristas, rich Zoka coffee beans— what more could you ask for? Maybe some tasty pastries, or a grilled panini from Mike's East Coast Sandwiches. The kids can chomp on PB&Js while you sit back and smell the coffee. *308 NE 72nd St. ☎ 206/523-5623. $*

7 ★ Seattle Public Theater at the Bathhouse. This 1920s-era bathhouse has been converted into a popular playhouse on the west side of the lake. Here, tucked away in the middle of Green Lake Park, Seattle Public Theater presents shows that are sometimes controversial and usually worth watching. *7312 W. Greenlake Dr. N. ☎ 206/524-1300. www.seattlepublictheater.org.*

Take a boat out on the lake, just like the locals do.

Washington Park **Arboretum**

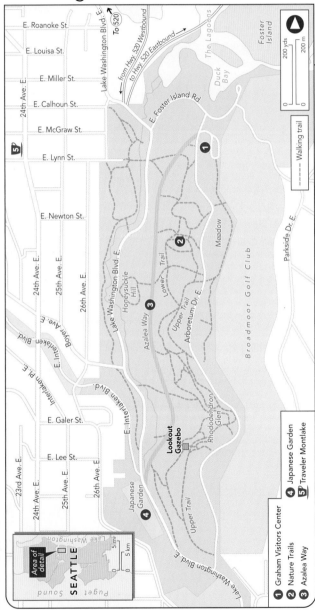

E. Roanoke St.

E. Louisa St.

E. Miller St.

E. Calhoun St.

E. McGraw St.

E. Lynn St.

E. Newton St.

E. Galer St.

E. Lee St.

24th Ave. E.

25th Ave. E.

26th Ave. E.

23rd Ave. E.

24th Ave. E.

25th Ave. E.

26th Ave. E.

Lake Washington Blvd. E.

Boyer Ave. E.

Interlaken Blvd

E. Interlaken Blvd.

Interlaken Pl. E.

Lake Washington Blvd. E.

To (520)

from Hwy 520 Westbound

to Hwy 520 Eastbound

E. Foster Island Rd.

The Lagoons

Duck Bay

Foster Island

Broadmoor Golf Club

Parkside Dr. E.

Meadow

Lower Trail

Upper Trail

Arboretum Dr. E.

Honeysuckle Hill

Azalea Way

Rhododendron Glen

Lookout Gazebo

Japanese Garden

Upper Trail

Lake Washington Blvd. E.

200 yds
200 m

---- Walking trail

① Graham Visitors Center
② Nature Trails
③ Azalea Way
④ Japanese Garden
5 Traveler Montlake

SEATTLE

Area of detail

Lake Washington

Puget Sound

5 km
5 miles

This is Seattle's garden, sprawled along 200 acres of lush property, with Lake Washington winding its way around the northern edge. Breathtaking any time of year, the arboretum is especially stunning in the spring and early summer. Thousands of exotic plants have been gathered from every corner of the world. START: **2300 Arboretum Dr.**

Get lost in a sea of color along Azalea Way.

① **Graham Visitors Center.** Stop here for a map of the trails, then wander among the trees, ponds, and shrubs of the Arboretum (open daily dawn to dusk) at your leisure. *2300 Arboretum Dr.* ☎ *206/543-8800. www.depts. washington.edu/uwbg/gardens/wpa. shtml. Daily 9am–5pm.*

② **★★ kids Nature Trails.** Pick a trail on your map and start hiking! It's a good idea to bring along a light backpack for snacks and water. These trails are all easy walks with no hills to scale. My favorite is the 3.5-mile Foster Island trail, which winds along a boardwalk through an emerald-green wetland area, and leads to two islands. You'll be rewarded with spectacular views of Lake Washington. *2300 Arboretum Dr.*

③ **Azalea Way.** This garden near Graham Visitors Center comes alive in the springtime, when it is transformed into a riotous ¾-mile promenade of azaleas and cherry blossoms. *2300 Arboretum Dr.*

④ **★★★ Japanese Garden.** The centerpiece of the Arboretum, this exquisite garden is the perfect place to relax and contemplate life. World-famous garden artist Juki Iida designed it with nearly divine beauty. Formal tea ceremonies cost $10 per person and are held at the Shoseian Teahouse inside the garden, from April to October (check dates on the Urasenke Foundation's website: www.urasenkeseattle. org). *1075 Lake Washington Blvd. E.* ☎ *206/684-4725. www.seattle japanesegarden.org. $6 adults, $4 seniors & ages 6–17. Open Mar–Nov. Daily 10am–dusk (closed Mon Mar & Oct–Nov).*

⑤ **Traveler Montlake.** This friendly bar-restaurant, which opened in 2014, pours good libations to accompany new versions of comfort food, like buffalo meatloaf, wild boar sloppy joes, and roasted goose pot pie. *2307 24th Ave. E.* ☎ *206/726-5968. $*

The best time to visit is in the spring, when everything is in bloom, but the arboretum is gorgeous year-round.

Woodland Park

1 Woodland Park Zoo
2 Woodland Park Rose Garden
3 ZooTunes
4 Woodland Park

The focal point of this park, of course, is the **Woodland Park Zoo, a must stop for families with kids.** It's surrounded by grassy hills that are perfect for picnics and afternoons of fun. The part west of S.R. 99 (Aurora Avenue) is occupied mainly by the zoo; to the east of the highway stretch the parklands, which adjoin Green Lake Park. START: **Bus 5 or 82 to Phinney Ave. N. & N. 50th Street, walk to 750 N. 50th St.**

1 ★★★ Kids **Woodland Park Zoo.** There's never a dull moment at this zoo, where the tenants range from red pandas to Komodo dragons. Though a zoo of some sort has occupied Woodland Park since the 1890s, the animal habitats at the present-day facility are on the cutting edge of zoo technology. The Humboldt penguin exhibit, which opened in 2009, won the national zoo association's best-exhibit award. The next year, the zoo

added eight playful meerkats to its menagerie. *750 N. 50th St.* ☎ *206/684-4800. www.zoo.org. Admission May–Sept: $19 ages 13–64, $17 ages 65 & older, $12 ages 3–12; Oct–Apr: $13 ages 13–64, $ 11 ages 65 & older, $8.75 ages 3–12. May–Sept daily 9:30am–6pm; Oct–Apr: daily 9:30am–4pm. See p 37.*

2 ★★ **Woodland Park Rose Garden.** Roses love the Pacific Northwest, and even non-flower-lovers will be captivated by the

Come visit the local fauna, such as grizzly bears, along with more exotic species, at the Woodland Park Zoo.

beauty and diversity packed into this 2½-acre garden. Although it's no longer an All-America Rose Selections test site, the Woodland Park Rose Garden displays the very latest prize-winning varieties. It's no wonder the garden is always in great demand for weddings. You'll find it east of the zoo's south entrance gate, but in the summertime your nose will lead you there. *700 N. 50th St. Free. Daily 7am–dusk.*

③ ★★ kids ZooTunes. Summertime means outdoor concert season at Woodland Park Zoo, and they're always great fun, whether it's a time-honored act like Art Garfunkel or something a bit hipper, like Pink Martini. Bring a blanket or a low beach chair—yours might actually be measured if it looks too tall—and settle in on the meadow, just inside the zoo's north entrance. Kids are welcome and dancing is encouraged! If you plan to visit Seattle from mid-June through August, check the schedule (www.zoo.org/zootunes) in early May. If you see a concert you like, book early because they sell out fast. The website explains how to buy tickets online. The prices are quite reasonable compared to most venues, averaging around $22 a ticket, plus service fee for web sales. *N. 59th & Evanston Ave.* ☎ *206/615-0076.*

④ kids Woodland Park. This large urban park is a favorite picnic spot. Sheltered areas hold from 50 to 300 people, and these may be rented starting at $90 per day from April 1 to September 30 (other times they're free and first-come-first-served). You'll also find tennis courts, horseshoes, a ball field, playground, and an off-leash dog area. *Aurora Ave. N. & N. 59th St.* ☎ *206/684-4081.*

The Woodland Park Rose Garden.

Seattle Center

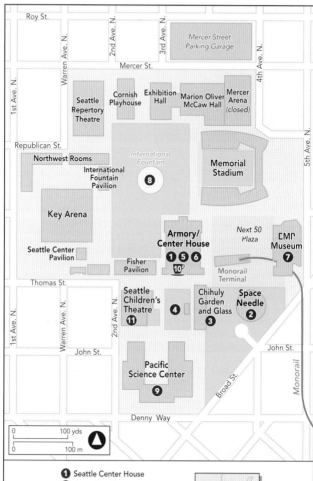

Roy St.

Mercer Street Parking Garage

Mercer St.

Seattle Repertory Theatre

Cornish Playhouse

Exhibition Hall

Marion Oliver McCaw Hall

Mercer Arena *(closed)*

Republican St.

Northwest Rooms

International Fountain Pavilion

International Fountain

8

Memorial Stadium

Key Arena

Seattle Center Pavilion

Armory/ Center House

1 5 6

10½

Fisher Pavilion

Next 50 Plaza

EMP Museum **7**

Monorail Terminal

Thomas St.

Seattle Children's Theatre **11**

4

Chihuly Garden and Glass **3**

Space Needle **2**

John St.

Pacific Science Center

9

Denny Way

0   100 yds
0   100 m

1 Seattle Center House
2 Space Needle
3 Chihuly Garden and Glass
4 Movies at the Mural
5 Seattle Children's Museum
6 Winterfest
7 Experience Music Project
8 International Fountain
9 Pacific Science Center
10½ Seattle Fudge
11 Seattle Children's Theatre

Seattle Center

SEATTLE

Puget Sound

Lake Washington

0   5 mi
0   5 km

This is where Seattle comes to party. From the spectacular fountain—where Northwesterners "cool off" as soon as it hits the 60s—to the myriad festivals that mark summertime in Seattle, there's always fun to be had here. Even in the winter, the grounds are a lovely place to enjoy a book on a sunny day. If it gets too chilly, pop into the Center House for a hot chocolate. START: **Monorail or bus 3, 4, 8, 16 or 30 to Seattle Center.**

❶ ★ kids Seattle Center Armory. This huge building is a focal point of Seattle Center, offering indoor activities that go hand-in-hand with the festivities outside, often hosting art shows and cultural activities, and musical performances on stage. The inside perimeter is lined with restaurants, cafes, and a candy shop. There are indoor tables, but on a nice day, it's much more fun to take your food outside and people-watch while you eat! *See p 36.*

❷ ★★★ kids Space Needle. Take a ride to the observation deck. On a clear day, you'll see all of Seattle (and Mt. Rainier) at your feet. ① *1 hr. Summer weekends are busiest. 400 Broad St.* ☎ *206/905-2100. Observation deck tickets: $18 adults, $16 seniors, $11 ages 4–13. Mon–Thurs 10am–9pm; Fri–Sat 9:30pm–10:30pm; Sun 9:30am–9:30pm. See p 48,* **⓮**.

❸ ★★★ Chihuly Garden and Glass. This museum and landscaped garden showcases the extraordinary glass art of Tacoma native Dale Chihuly. *See p 27,* **❸**.

❹ kids Movies at the Mural. Every August weekend, families bring their blankets and low folding chairs to the Mural Amphitheatre, to lounge on the lawn and watch a free movie projected onto a giant screen. Outdoor cinema on a perfect Seattle evening with the Space Needle as a backdrop is a little slice of heaven. Check the website for the schedule (www.seattlecenter.

com; click "Events & Programs," then "Film and Movies").

❺ ★ kids Seattle Children's Museum. Crafts and exhibits for the younger set transform education into playtime. ① *1 hr. 305 Harrison St.* ☎ *206/441-1768. www.thechildrensmuseum.org. $8.25 adults & children, free under age 1. Mon–Fri 10am–5pm; Sat–Sun 10am–6pm. See p 36,* **❹**.

❻ ★ kids Winterfest. From Thanksgiving weekend through December, this celebration puts a little magic into the cold season. An antique carousel is set up outside the Center House, and rides

Yes, it's indoors, but the Experience Music Project shouldn't be missed.

The Pacific Science Center.

are just $1. There are also bonfires, choirs, ice sculpting, and storytelling. If you get chilly, duck inside and admire the huge train set, complete with an oversized turn-of-the-20th-century village, set up in the Center House. Outside, Fisher Pavilion becomes an ice rink (Sun–Thurs 11am–8pm; Fri–Sat 11am–10pm. $5 adults, $3 ages 6–12), open through the first weekend of January. *305 Harrison St.* ☎ *206/684-7200. www. seattlecenter.com.*

⑦ ★ Experience Music Project. Rock-music fans flock to Microsoft co-founder Paul Allen's museum, designed by Frank Gehry. ⏱ *1 hr. 325 5th Ave. N. (at Seattle Center).* ☎ *206/770-2700. www. empsfm.org. Admission $20 adults, $17 seniors, $14 ages 5–17. Late May–early Sept daily 10am–7pm; early Sept–late May 10am–5pm. See p 47, ⑬.*

⑧ ★ kids International Fountain. It's hard to match Seattle on a summer day for sheer joy, and you'll see plenty of it on the faces of kids, grownups and a dog or two at this colossal fountain just north of the Center House. Water-lovers charge down the concrete ramp to splash through the glorious spray, while sunbathers arrange themselves around the fountain to soak up the rays. At night, the waters dance to rainbow colors.

⑨ ★★ kids Pacific Science Center. Spend some time with the cool outdoor exhibits before you go inside. Walk through a giant water wheel, spin a 2-ton granite ball, or ride a high-rail bicycle (weather permitting). This hands-on approach to science is fun for everyone. ⏱ *2 hr. 200 2nd Ave. N.* ☎ *206/443-2001. www.pacsci.org. Admission $18 adults, $16 seniors, $13 ages 6–15, $10 ages 3–5. IMAX: $9–$14 adults, $8–$12 seniors, $7–$11 ages 6–15, $6–$9 ages 3–5; Mon & Wed–Fri 10am–5pm; Sat–Sun 10am–6pm. See p 36, ⑤.*

⑩ ★ Seattle Fudge. Don't even pretend to look for a healthy snack here (unless popcorn counts?) Just go ahead and indulge in the rich, creamy fudge. The kids can watch taffy being pulled—hey, consider it an educational experience! *Center House.* ☎ *206/441-0524. $*

⑪ ★★★ kids Seattle Children's Theatre. The shows at this first-rate playhouse are based on beloved classic and contemporary books and movies. *201 Thomas St. at Seattle Center.* ☎ *206/441-3322. www.sct.org. Ticket prices vary. See p 35, ②.* ●

Dining Best Bets

Best **French**
★★ Café Campagne $$–$$$ 1600 Post Alley (p 124)

Best **Brunch**
★★ Salty's on Alki Beach $$$ 1936 Harbor Ave SW. (p 131)

Best **Special Occasion**
★★★ Canlis $$$$–$$$$$ 2576 Aurora Ave N. (p 124)

Best **Steak**
★★★ Metropolitan $$$$ 820 2nd Ave. (p 129)

Most Exciting **Fusion Cuisine**
★★★ Poppy $$–$$$ 622 Broadway E. (p 130)

Best **Waterfront Dining**
★★ Ray's Boathouse $$$–$$$$$ 6049 Seaview Ave NW. (p 131)

Best for **Vegetarians**
★★ Wild Ginger $$–$$$ 1401 3rd Ave. (p 134)

Best **Dim Sum**
★ Jade Garden $–$$ 424 7th Ave S. (p 127)

Best **Hotel Fine Dining**
★★★ Hunt Club $$$ 900 Madison St. (p 126)

Best **Pre-Theater**
★★ Tulio $$$ 1100 5th Ave. (p 134)

Best **Sushi**
★★ Shiro's $$ 2401 2nd Ave. (p 132)

Best **Tapas**
★★ List $$–$$$ 2226 1st Ave. (p 128)

Best **Italian**
★★ Assaggio $$–$$$ 2010 4th Ave. (p 123)

Best **Late-Night**
★★ Ten Mercer $$–$$$ 10 Mercer St. (p 133)

Best **Fine Dining with Kids**
★★ Cutters Crabhouse $$$ 2001 Western Ave. (p 124)

Best **Seafood Spot**
★★ Blueacre $$–$$$ 1700 7th Ave., Ste. 100 (p 124)

Most Fun **Near the Market**
★★ Steelhead Diner $$–$$$ 95 Pine St. (p 133)

Best **Italian Menu**
★★ Il Fornaio $$–$$$ 600 Pine St., Ste. 132 (p 127)

Best **Organic**
★★★ Tilth $$–$$$ 1411 N. 45th St. (p 134)

Best **Pizza**
★★ Pagliacci Pizza $–$$ 426 Broadway Ave. E. (p 130)

Most Likely to **Delight the Whole Crowd**
★★ MistralKitchen $$$–$$$$ 2020 Westlake Ave. (p 129)

Best Marriage of **Tuscany & the Northwest**
★★ Volterra $$–$$$ 5411 Ballard Ave NW. (p 134)

Salty's is a shellfish lover's dream come true. Previous page: A dessert from Relish Burger Bistro (Westin Seattle).

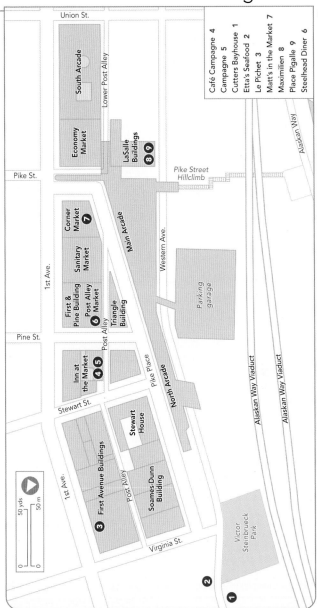

Pike Place Market Dining

Union St.

South Arcade

Lower Post Alley

Economy Market

LaSalle Buildings **8 9**

Pike St.

Pike Street Hillclimb

Corner Market **7**

Main Arcade

Sanitary Market

Western Ave.

First & Pine Building

Post Alley Market **6**

Triangle Building

Parking garage

1st Ave.

Pine St.

Post Alley

Inn at the Market **4 5**

Pike Place

North Arcade

Stewart St.

Stewart House

First Avenue Buildings **3**

1st Ave.

Post Alley

Soames-Dunn Building

Virginia St.

Victor Steinbrueck Park

Alaskan Way

Alaskan Way Viaduct

Alaskan Way Viaduct

2

1

50 yds

50 m

0

0

Dining **Best Bets**

Café Campagne **4**
Campagne **5**
Cutters Bayhouse **1**
Etta's Seafood **2**
Le Pichet **3**
Matt's in the Market **7**
Maximilien **8**
Place Pigalle **9**
Steelhead Diner **6**

Downtown/Pioneer Square

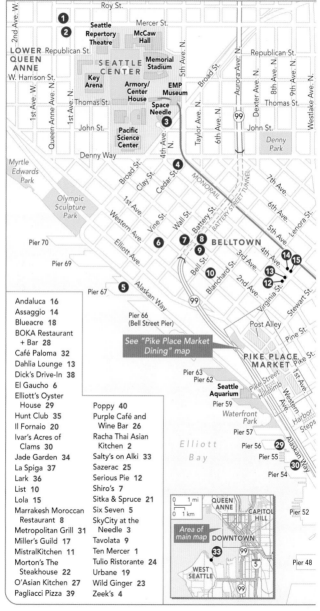

Andaluca 16
Assaggio 14
Blueacre 18
BOKA Restaurant + Bar 28
Café Paloma 32
Dahlia Lounge 13
Dick's Drive-In 38
El Gaucho 6
Elliott's Oyster House 29
Hunt Club 35
Il Fornaio 20
Ivar's Acres of Clams 30
Jade Garden 34
La Spiga 37
Lark 36
List 10
Lola 15
Marrakesh Moroccan Restaurant 8
Metropolitan Grill 31
Miller's Guild 17
MistralKitchen 11
Morton's The Steakhouse 22
O'Asian Kitchen 27
Pagliacci Pizza 39

Poppy 40
Purple Café and Wine Bar 26
Racha Thai Asian Kitchen 2
Salty's on Alki 33
Sazerac 25
Serious Pie 12
Shiro's 7
Sitka & Spruce 21
Six Seven 5
SkyCity at the Needle 3
Tavolata 1
Ten Mercer 1
Tulio Ristorante 24
Urbane 19
Wild Ginger 23
Zeek's 4

Dining

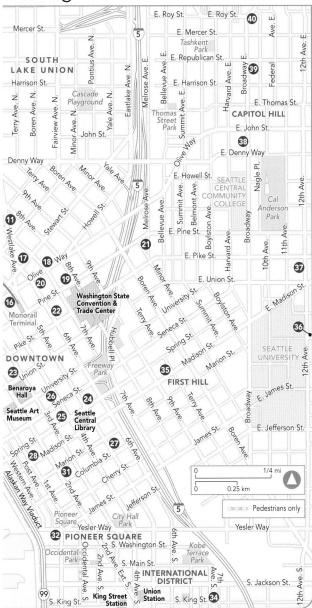

North Seattle Dining

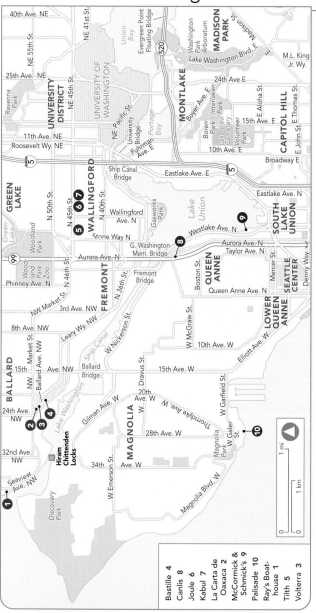

Bastille **4**

Canlis **8**

Joule **6**

Kabul **7**

La Carta de
Oaxaca **2**

McCormick &
Schmick's **9**

Palisade **10**

Ray's Boat-
house **1**

Tilth **5**

Volterra **3**

Seattle Restaurants A to Z

★★ **Andaluca** DOWNTOWN
MEDITERRANEAN Spain meets
the Northwest in perfectly spiced
paellas and other Mediterranean-
influenced choices. The romantic
Andaluca is at the Mayflower Park
Hotel. *407 Olive Way.* ☎ *206/382-
6999. www.andaluca.com. Entrees
$23–$38. AE, DC, DISC, MC, V.
Breakfast daily, lunch Mon–Fri, dinner
Tues–Sun. Bus: 25, 79,123, 202.
Map p 120.*

★★ **Aqua** WATERFRONT *SEA-
FOOD* From a seasonal variety of
local oysters to crispy-skinned
salmon to king crab legs in truffle
aioli, Chef Wesley Hood's seafood
is always fresh and delicious. And,
being the sister restaurant to El
Gaucho steakhouse, this is one seafood spot where landlubbers are
just as happy. One favorite signature side dish: lobster mashed
potatoes. *2801 Alaskan Way, Pier 70.*
☎ *206/956-9171. www.elgaucho.
com. Entrees $28–$89. Dinner daily.
Bus: 99.*

★★ **Assaggio** DOWNTOWN *ITAL-
IAN* From the Michelangelo-inspired
art (look up!) to the personal welcome by gregarious owner/chef
Mauro Golmarvi to the melt-in-your-
mouth veal dishes, there's no doubt
you've entered a world where food is
a passion. The boisterous back room
is a fun place to meet friends; the
front room has more private spaces.
Everything from the simple Margarita
pizza to the sophisticated osso buco
is fresh and memorable. Don't pass
on dessert. *2010 4th Ave.* ☎ *206/441-
1399. www.assaggioseattle.com.
Entrees $15–$29. AE, MC, V. Lunch
Mon–Fri, dinner Mon–Sat. Bus: 1, 13,
15, 16, 17. Map p 120.*

★★ **Bastille** BALLARD *FRENCH*
The best choices at this fasionable
Parisian-style brasserie are the *plats
du jour*, such as tender-crisp bone-
less quail. Or come for Sunday
brunch when the Ballard Farmers'
Market adds spice to the scene and
you can people-watch from the
enclosed patio while enjoying a fluffy
omelet. *5307 Ballard Ave. NW.*
☎ *206/453-5014. www.bastilleseattle.
com. Entrees $15–$25. AE, MC, V. Dinner daily, Sun brunch. See map p 122.*

The art on the walls is as inventive as the cuisine at Assaggio.

Be sure to leave room for dessert at Canlis.

★★ Blueacre DOWNTOWN *SEAFOOD* Northwest cuisine shines at this friendly but elegant spot, where the oyster bar serves up a variety of tender, buttery local offerings. The dinner menu offers inventively prepared, sustainably caught seafood. My favorite is the lemon-crusted salmon with horseradish brown butter. When available, don't miss the lightly battered local chanterelle mushrooms in hot-sweet mustard vinaigrette. *1700 7th Ave., Ste. 100.* ☎ *206/659-0737. www.blueacreseafood.com. Entrees $16–$36. AE, MC, V. Lunch & dinner daily. Bus: 25, 66, 70, 73, 123. Map p 120.*

★★ BOKA Restaurant + Bar DOWNTOWN *NEW AMERICAN* Food is art, and art is food for the soul at this stylish cafe in the ultra-hip Hotel 1000. It's hard to decide whether to take a bite or a picture—take a bite! The flavorful, inventive menu shifts with the season. The petrale sole is fabulous. *1010 1st Ave.* ☎ *206/357-9000. www.bokaseattle.com. Entrees $14–$31. AE, MC, V. Breakfast daily, lunch Mon–Fri, dinner daily. Bus: 12, 16, 66, 99. Map p 120.*

★★ Café Campagne PIKE PLACE MARKET *FRENCH* Come here for a casual, oh-so-French bistro experience. You won't find a better *croque-monsieur* outside Paris. *1600 Post Alley.* ☎ *206/728-2233. www.cafecampagne.com. Entrees $15–$23. AE, DISC, MC, V. Lunch Mon–Fri, brunch Sat–Sun, dinner daily. Bus: 10, 99, 113, 121, 122. Map p 119.*

★ Café Paloma PIONEER SQUARE *MEDITERRANEAN* At this intimate Turkish cafe, you'll find the Mediterranean standards, plus some creative choices—think gorgonzola panini. *93 Yesler Way.* ☎ *206/405-1920. www.cafepaloma. com. Entrees $6–$12. MC, V. Lunch Mon–Sat, dinner Tues–Sat. Bus: 99, 143, 157, 158. Map p 120.*

★★★ Canlis DOWNTOWN *NORTHWEST* Dining here is more an experience than a meal. The food is fabulous—fresh and inventive—and the wine list outstanding. The seasonal salad features creative pairings—mango with prawns; beets with pears—and the lamb chops with couscous are among my favorites. But it's the service, impeccable without being stuffy, that makes Canlis perfect for a special occasion. Plan to spend longer than usual for dinner, because you won't want the pampering—or the view of Lake Union—to end. *2576 Aurora Ave N.* ☎ *206/283-3313. www.canlis.com. Entrees $36–$68. AE, DISC, MC, V. Dinner Mon–Sat. Bus: 5, 16, 28. Map p 122.*

★★ 🧒 Cutters Crabhouse PIKE PLACE MARKET *NORTHWEST* This lovely restaurant is just steps from Pike Place Market. With sweeping views of Elliott Bay and friendly service, it's the perfect place to relax after shopping—and you won't feel uncomfortable bringing the kids. (There's a children's menu.) The seafood shines; try the tasty crab cakes. *2001 Western Ave.* ☎ *206/448-4884. www.cuttersbayhouse.com. Entrees $15–$49. AE, DISC, MC, V. Lunch & dinner daily. Bus: 99, 113, 121, 122. Map p 119.*

★★★ **Dahlia Lounge** BELL-TOWN *NORTHWEST* The menu at this quintessential Seattle restaurant never fails to enchant with unique flavor combinations. Think five-spice Peking duck with curry fried rice and orange chili dip. Beautiful and classy, the Dahlia is owned by legendary chef Tom Douglas, who runs a steadily growing number of Seattle establishments, including a bakery. Desserts are memorable. *2001 4th Ave.* ☎ *206/682-4142. www.tomdouglas. com/restaurants/dahlia-lounge. Entrees $27–$38. AE, DISC, MC, V. Lunch Mon–Fri, brunch Sat–Sun, dinner daily. Bus: 1, 13, 15, 26, 202. Map p 120.*

kids Dick's Drive-In CAPITOL HILL *BURGERS* Seattle's iconic burger joint still has the orange awnings from the '50s, though the drive-up service has ended. Many locals won't eat burgers anywhere else. *115 Broadway Ave. E.* ☎ *206/323-1300. www.dicksdrivein.com.*

Entrees $1.50–$2.85. Lunch & dinner daily. Bus: 8, 43, 49, 60. Map p 120.

★★ **El Gaucho** BELLTOWN *STEAK* The steaks are perfection, the service attentive at this upscale, supperclub-style steakhouse. For a special occasion, order the chateaubriand for two. *2505 1st Ave.* ☎ *206/728-1337. www.elgaucho. com. Entrees $17–$75. AE, DISC, MC, V. Dinner daily. Bus: 19, 24, 81, 99. Map p 120.*

★★ **kids Elliott's Oyster House** WATERFRONT *SEAFOOD* This is an oyster-lover's nirvana, with a huge selection of local oysters, raw, steamed, or pan-fried. The seafood is fresh and local, with standouts including the salmon (always non-farmed) and the Dungeness crab with chili-lime sauce. If it's a nice day, dine outside on the deck overhanging Elliott Bay. *1201 Alaskan Way, Pier 56.* ☎ *206/623-4340. www.elliotts oysterhouse.com. Entrees $18–$38. AE, DISC, MC, V. Lunch & dinner daily. Bus: 12, 99, 113, 121. Map p 120.*

★★ **Etta's Seafood** PIKE PLACE MARKET *SEAFOOD* Casual but classy, Etta's caters to the tourist crowd (you can even get a burger) but also has a loyal local following. Owned by chef Tom Douglas,

The decor is nearly as big a draw as the food at Dahlia Lounge.

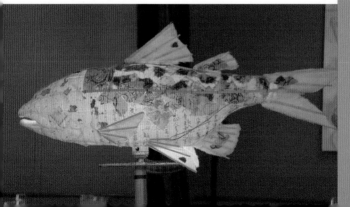

Seattle: A Locavore's Dream

Washington state's temperate climate is ideal for growing everything from apples to zucchinis. Small farms grow such a wide variety of fresh produce throughout the year that the locavore movement (eating locally as much as possible) has rapidly gained ground among chefs at top restaurants like Tilth.

Seafood Silvery salmon, hefty Dungeness crabs, clams, mussels, and dozens of varieties of oysters are the seafood stars in this city on the shores of Puget Sound. Salmon, although not always local, is a Northwest icon that shows up both fresh and smoked on Seattle menus. Wish you could take some home? Not a problem. Pike Place Market fishmongers will pack fresh salmon for you to take home on the plane, and some vacuum-packed smoked salmon doesn't even need to be refrigerated.

Chocolate Seattle's **Theo Chocolate** (☎ 206/632-5100; www. theochocolate.com), a company that gives tours of its chocolate factory, roasts its own organic and fair-trade cocoa beans. Finally, guilt-free chocolate!

Coffee Of course, as nearly everyone on the planet knows, Starbucks got its start in Seattle, and espresso here has been raised to an art form. Even espresso stands around town have jumped on the wagon, serving organic, fair-trade, and shade-grown coffees.

Wine & Beer Many of Washington state's best and biggest wineries are in the town of Woodinville, just a 30-minute drive north of Seattle. Washington wineries are best known for their cabernet sauvignon and merlot, but you should also keep an eye out for excellent syrahs and semillons. Seattle is also home to quite a few craft breweries. Check out **Big Time Brewery & Alehouse** (☎ 206/545-4509; www.bigtime brewery.com) and the **Elysian Brewing Company** (p 140).

—Karl Samson

Etta's is my favorite destination for salmon. Another sure bet: Tom's famous Dungeness crab cakes. *2020 Western Ave.* ☎ *206/443-6000. www.tomdouglas.com. Entrees $16–$36. AE, DISC, MC, V. Lunch Mon–Fri, brunch/breakfast Sat–Sun, dinner daily. Bus: 19, 21, 99, 113. Map p 119.*

★★★ **Hunt Club** FIRST HILL *NORTHWEST/MEDITERRANEAN* Inside the elegant Sorrento Hotel, this warm, sophisticated restaurant delivers classic cuisine with imaginative touches, especially in its sauces. The duck with huckleberry sauce is a standout, and the black truffle mashed potatoes are not to be missed. Do yourself a favor and order the croissant bread pudding for dessert. *900 Madison St.* ☎ *206/343-6156. www.hotelsorrento.com/food-drink/hunt-club. Entrees $23–$49. AE, DISC, MC, V. Breakfast,* lunch & dinner daily, brunch Sat–Sun. Bus: 12, 60. Map p 120.

★★ Il Fornaio DOWNTOWN *ITALIAN* By exploring a different region of Italy each month, this stylish eatery keeps things fresh. The breads, baked on site, are divine; the sauces scrumptious; and many of the wines come from Il Fornaio's own vineyard in Tuscany. My favorite: the ravioli stuffed with butternut squash and walnuts. The bakery and cafe are downstairs; climb up the spiral staircase to the classy dining room. *600 Pine St., Ste. 132.* ☎ *206/264-0994. www.ilfornaio. com. Entrees $14–$40. AE, MC, V. Breakfast, lunch & dinner daily. Bus: 10, 11, 14, 43, 49. Map p 120.*

★★ kids Ivar's Acres of Clams WATERFRONT *SEAFOOD* This iconic Seattle establishment, perched on Pier 54, has been in business in various forms since 1947. The clam chowder is arguably the best in the universe. It's a charming place to eat fresh seafood and watch the ferries cross the sound. *1001 Alaskan Way.* ☎ *206/624-6852. www.ivars.com. Entrees $15–$50. AE, DISC, MC, V. Lunch Mon–Sat, brunch Sun, dinner daily. Bus: 16, 66, 99. Map p 120.*

★ kids Jade Garden INTERNATIONAL *ASIAN* In a town blessed with a number of good dim sum spots, this is one of the best for variety, freshness, and ambience. If you're new to dim sum, start with some basics like *humbow* (steamed buns stuffed with sweet barbecued pork), *ha gao* (shrimp dumpling) and sticky rice wrapped in lotus leaves. *424 7th Ave. S.* ☎ *206/622-8181. Entrees $5–$13. MC, V. Lunch & dinner daily. Bus: 7, 14, 36, 99. Map p 120.*

★★★ Joule WALLINGFORD *KOREAN/FRENCH FUSION* Though Asian influence is common in the Seattle culinary world, there is nothing common about the cuisine at Joule. The owners blend French, Korean, and American flavors in delightful ways. The names are exotic—black bean and squid pancake, Kabocha rice grits, octopus and smoked pork belly salad—the tastes divine. On a chilly day, don't miss the roasted apple bisque with curry. *1913 N. 45th St.* ☎ *206/632-1913. www.joule restaurant.com. Entrees $17–$30. AE, DC, DISC, MC, V. Brunch Sat–Sun, dinner daily. Bus: 16, 44. Map p 122.*

★ Kabul NORTH SEATTLE *AFGHAN* Kabul transforms the humble eggplant into a dish so flavorful, I come back here again and again. Finish the night with a cup of cardamom tea. *2301 N. 45th St.* ☎ *206/545-9000. www.kabul restaurant.com. Entrees $10–$25. AE, DISC, MC, V. Dinner daily. Bus: 16, 44. Map p 122.*

★★ Lark CAPITOL HILL *INTERNATIONAL* This trendy bistro has earned a name for service and quality. The eclectic menu ranges from scrambled eggs with truffles to caviar with potatoes and cream, served on small to medium plates for sharing. *926 12th Ave.* ☎ *206/323-5275. www.larkseattle.com. Entrees $16–$25. MC, V. Dinner Tues–Sun. Bus: 2, 9, 12. Map p 120.*

★ La Carta de Oaxaca BALLARD *MEXICAN* Seattle's most authentic Mexican restaurant is known for its yummy, hand-mashed guacamole with house-fried tortilla chips and the tender chicken in Oaxaca's signature sweet-spicy black mole. *5431 Ballard Ave NW.* ☎ *206/782-8722. www.lacartade oaxaca.com. Entrees $13–$18. Lunch Tues–Sat, dinner Mon–Sat. Map p 122.*

★★ La Spiga CAPITOL HILL *ITALIAN* Lovingly prepared

Northern Italian cuisine takes the spotlight at this contemporary, inviting spot. The delicate hand-made gnocchi is a standout, served in a cream and truffle sauce spiced with Italian sausage that transforms the dumplings into comfort food at its best. *1429 12th Ave.* ☎ *206/323-8881. www.laspiga.com. Entrees $16–$29. AE, DC, DISC, MC, V. Lunch Mon–Fri, dinner daily. Bus: 2, 12. Map p 120.*

★★ **Le Pichet** PIKE PLACE MARKET *FRENCH* This casual bistro serves a classic French menu that would make a Parisian feel right at home. The ingredients are simple and fresh, the sauces superb. *1933 1st Ave.* ☎ *206/256-1499. Entrees $12–$20. DISC, MC, V. Lunch & dinner daily. Bus: 10, 99, 113, 121. Map p 119.*

★★ **List** BELLTOWN *TAPAS/ITAL-IAN* There's a nice, relaxed vibe to this affordable wine bar and tapas spot. Share a few small plates—maybe the delectable gnocchi with black truffle cream, or the sea salt and pepper calamari—with a bottle of your favorite vintage (they also have good and inexpensive bottles of house red and white) and go on from there. During Happy Hour (all day Sun–Mon, 4–6:30pm & 9pm–midnight Tues–Thurs, 4–6:30pm Fri–Sat) many dishes are half price. *2226 1st Ave.* ☎ *206/441-1000. www.listbelltown.com. Tapas $6–$14. AE, MC, V. Dinner daily. See map p 120.*

★★★ **Lola** BELLTOWN *GREEK* If you love Greek food, you probably love lamb, and if you're a lamb fan, well, you're going to love Lola. Try the lamb ravioli with yogurt, Aleppo pepper, and pine nuts; lamb kebab with caramelized garlic and red wine; lamb burger; or the slow-cooked and succulent lamb shank. And if you're just hankering for a

fresh Greek salad with tomatoes, olives, and feta cheese, this is the place to find it. *2000 4th Ave.* ☎ *206/441-1430. Entrees $17–$37. Breakfast Mon–Fri, brunch daily, lunch Mon–Fri, dinner daily. AE, MC, V. Map p 120.*

★ **Marrakesh Moroccan Restaurant** BELLTOWN *MOROCCAN* This cozy spot has the exotic feel of an Arabian tent. Diners sit on cushions or benches at round tables as tantalizing aromas and belly dancers (Wed–Sun) drift through the room. *2334 2nd Ave.* ☎ *206/956-0500. Entrees $12–$15. MC, V. Dinner daily. Bus: 1, 13, 15, 19, 24. Map p 120.*

★★ **Matt's in the Market** PIKE PLACE MARKET *NORTHWEST* Chef Shane Ryan doesn't have far to go to get market-fresh produce and seafood. Matt's expanded location is right above Pike Place Market. *94 Pike St., Ste. 32.* ☎ *206/467-7909. www.mattsinthemarket.com. AE, MC,*

Metropolitan Grill.

Cozy Tilth, located in a Craftsmen house, shows off the region's organic bounty.

V. Entrees $28–$39. Lunch & dinner Mon–Sat. Bus: 99, 113, 121, 122. Map p 119.

★★ **Maximilien** PIKE PLACE MARKET *FRENCH* Watch the sun set over Elliott Bay through panoramic windows as you dine on classic French fare. *81A Pike St.* ☎ *206/ 682-7270. www. maximilienrestaurant.com. AE, DISC, MC, V. Entrees $30–$40. Lunch & dinner daily, brunch Sun. Bus: 99, 113, 121, 122. Map p 119.*

The pizza at Pagliacci is some of the best in town.

★ **McCormick & Schmick's** LAKE UNION *SEAFOOD* With a spectacular view of Lake Union and an outside deck, this elegant restaurant is a great spot for dinner. But it's also popular at lunchtime, when you can watch the seaplanes take off. Seafood is the star, and the "fresh list" is impressively long. Don't miss the bay shrimp cake appetizers. *1200 Westlake Ave. N.* ☎ *206/270-9052. www.mccormick andschmicks.com. Entrees $16–$34. AE, DISC, MC, V. Lunch & dinner daily. Bus: 17, 30. Map p 122.*

★★★ **Metropolitan Grill** DOWNTOWN *STEAKS* This historic Seattle restaurant could make a beef-eater out of anyone. If you're in the mood for extravagance, order the prized wagyu beef. But the steak on the regular menu is so flavorful, and cooked to such perfection, there's no need to look further. At lunchtime, it's very popular with the business crowd. *820 2nd Ave.* ☎ *206/624-3287. www.the metropolitangrill.com. Entrees $20–$74. AE, MC, V. Lunch Mon–Fri, dinner daily. Bus: 143, 157, 158, 159. Map p 120.*

★★ **Miller's Guild** DOWNTOWN *PACIFIC NORTHWEST* A giant mesquite-burning stove in the open kitchen grills ribs, steaks, chops, and seafood at this spot, which opened at Hotel Max in 2014. Whet your appetite with a craft cocktail and an appetizer like the coal-roasted beets with dill, mint, caraway salt and horseradish. Then try the melt-in-your-mouth short ribs with a couple of sides, accompanied by a glass of local beer or wine. *612 Stewart St.* ☎ *206/443-3663. www.millersguild.com. Entrees $18–$63. AE, MC, V. Breakfast, lunch & dinner daily. Map p 120.*

★★ **MistralKitchen** DOWNTOWN *CONTEMPORARY AMERICAN/GLOBAL* They say you can't please everyone, but chef/owner William Belickis does his best, mingling influences from Africa, France, Spain, Japan, and the U.S. Food is prepared at four stations: a wood-fired/tandoor oven, traditional kitchen, pastry kitchen, and a high-tech kitchen. Don't miss the heavenly foie gras or the tropical *baba* dessert. Both the wine and cocktail lists are excellent. *2020 Westlake Ave.* ☎ 206/623-1922. *www.mistral-kitchen.com. Entrees $21–$38. AE, DISC, MC, V. Lunch Mon–Fri, brunch Sat–Sun, dinner & happy hour daily. Bus: 25, 98, 250, 252, 257. Map p 120.*

★★ **Morton's The Steakhouse** DOWNTOWN *STEAKS* This classic steakhouse is reminiscent of a glamorous era of crisp, white linens, rich cherry wood, and tuxedoed waiters. The service is excellent without being obtrusive; the steaks divine. My favorite? The melt-in-your-mouth filet mignon. The lengthy wine list includes an unusually interesting by-the-glass selection. *1511 6th Ave.* ☎ 206/223-0550. *www.mortons.com. Entrees $33–$64. AE, DC, DISC, MC, V. Dinner daily. Bus: 10, 11, 14, 306, 312, Map p 120.*

★ **O'Asian Kitchen** DOWNTOWN *CHINESE* The best thing at this stylish restaurant is the dim sum, popular with the office lunch crowd, which comes delicious and

Ray's Boathouse is a Seattle institution, thanks to its superb seafood.

steaming-hot from the kitchen on traditional carts. *800 5th Ave.* ☎ 206/264-1789. *Dim sum $3–$6. AE, MC, V. Lunch, dinner & dim sum daily. Bus: 250, 252, 257, 260. Map p 120.*

★★ **kids Pagliacci Pizza** CAPITOL HILL *PIZZA* The pies here come with thin, crunchy crusts and bold, tasty toppings. Pies come in three sizes to accommodate your group—or appetite. *426 Broadway Ave. E.* ☎ 206/726-1717. *www.pagliacci.com. Entrees $14–$24. AE, MC, V. Lunch & dinner daily. Bus: 9, 49. Map p 120.*

★★ **Palisade** NORTH SEATTLE *NORTHWEST/POLYNESIAN* This landmark Seattle restaurant has a Polynesian influence. The panoramic views of Elliott Bay, Mt. Rainier, and the city are stunning, and the seafood is fresh and expertly prepared. Start with the lemongrass calamari and finish with a clever bento box dessert, packed with goodies such as jasmine rice and mango tapioca "sushi." *2601 W. Marina Place.* ☎ 206/285-1000. *www.palisaderestaurant.com. Entrees $20–$43. AE, DC, DISC, MC, V. Lunch Mon–Sat, dinner daily, brunch Sun. Bus: 19, 24, 33. Map p 122.*

★★ **Place Pigalle** PIKE PLACE MARKET *FRENCH* You can't beat the mussels at this romantic spot perched above the Sound. Dine to the strains of Edith Piaf. *81 Pike St.* ☎ 206/624-1756. *www.placepigalle-seattle.com. Entrees $26–$31. AE, DISC, MC, V. Lunch & dinner daily. Bus: 99, 113, 121, 122. Map p 119.*

★★★ **Poppy** CAPITOL HILL PACIFIC *NORTHWEST/INDIAN* A foodie mecca in Capitol Hill, this innovative, award-winning restaurant created by Chef Jerry Traunfeld presents a fresh local take on the Indian *thali,* a compartmentalized platter holding various

Six Seven offers the best of both worlds: excellent food and excellent views.

dishes with many different tastes. The extraordinary medley of textures, herbs, and spices is surprising and satisfying. *622 Broadway E. ☎ 206/324-1108. www.poppy seattle.com. Thalis $24–$28. AE, MC,V. Dinner daily. Bus 8, 49. See map p 120.*

★★ Purple Café and Wine Bar
DOWNTOWN *PACIFIC NORTH-WEST/INTERNATIONAL* With its huge glass windows and floor-to-ceiling wine storage tower, the dining room dwarfs the diners, but no one seems to mind because the food is always good and the atmosphere is lively and loud. Wine is a big feature here, and wine pairings with your various plates can be surprisingly inexpensive compared to other Seattle restaurants. The menu gives a nod to international influences but makes abundant use of the bounty of the Pacific Northwest in dishes like Dungeness crab and chanterelle mushroom pasta but you can also order crispy-crust pizzas or a burger made from free-range beef. *1225 4th Ave. ☎ 206/ 829-2280. www.purplecafe.com. Entrees $22–$35. AE, MC, V. Lunch & dinner daily. Map p 120.*

★★ Racha Thai & Asian Kitchen
QUEEN ANN *ASIAN* Sure, you can get a delicious pad Thai at this elegant spot, but with so many more inventive items on the menu, consider branching out. The catfish Panang and Golden Duck with ginger sauce are real standouts. *23 Mercer St. ☎ 206/281-8883. Entrees $10–$14. AE, M, V. Lunch & dinner daily. Bus: 1, 8, 13, 15, 18. Map p 120.*

★★ Ray's Boathouse
NORTH SEATTLE *SEAFOOD* An iconic seafood restaurant in the Ballard neighborhood, Ray's menu is as fresh and delicious as ever. The view, looking out over Puget Sound, is jaw-dropping. Families with kids may opt for the more casual cafe. *6049 Seaview Ave. NW. ☎ 206/789-3770. www.rays.com. Entrees $24–$50. AE, DISC, MC, V. Lunch & dinner daily cafe, dinner daily Boathouse. Map p 122.*

★★ kids Salty's on Alki
WEST SEATTLE *SEAFOOD* The panoramic view looking across the bay at Seattle is an eye-popper—but so is the brunch buffet, laden with fresh seafood (basics along with inventive dishes like Vietnamese

catfish with red pepper sauce), pasta and omelets to order (try the lobster-filled pasta), meats, and more. The gingerbread pancakes are addictive! But save room for the dessert buffet, starring a chocolate fountain. Or come for a sunset dinner. *1936 Harbor Ave. SW.* ☎ *206/937-1600. www.saltys.com/ seattle. Entrees $14–$56. AE, DC, DISC, MC, V. Lunch Mon–Fri, dinner daily, brunch Sat–Sun. Bus: 37. Map p 120.*

★★ **Sazerac** DOWNTOWN *AMERICAN/SOUTHERN* The focus at this New Orleans–influenced spot in the beautiful Monaco Hotel is as much on fun as it is on food; Sazerac gets them both right. You won't get better catfish this side of the Mississippi. And order whatever bread pudding is on the menu. *1101 4th Ave.* ☎ *206/624-7755. www.sazeracrestaurant.com. Entrees (small & big plates): $11–$26. AE, DISC, MC, V. Breakfast & lunch Mon– Fri, dinner Mon–Sat (lounge service Sun), brunch Sat–Sun. Bus: 7, 39, 124, 202, 554. Map p 120.*

★★ **Serious Pie** DOWNTOWN *PIZZA* Chef Tom Douglas is serious about food, and that includes pizza. His applewood-burning oven turns out artisan-quality pies. My mouth waters for the Yukon gold potato pizza with rosemary and pecorino. Of course, you can order a gourmet appetizer and wine. *316 Virginia St.* ☎ *206/838-7388. www.tomdouglas. com. Entrees $15–$17. AE, DISC, MC, V. Lunch & dinner daily. Bus: 1, 13, 15, 16, 17. Map p 120.*

★★ **Shiro's** BELLTOWN *SUSHI* Try to get a seat at the sushi bar, where you can watch legendary sushi Chef Shiro Kashiba work his genial magic. *2401 2nd Ave.* ☎ *206/443-9844. www.shiros.com. Entrees $6.25–$17; assortments $17*

The Steelhead Diner offers one of the most creative menus in Seattle.

& up. AE, DISC, MC, V. Dinner daily. Bus: 19, 24, 116, 118. Map p 120.

★ **Sitka & Spruce** MELROSE *PACIFIC NORTHWEST* The lunches are great at Matt Dillon's locavore hotspot, where the focus is on fine, local foods accented with North African, Spanish, and Persian seasonings. A good choice for vegetarians. *1531 Melrose Ave.* ☎ *206/ 324-0662. www.sitkaandspruce.com. Entrees $13–$32. AE, MC, V. Lunch Mon–Fri, brunch Sat–Sun, dinner Tues–Sun. Map p 120.*

★★ **Six Seven** WATERFRONT *SEAFOOD* Located in the historic Edgewater Hotel (where the Beatles once stayed), the Six Seven feels like a cozy lodge. It showcases the best of the region's seafood. My favorite entree is the sea bass, cooked to juicy perfection with a crispy skin. Holiday brunches are spectacular. The view of Elliott Bay is dramatic; in the summertime you can eat outside. *2411 Alaskan Way.* ☎ *206/269-4575. www.edgewater hotel.com/edgewater_dining. Entrees $26–$48. AE, DISC, MC, V. Breakfast & dinner daily, lunch Mon–Sat, brunch Sun. Bus: 19, 24, 99. Map p 120.*

★ SkyCity at the Needle

DOWNTOWN *NORTHWEST* The menu features well-prepared local seafood, berries, and other produce, but the main attraction is the view. You'll see Seattle from every angle as you rotate around the Space Needle. Don't forget: Dinner includes observation deck admission. *400 Broad St.* ☎ *206/905-2100. www.spaceneedle.com/restaurant. Entrees $29–$59. AE, DISC, MC, V. Lunch Mon–Fri, brunch Sat–Sun, dinner daily. Monorail or Bus: 3, 4, 8, 16 or 30. Map p 120.*

★★ Steelhead Diner PIKE

PLACE MARKET *SEAFOOD/NEW AMERICAN* This lively spot features the cooking of Kevin Davis, who brings together influences of New Orleans, France, California, and the Northwest, making for a unique and exciting dining experience. Don't miss the crab and bay shrimp tater tots, or tortellini with truffle cream sauce. Other standouts: kasu-marinated Oregon black cod, and a fabulous veggie "meatloaf." *95 Pine St.* ☎ *206/625-0129. www.steelheaddiner.com. Entrees $17–$42. AE, DISC, MC, V. Lunch & dinner daily, brunch Sat–Sun. Bus: 10, 99, 113, 121, 122. Map p 119.*

★★ Tavolata BELLTOWN *ITAL-

IAN* This hip urban space serves up mouthwatering Italian dishes, always with more than a dash of ingenuity. The menu changes daily, so one day you'll find linguine with mussels; the next, it may come with chili and prosciutto. The mozzarella is homemade, as are the succulent pastas. *2323 2nd Ave.* ☎ *206/838-8008. www.tavolata.com. Entrees $14–$27. AE, DISC, MC, V. Dinner daily. Bus: 1, 15, 27, 19, 24. Map p 120.*

★★ Ten Mercer QUEEN ANNE

CONTEMPORARY AMERICAN Upstairs is elegantly formal; downstairs is more casual. Either way, it's

Dining Out of Town

Located in Woodinville, about 30 miles north of Seattle, The **Herbfarm** (☎ **425/485-5300;** www.theherbfarm.com) is known for its lavish, themed meals that change with the seasons. Wild gathered vegetables, Northwest seafood and meats, organic produce, wild mushrooms, and, of course, fresh herbs from the Herbfarm gardens are the ingredients from which the restaurant creates its culinary extravaganzas. Dinners are paired with complementary Northwest wines.

The restaurant is in a reproduction country inn beside a contemporary Northwest-style lodge. Dinner highlights might include paddlefish caviar on crisp salmon skin; rosemary-mussel skewers with cucumber kimchi; oysters with sorrel sauce; Dungeness crab and wild mushroom "handkerchiefs"; salmon in a squash blossom with lemon thyme; perch on salsify puree with parsley-lovage sauce; lamb served three ways; truffled cheese; and, for dessert, muscat-poached peaches with anise hyssop ice. If you're a foodie, you need to have a dinner like this at least once in your life.

—Karl Samson

a great spot for dinner before or after the opera or a play at Seattle Center—they're open 'til midnight! You can't beat the Washington chicken, juicy and tender with a perfect, crisp skin. *10 Mercer St.* ☎ *206/691-3723. www.tenmercer. com. Entrees $13–$28. AE, DISC, MC, V. Dinner daily. Bus: 1, 8, 13, 15, 18. Map p 120.*

★★★ **Tilth** NORTH SEATTLE *ORGANIC/NEW AMERICAN* This cozy restaurant in a Craftsman house showcases the organic and wild bounty of the region. Renowned chef Maria Hines whips up a mouthwatering menu of seasonal delicacies. If the savory apple soup with caramelized onion and fried shallots is available, don't miss it. *1411 N. 45th St.* ☎ *206/633-0801. www.tilthrestaurant.com. Entrees $15–$33. AE, MC, V. Dinner Mon–Sat, brunch Sat–Sun. Bus: 16, 44. Map p 122.*

★★ **Tulio Ristorante** DOWN-TOWN *ITALIAN* The pasta is painstakingly handmade at this warm, inviting spot, which I love to visit before a show at the 5th Avenue Theatre. Chef Walter Pisano is a maestro at Italian cooking with contemporary flair. One customer comes from Canada just for the sweet potato gnocchi, and when you taste it you'll know why. *1100 5th Ave. (at the Hotel Vintage).* ☎ *206/624-5500. www.tulio.com. Entrees $16–$33. AE, DISC, MC, V. Breakfast & lunch Mon–Fri, dinner daily, brunch Sat–Sun. Bus: 12, 143, 157, 158, 545. Map p 120.*

★★ **Urbane** DOWNTOWN *NORTHWEST* Blue lighting accents this chic bistro at the Hyatt at Olive 8, which manages to be both ultramodern and warmly inviting. The menu features sustainable Northwest bounty, and the chef is not afraid to mix up the flavors. Beets with melted goat cheese and pistachios? Steamed clams with bacon, mint, and jalapeno? Scrumptious! *1639 8th Ave.* ☎ *206/676-4600. www.urbaneseattle.com. Entrees $18–$38. AE, MC, V. Breakfast & lunch Mon–Fri, dinner daily, brunch Sat–Sun. Bus: 10, 11, 14, 49. Map p 120.*

★★ **Volterra** NORTH SEATTLE *ITALIAN* The rich flavors of a Tuscan village meld with the bounty of the Northwest on Don Curtiss' inventive menu. The signature dish, wild boar tenderloin with Gorgonzola sauce, is rich and creamy. The polenta with wild mushrooms is a standout appetizer. Don't pass on the chocolate orange cake. (Trust me.) *5411 Ballard Ave NW.* ☎ *206/789-5100. www.volterrarestaurant. com. Entrees $18–$34. AE, DC, DISC, MC, V. Dinner daily, brunch Sat–Sun. Bus: 17, 18, 44. Map p 122.*

★★ **Wild Ginger** DOWNTOWN *PAN-ASIAN* This wildly popular restaurant is sophisticated, glamorous, and boasts a very tempting menu emphasizing satay. You can't go wrong with the Wild Ginger fragrant duck. There's a terrific separate vegetarian menu. *1401 3rd Ave.* ☎ *206/623-4450. www.wild ginger.net. Entrees $7–$30. AE, DC, DISC, MC, V. Lunch & dinner daily. Bus: 1, 13, 14, 16, 17. Map p 120.*

★★ kids **Zeek's** BELLTOWN *PIZZA* The crust is to die for; the toppings unconventional. Try the Tree-Hugger, with mozzarella, sun-dried tomato, spinach, mushroom, artichoke hearts, broccoli, tomato, garlic, and olives. *419 Denny Way.* ☎ *206/285-8646. Entrees $14–$29. AE, MC, V. Lunch & dinner daily. Bus: 8, 30. Map p 120.* ●

Nightlife Best Bets

Best Fine-Dining Wine Bar
★★ Purple Café and Wine Bar,
1225 4th Ave. (p 141)

Best Place to Dance with the
Beautiful People
★★ Baltic Room, *1207 Pine St.*
(p 143)

Best Bartenders
★★ ZigZag Café, *1501 Western*
Ave. (p 142)

Best Date Spot
★★ BOKA Restaurant + Bar, *1010*
1st Ave. (p 140)

Best Brewpub
★★ Elysian Brewing Company,
1221 E. Pike St. (p 140); and ★ The
Pike Pub & Brewery, *1415 1st Ave.*
(p 141)

Best Mariners Game-Day
Hangout
★ Pyramid Alehouse, *1201 1st Ave.*
S. (p 142)

Best Jazz Club
★★★ Dimitriou's Jazz Alley, *2033*
6th Ave. (p 144)

Best Happy Hour
★ Contour, *807 1st Ave. (p 143)*

Best Hotel Bar
★★ Oliver's Lounge, *405 Olive*
Way (p 141)

Best Bar Burger
Two Bells, *2313 4th Ave. (p 142)*

Best Bar to Run into Your
Roommate from Harvard
★★ Bookstore Bar, *1009 1st Ave.*
(p 140)

Best Spot for a Romantic
Cocktail
★★ Fireside Room, *900 Madison St.*
(p 140)

Best Bavarian-style Beer Hall
★★ Von Trapp's, *912 12th Ave.*
(p 142)

Best (and Only) Lesbian Bar
Wild Rose, *1021 E. Pike St. (p 143)*

Best Place to See & Be Seen
★★ Black Bottle Gastro-Tavern,
2600 1st Ave. (p 140)

Best Martinis
★ Karma Martini Lounge & Bistro,
2318 2nd Ave. (p 141)

Best Gay-Friendly Bar
★ Neighbours, *1509 Broadway*
(p 143)

Elysian Brewing Company. Previous page: Vintage neon sign in Fremont.

Pioneer Square

88 Keys Dueling Piano
Sports Bar **21**
Alibi Room **5**
BOKA Restaurant
+ Bar **11**
Bookstore Bar **12**
The Central Saloon **19**
Contour **13**
Fado Irish Pub **15**
Kells Irish Restaurant
& Pub **3**
New Orleans **18**
Oliver's Lounge **1**
Owl 'N Thistle **14**

The Pike Pub
& Brewery **6**
Polar Bar **16**
Purple Café and
Wine Bar **8**
Pyramid Alehouse **23**
Slugger's **22**
Tap House Grill **2**
Temple Billiards **20**
Trinity Nightclub **17**
The Triple Door **7**
Von's 1000 Spirits **10**
W Bar **9**
ZigZag Café **4**

Downtown

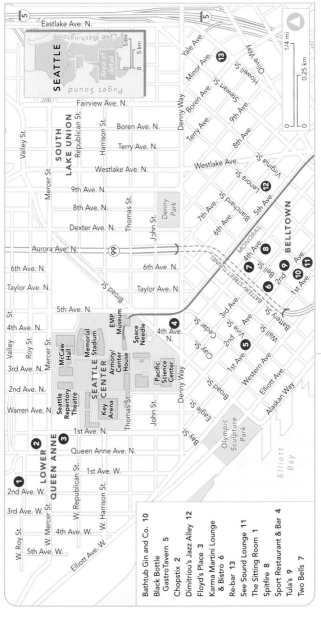

Bathtub Gin and Co. 10
Black Bottle
GastroTavern 5
Chopstix 2
Dimitriou's Jazz Alley 12
Floyd's Place 3
Karma Martini Lounge
& Bistro 6
Re-bar 13
See Sound Lounge 11
The Sitting Room 1
Spitfire 8
Sport Restaurant & Bar 4
Tula's 9
Two Bells 7

Capitol Hill

Denny Way
E. Denny Way
Olive Way
E. Howell St.
E. Howell St.

SEATTLE CENTRAL COMMUNITY COLLEGE
Cal Anderson Park

CAPITOL HILL

E. Pine St.
E. Olive St.
E. Pike St.
E. Union St.
E. Madison St.
E. Union St.
E. Spring St.

SEATTLE UNIVERSITY

FIRST HILL

Madison St.
To Downtown

Artusi **9**	Elysian Brewing Company **11**	Raygun Lounge **3**
Baltic Room **2**	Fireside Room **1**	Von Trapp's **13**
Cha Cha Lounge **5**	Madison Pub **12**	The Wild Rose **6**
Chop Suey **10**	Neighbours **4**	
The Cuff Complex **7**		

Seattle Nightlife A to Z

Bars/Lounges

★ **Alibi Room** PIKE PLACE MARKET Tucked away underneath the market, this hip pub serves up potent drinks and very good food. Club nights with dance DJs are Fridays and Saturdays, in the downstairs room. *85 Pike St., Ste. 410.* ☎ *206/623-3180. www.seattlealibi. com. Bus: 19, 21, 99, 113, 157. Map p 137.*

★ **Artusi** CAPITOL HILL When you need a hit of Italy, head for this lively, minimalist *aperitivo* bar for a grappa or amaro accompanied by excellent *stuzzichini* ("little nibbles"). *1535 14th Ave.* ☎ *206/678-2516. www.artusibar.com. Bus: 2, 10, 11. Map p 139.*

★ **Bathtub Gin and Co.** BELLTOWN All that's missing in this dimly lit, speakeasy atmosphere is the cigarette smoke. Come here for a great cocktail or, on a chilly evening, a signature hot toddy. *2205 2nd Ave.* ☎ *206/728-6069. www. bathtubginseattle.com. Bus: 19, 24, 99. Map p. 138.*

The Central Saloon is a Seattle institution.

Von Trapp's.

★★ Black Bottle Gastro-Tavern BELLTOWN Seattleites make the scene here as much for the food as the drinks. The sleek bar with its wood floor and blond tables is *au courant,* and the small plates are wonderfully inventive and tasty, even if they are healthy. *2600 1st Ave.* ☎ *206/441-1500. www.blackbottleseattle.com. Bus: 1, 13. Map p 138.*

★★ BOKA Restaurant + Bar DOWNTOWN This contemporary bar is a beautiful place to relax and enjoy gourmet bar food—the pear and blue cheese bruschetta, perhaps, or the sugar cane-skewered crab cakes. The seasonal cocktails are fun and delicious. *1010 1st Ave.* ☎ *206/357-9000. www.bokaseattle. com. Bus: 12, 16, 66, 99. Map p 137.*

★★ Bookstore Bar DOWNTOWN This elegant bar at the Alexis Hotel makes you feel like you're enjoying drinks in a well-heeled friend's private library. *1009 1st Ave.* ☎ *206/624-3646. www. librarybistro.com. Bus: 12, 16, 66, 99. Map p 137.*

The Central Saloon PIONEER SQUARE The oldest saloon in Seattle, the Central is a favorite neighborhood hangout. The food is good, and the live rock can be fabulous. *207 1st Ave. S.* ☎ *206/622-0209. www.centralsaloon.com. Cover*

$5–$10 (or joint Pioneer Square cover $12 Fri–Sat, check www.seattlejoint cover.com). Bus: 85, 99, 143, 157, 158. Map p 137.

Cha Cha Lounge CAPITOL HILL Red lighting, kitschy velvet paintings, piñatas hanging from the ceiling. Punk and heavy metal shake the rafters. Get your nachos upstairs at Bimbo's Cantina. *1013 E. Pike St.* ☎ *206/322-0703. www.chachalounge. com. Bus: 2, 10, 11. Map p 139.*

★★ Elysian Brewing Company CAPITOL HILL This award-winning microbrewery offers great beer and great food. A customer favorite is the Avatar Jasmine, an Indian pale ale brewed with jasmine flowers. *1221 E. Pike St.* ☎ *206/860-1920. www.elysianbrewing.com. Bus: 2, 10, 11. Map p 139.*

★ Fado Irish Pub DOWNTOWN Throw back a pint of Irish ale with the regulars at this popular after-work tavern. They also serve up a mean corned beef and cabbage. Irish bands play frequently. *801 1st Ave.* ☎ *206/264-2700. www.fado irishpub.com/seattle. Bus: 99, 143, 157, 158. Map p 137.*

★★ Fireside Room FIRST HILL This elegant lounge at the Sorrento Hotel is a romantic spot to stop for a drink, especially on Friday and Saturday nights, when you can hear live music, often jazz. *900 Madison*

St. ☎ 206/622-6400. Bus: 12. Map p 139.

★ Karma Martini Lounge & Bistro
BELLTOWN You've probably never had martinis like these. Think cucumber. Think Washington apple. Think delicious. *2318 2nd Ave.* ☎ *206/838-6018. www.karma seattle.com. Bus: 1, 13, 17, 19, 24. Map p 138.*

★ Kells Irish Restaurant & Pub
PIKE PLACE MARKET If it's a nice day, settle in on the patio with a shepherd's pie and a pint, and enjoy the lively mixed crowd of tourists and students. Live Irish music. *1916 Post Alley.* ☎ *206/728-1916. www.kellsirish.com. Cover free to $5. Bus: 10, 99, 113, 121, 122. Map p 137.*

★★ Oliver's Lounge
DOWNTOWN This relaxing bar at the elegant Mayflower Park Hotel serves award-winning martinis and upscale bar food. *405 Olive Way.* ☎ *206/623-8700. Bus: 25, 79, 123, 355. Map p 137.*

★ Owl N' Thistle
DOWNTOWN This popular Irish bar offers an eclectic mix of bands, including its own house Irish folk band, and a dance area. *808 Post Ave.* ☎ *206/621-7777. www.owlnthistle.com. Cover*

free to $5. Bus: 12, 16, 66, 99. Map p 137.

★ The Pike Pub & Brewery
PIKE PLACE MARKET One of the largest breweries in the state, Pike keeps customers coming back for labels like the Scotch Style Pike Kilt Lifter and Naughty Nellie. *1415 1st Ave.* ☎ *206/622-6044. Bus: 99, 113, 121, 143, 157. Map p 137.*

★★ Polar Bar
PIONEER SQUARE Watched over by a rearing polar bear (don't worry, it's art), this Art Deco lobby bar in the wonderfully restored Arctic Club Hotel, once an exclusive men's club, is a cool and civilized place for evening drinks and conversation beside the fireplace. *700 3rd Ave.* ☎ *206/340-0340. Bus: 99, 143. Map p 137.*

★★ kids Purple Café and Wine Bar
DOWNTOWN Boasting an amazing focal point—a soaring wine tower with wraparound spiral staircase—Purple has an impressive selection of vino. If you're hungry, order a cheese and wine flight, or try several small plates. Though it's a sophisticated space, children are welcome to dine. *1225 4th Ave.* ☎ *206/829-2280. www.thepurple cafe.com. Bus: 14, 21, 22, 202, 210. Map p 137.*

Kells is one of Seattle's best Irish pubs and the perfect place for a pint.

★ **Pyramid Alehouse** PIONEER SQUARE There are two big draws here: the location (across the street from Safeco Field) and the beer (including the award-winning Pyramid Hefe Weizen). On Mariners game days, it fills up fast. *1201 1st Ave. S.* ☎ *206/682-3377. Bus: 12, 21, 54, 56, 99. Map p 137.*

★ **Raygun Lounge** CAPITOL HILL It looks kind of unfinished, but that's part of the brainy charm of this super-friendly spot offering dozens of board games. While you're playing, you can order food, sip a spirit or something non-alcoholic, and never feel like you're being rushed. *501 E. Pine St.* ☎ *206/852-2521. Bus: 2, 10, 11. Map p. 139.*

See Sound Lounge BELLTOWN Trendy and lively, See Sound's crowd tends toward the younger side. A smaller club, See Sound has DJs from around the world, and cool visual projections on the walls. *115 Blanchard St.* ☎ *206/374-3733. www.seesoundlounge.com. Bus: 19, 24, 99. Map p 138.*

Fans of jazz should plan to spend an evening at Dimitriou's Jazz Alley.

★★ **The Sitting Room** QUEEN ANNE A cozy spot with more than a dash of Euro-style, the Sitting Room serves yummy specialty drinks and gourmet eats at intimate candlelit tables. *108 W. Roy.* ☎ *206/285-2830. www.the-sitting-room.com. Bus: 1, 2, 8, 13, 15. Map p 138.*

★ **Smith** CAPITOL HILL This dark, rustic tavern is a fave with locals who come for a drink and appetizers like salted cod fritters. *332 15th Ave E.* ☎ *206/709-1900. Bus: 99, 143.*

★ **Tap House Grill** DOWNTOWN With more than 150 beers

on tap and an excellent menu that includes steaks and sushi, this upscale spot is a fun place to watch a game. *1506 6th Ave.* ☎ *206/816-3314. www.taphousegrill.com. Bus: 10, 11, 14, 43, 545. Map p 137.*

Two Bells DOWNTOWN A favorite neighborhood hangout, Two Bells serves beer, wine, and some of the best burgers in Seattle. *2313 4th Ave.* ☎ *206/441-3050. www.thetwobells.com. Bus: 1, 13, 15, 16, 17. Map p 138.*

★ **Von's 1000 Spirits** DOWNTOWN Von's famous Scratch Martini ($5) is reason enough to visit this purveyor of fine spirits and fab finger foods (plus primo burgers and pizzas baked over almond wood). *1225 1st Ave* ☎ *206/621-8667. Bus: 12, 16, 99. Map p 137.*

★★ **Von Trapp's** CENTRAL DISTRICT Beer, brats ,and bocce are the three Bs that make this Bavarian-inspired beer hall and garden so popular and fun. The wursts and breads are made from scratch daily. *912 12th Ave.* ☎ *206/325-5409. Bus 2, 10, 11. Map p 139.*

★ **W Bar** DOWNTOWN With a classy decor, great happy hour, and gourmet bar food, the W is a favorite after-work gathering spot. *1112 4th Ave.* ☎ *206/264-6000. Bus: 202, 210, 214, 215, 554. Map p 137.*

★★ **ZigZag Café** PIKE PLACE MARKET The bartenders at this friendly and comfortable lounge are practically magicians and more than happy to fill you in on all their amazing cocktails, many made with fresh-squeezed juices. The food's great, too—try the Sangrita pork, flamed in tequila. *1501 Western*

Ave. ☎ 206/625-1146. www.zigzag
seattle.com. Bus: 12, 99, 113, 121,
122. Map p 137.

Dance Clubs

★★ **Baltic Room** CAPITOL HILL
This classy, romantic club plays
themed music from around the
globe. A fun clientele of various
ethnicities and sexual persuasions
packs the small dance floor. 1207
Pine St. ☎ 206/625-4444. www.
balticroom.com. Cover free to $10.
Bus: 10, 11, 14, 43, 49. Map p 139.

Chop Suey CAPITOL HILL The
dance floor is usually packed at this
eclectic bar. Bands and DJs range
from punk to techno. 1325 E. Madison. ☎ 206/324-8005. www.chop
suey.com. Cover free to $30. Bus: 2,
10, 11, 12. Map p 139.

★ **Contour** DOWNTOWN This is
where serious partiers dance till
dawn to DJs and live bands. Happy
hour on Friday lasts 6 hours, ending
at 9pm. 807 1st Ave. ☎ 206/447-
7704. www.clubcontour.com. Cover
free to $10. Bus: 12, 16, 66. Map
p 137.

★ **Trinity Nightclub** PIONEER
SQUARE A young clientele dances
its way through three areas, each
with a different type of music, at
this multi-level dance club. The
dance floor is one of the largest in
town. 111 Yesler Way. ☎ 206/447-
4140. Cover free to $15. www.trinity
nightclub.com. Bus: 99, 143, 157,
158, 161. Map p 137.

Gay & Lesbian-Friendly
The Cuff Complex CAPITOL
HILL This very popular gay bar
draws mostly men. It has pool
tables, pinball, a small dance floor,
and nice outdoor deck in the back.
1533 13th Ave. ☎ 206/323-1525.
Bus: 2, 10, 11, 12. Map p 139.

Disco balls light up the room at Trinity.

Madison Pub CAPITOL HILL The
crowd at this low-key pub is mixed,
but mostly gay and male. It's a
down-to-earth place with welcoming bartenders. 1315 E. Madison St.
☎ 206/325-6537. Bus: 2, 10, 11, 12.
Map p 139.

★ **Neighbours** CAPITOL HILL
This longtime favorite disco is gay-
friendly but attracts a mixed group
to bump and grind on its large,
popular dance floor. 1509 Broadway. ☎ 206/324-5358. www.
neighboursnightclub.com. Bus: 2,
10, 11, 49. Map p 139.

Re-bar BELLTOWN There's always
something going on at this funky
club, which attracts a mixed
straight/younger gay (some in drag)
clientele. There's dancing every
night. 1114 Howell St. ☎ 206/233-
9873. www.rebarseattle.com. Bus:
70, 71, 72, 73, 83. Map p 138.

The Wild Rose CAPITOL HILL
Everyone is welcome at Seattle's
only real lesbian bar, as long as
they're tolerant and don't gawk at
the ladies. The drinks are strong, the
bar food is good, and the atmosphere is laid-back. 1021 E. Pike St.
☎ 206/324-9210. www.thewildrose
bar.com. Bus: 2, 10, 11. Map p 139.

Live Jazz & Blues

★★★ Dimitriou's Jazz Alley

BELLTOWN With consistently great acts from around the globe, this beautiful club is Seattle's premier jazz spot. *2033 6th Ave.* ☎ *206/441-9729. www.jazzalley.com. Ticket prices vary; check website. South Lake Union Street Car 98, Bus: 25, 66, 70, 73, 250. Map p 138.*

★ New Orleans PIONEER

SQUARE The New Orleans is hopping every night with live jazz, zydeco, and blues. Chow down on some Cajun food while you listen. Kids are allowed until 10pm. *114 1st Ave. S.* ☎ *206/622-2563. www. neworleanscreolerestaurant.com. Cover free to $10 Fri–Sat. Bus: 99, 143, 157, 158, 159. Map p 137.*

★★★ The Triple Door DOWN-

TOWN This former vaudeville theater attracts an upscale, friendly crowd. Hear music from around the world upstairs in the Musiquarium (a bar with a huge fish tank) or buy a ticket to watch the show in the Mainstage Theatre. Shows that start before 9pm are open to children. *216 Union St.* ☎ *206/838-4333. www.tripledoor.com. Ticket prices vary. Bus: 143, 157, 158, 159, 162. Map p 137.*

★ Tula's BELLTOWN You'll find

live jazz nightly at this intimate club, plus a tasty Mediterranean menu. All ages welcome until 10pm. *2214 2nd Ave.* ☎ *206/443-4221. www. tulas.com. Cover $5–$15. Bus: 19, 21, 24, 56. Map p 138.*

Piano Bars

★ 88 Keys Dueling Piano

Sports Bar PIONEER SQUARE An unlikely combination of dueling pianists and sports makes this a unique and entertaining spot. The show starts at 9pm. *315 2nd Ave. S.*

☎ *206/839-1300. Cover free to $10. Bus: 13, 99, 522. Map p 137.*

★ Chopstix QUEEN ANNE The

fun starts at 8pm, when dueling performers play their hearts out on a pair of grand pianos. *11 Roy St.* ☎ *206/270-4444. www.chopstix pianobar.com. Cover free to $7. Bus: 1, 2, 8, 13, 15. Map p 138.*

Sports Bars

Floyd's Place QUEEN ANNE Savor some of the best barbecue in town while you watch a game at this neighborhood hangout. Pool tables are in the back. *521 1st Ave. N.* ☎ *206/284-3542. Bus: 1, 2, 8, 13, 15. Map p 138.*

★ Slugger's PIONEER SQUARE

Across from CenturyLink Field, this convenient location draws lots of pre- and post-game fans. *538 1st Ave. S.* ☎ *206/654-8070. Bus: 13, 70, 85, 99, 522. Map p 137.*

★ Spitfire BELLTOWN Lots and

lots of TV sets airing lots and lots of events. Grab a bowl of yummy tortilla soup, loaded with avocado, or a pulled pork sandwich, and settle in. *2219 4th Ave.* ☎ *206/441-7966. Bus: 1, 13, 17, 56, 202. Map p 138.*

★ Sport Restaurant & Bar

QUEEN ANNE If you get a booth, you can control your own TV set. If not, you'll have plenty of options, including the gargantuan HD screen over the lounge. *140 4th Ave. N., Ste. 130.* ☎ *206/404-7767. Bus: 3, 8, 13, 16, 30. Map p 138.*

★ Temple Billiards PIONEER

SQUARE A friendly place with great pool tables and sticks, Temple also has a DJ and dancing downstairs. And it's open for lunch. *126 S. Jackson St.* ☎ *206/682-3242. Bus: 10, 13, 99. Map p 137.* ●

Arts & Entertainment Best Bets

Most **Jaw-Dropping Show with Dinner**
★★★ Teatro ZinZanni, *222 Mercer St. (p 146)*

Best **Place to Go for a Chuckle**
★ The Comedy Underground, *109 S. Washington St. (p 148)*

Best **Family Entertainment**
★★ Zootunes, *N. 59th St. and Evanston Ave. (p 149)*

Best **Popular Music**
★★★ Showbox, *1426 1st Ave. (p 152)*

Best **Orchestra**
★★★ Seattle Symphony, *200 University St. (p 148)*

Most **Eclectic Theater Calendar**
★★ The Moore Theatre, *1932 2nd Ave. (p 151)*

Best **Place to Hear Chamber Music One Night and a Talk on Religion in Politics the Next**
★★ Town Hall, *1119 8th Ave. (p 148)*

Best **Theater to Take Your Date before Popping the Question**
★★★ Paramount Theatre, *911 Pine St. (p 152)*

Best **Place to Watch an Arabesque**
★★★ Pacific Northwest Ballet, *321 Mercer St. (p 149)*

Most **Eclectic Musical Lineup**
★★★ The Triple Door, *216 Union St. (p 150)*

The Pacific Northwest Ballet. Previous page: Entertainment at Teatro ZinZanni.

Seattle Arts & Entertainment

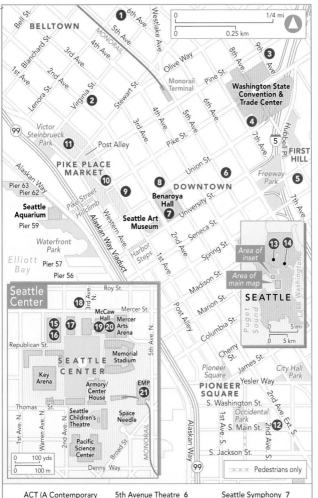

ACT (A Contemporary
  Theatre) 4
Can Can 10
The Comedy
  Underground 12
Cornish Playhouse 17
Dimitriou's Jazz Alley 1
Experience Music
  Project 21

5th Avenue Theatre 6
The Moore Theatre 2
Pacific Northwest Ballet 19
Paramount Theatre 3
The Pink Door Cabaret 11
Seattle Gilbert & Sullivan
  Society 16
Seattle Opera 20
Seattle Repertory Theatre 15

Seattle Symphony 7
Showbox 9
Teatro ZinZanni 18
Town Hall 5
The Triple Door 8
UW World Series 14
Zootunes 13

Arts & Entertainment A to Z

Feeling daring? Head to Can Can.

Classical Music

★★★ Seattle Symphony

DOWNTOWN The 85-person orchestra is beloved in the community, and has been going strong for more than a century. The Seattle Symphony is internationally respected and known for pushing the envelope musically and showcasing contemporary, as well as classical works. It performs in the beautiful and acoustically outstanding Benaroya Hall. *200 University St.* ☎ *206/215-4800. www.seattlesymphony.org. Ticket prices vary. Bus: 212, 216, 217, 218, 225. Map p 147.*

Comedy Clubs

★ The Comedy Underground

PIONEER SQUARE Comics from around the country keep the audience in stitches here every night of the week. The roster includes winners of regional comedy contests, late-night TV guests, and up-and-comers. The historic club is headquarters for the Seattle International Comedy Competition. *109 S. Washington St.* ☎ *206/628-0303. www.comedyunderground.com. Ticket prices vary. Bus: 85, 99. Map p 147.*

Concert Venues

★ Experience Music Project

The EMP hosts live concerts in its beautiful Sky Church auditorium; check the website for a calendar of events and ticket prices. *325 5th Ave. N.* ☎ *206/770-2700. Ticket prices vary. Monorail or Bus: 3, 16, 30, 82. Map p 147.*

★★ Town Hall FIRST HILL From

chamber music to science lectures to political discussions, you never know what you might hear at Town Hall, Seattle's cultural gathering place—despite the name, it is not connected to city government. The beautifully restored Roman-revival building houses two performance halls. *1119 8th Ave.* ☎ *206/652-4255.*

The Seattle Symphony Orchestra.

www.townhallseattle.org. *Ticket prices vary. Bus: 2, 12. Map p 147.*

★★ **Zootunes** FREMONT Every summer, locals head to Woodland Park Zoo one evening during the week to lounge on a grassy meadow and hear concerts by old favorites and new groups. You might hear anyone from Art Garfunkel to Roseanne Cash. The concert starts at 6, just inside the northern zoo gate. Lots of folks bring picnic baskets and low chairs or towels, but food is also available. You can buy tickets at the zoo, but many concerts sell out, so check the website in advance. *N. 59th St. & Evanston Ave.* ☎ *206/548-2500, ext.1164. www.zoo.org/zootunes. Prices vary but are reasonable; kids 12 & under free. Bus: 5, 82. Map p 147.*

Dance

★★★ **Pacific Northwest Ballet** QUEEN ANNE One of the country's largest and most acclaimed ballet companies, the PNB gives more than 100 performances a year, mostly at the beautiful Marion Oliver McCaw Hall, culminating in the beloved *Nutcracker*—complete with spectacular Maurice Sendak sets—over the holidays. *321 Mercer St.* ☎ *206/684-7200. www.pnb.org. Ticket prices vary. Bus: 3, 16, 82. Map p 147.*

★★ **UW World Series** UNIVERSITY DISTRICT The University of Washington brings in world-class dancers, musicians, and other artists from around the globe to perform at Meany Hall on the UW campus. The season runs October through May. UW Arts Ticket Office: 3901 University Way NE. Meany Hall is on the west side of the UW campus. *15th Ave. NE & NE 40th.* ☎ *206/543-4880. www.uwworldseries.org. Tickets $30–$55; $20 students (advance). Bus: 25, 43, 49, 70. Map p 147.*

The Paramount Theatre.

Dinner Theatre

★ **Can Can** PIKE PLACE MARKET This avant-garde cabaret venue is for the daring and open-minded. It's on the cutting edge of neo-burlesque. Dinner/show packages are available, and there is also a happy hour menu. Can Can brings in local and national acts, and also has its own house cabaret troupe. Almost anything can happen here! *94 Pike St.* ☎ *206/652-0832. www.thecan can.com. Show $5–$10. Bus: 19, 99, 113, 121, 122. Map p 147.*

★★ **The Pink Door Cabaret** PIKE PLACE MARKET There's almost always something out of the ordinary going on here, be it a trapeze artist or accordion player. But Saturday nights are reserved for the fun and naughty burlesque show in the lounge, which starts at 11pm and incorporates cross-dressing and elements of striptease. Come earlier and you can enjoy a delicious Italian meal in the dining room before the show. *1919 Post Alley.* ☎ *206/443-3241. www.thepinkdoor.net. Cover for burlesque show $15. Bus: 10, 99, 113, 121, 122. Map p 147.*

A performer at Teatro ZinZanni.

★★★ Teatro ZinZanni QUEEN ANNE
Talk about overstimulation! This incredible spectacle of sights and sounds, set inside a huge tent, is accompanied by a first-class five-course meal by none other than legendary Seattle Chef Tom Douglas. This 3-hour mix of acrobatics, circus acts, cabaret, comedy, and audience interaction must be experienced to be believed. Teatro is housed in a spectacular building just across from McCaw Hall. *222 Mercer St.* ☎ *206/802-0015. www.zinzanni.com. Showtimes 6:30pm Thurs–Sat (& some Wed); 5:30pm Sun. Tickets $99–$165 depending on day & seating area. ($10/ticket more in Dec.) Bus: 1, 2, 8, 13, 15. Map p 147.*

Jazz

★★★ Dimitriou's Jazz Alley
BELLTOWN If you're a jazz-lover, don't miss Dimitriou's while you're in town. The lineup of world-class performers at this large, yet somehow intimate, dinner/jazz club never fails to amaze. *2033 6th Ave.* ☎ *206/441-9729. www.jazzalley. com. Ticket prices vary; check website. South Lake Union Street Car 98, Bus: 25, 123, 250, 252. Map p 147.*

★★★ The Triple Door DOWNTOWN
Jazz is just part of the attraction at this hot club, known for its eclectic roster of performers. Its offerings even include chamber music by a group of musicians from the Seattle Symphony. *216 Union St.* ☎ *206/838-4333. www.tripledoor. com. Ticket prices vary. Bus: 143, 157, 158, 159, 161. Map p 147.*

Opera

★ Seattle Gilbert & Sullivan Society FIRST HILL
This is an amateur group, but it does the Victorian opera writers proud. The shows

Dimitriou's Jazz Alley hosts some of jazz's finest acts.

are fun, colorful, and fast-paced. The group uses different venues and ticket prices vary; check the website. ☎ 206/682-0796. www.pattersong.org. Map p 147.

★★★ **Seattle Opera** QUEEN ANNE Housed in the Marion Oliver McCaw Hall, this fine company performs the great operatic repertoire and an acclaimed "Ring" cycle every 4 years. *321 Mercer St.* ☎ *206/389-7676. www.seattleopera.org. Ticket prices vary. Bus: 3, 16, 82. Map p 147.*

Plays

★★★ **5th Avenue Theatre** DOWNTOWN This elegant playhouse produces some of the liveliest theater in Seattle, including original and Broadway-bound shows and Broadway musicals. *1308 5th Ave.* ☎ *206/625-1900. www.5thavenue.org. Ticket prices vary. Bus: 250, 252, 257, 260, 261. Map p 147.*

★★ **ACT (A Contemporary Theatre)** DOWNTOWN The focus at this energetic venue is on newer plays and playwrights, rather than the classics. *700 Union St.* ☎ *206/292-7676. www.acttheatre.org. Ticket prices vary. Bus: 306, 312, 522. Map p 147.*

The Triple Door features a broad range of acts.

★★ **Intiman Theatre** Serious drama-lovers will love the Tony award–winning Intiman. This gem of a regional theater, on the north side of Seattle Center, has produced international classics as well as contemporary plays—including some world premieres—for over 3 decades. Prices vary; check box office and website. *201 Mercer St.* ☎ *206/443-2222. www.intiman.org. Bus: 1, 2, 8, 13.*

★★ **The Moore Theatre** DOWNTOWN Seattle's oldest theater, the Moore hosts some of its edgier acts. It's always a diverse lineup; you might see anyone from cross-dressing Dame Edna to Ladysmith Black Mambazo—with

A performance by the Seattle Opera.

Cheap Tickets

If you want to catch a show in town but don't have tickets, try the theater box office—you can sometimes score a great deal an hour before a performance. But first try www.goldstar.com (click on "Seattle" at the bottom of the page), where you can get discounted deals on many local shows, as well as on lake and harbor cruises.

perhaps a children's play scheduled in between. *19322ndAve.* ☎ *206/467-5510. www.stgpresents.org. Ticket prices vary. Bus: 10, 25, 99, 113, 121. Map p 147.*

★★★ Paramount Theatre

DOWNTOWN From Broadway to rock shows, the Paramount offers superb entertainment in a glamorous historic setting. *911 Pine St. ☎ 206/467-5510. www.stgpresents. org. Ticket prices vary. Bus: 10, 11, 14, 43, 49. Map p 147.*

★★ Seattle Repertory Theatre

The Rep's offerings tend to be important, beautifully performed literary and artistic productions. The theater itself is an elegant venue, located at Seattle Center. *155 Mercer St. ☎ 206/443-2222. www.seattlerep.org. Prices vary;* check with box office or on the website. Bus: 1, 2, 8, 13, 15. Map p 147.

Popular Music

★★★ Showbox

PIKE PLACE MARKET One of Seattle's premier music clubs, the legendary Showbox has a lot going for it: great bands, elbowroom, good acoustics, and lots of all-ages shows. (The under-21s have their own section.) Around since 1939, the ballroom has hosted everyone from Duke Ellington to Pearl Jam. There is also a Showbox in the Sodo district. *Market location: 1426 1st Ave. Sodo: 1700 1st Ave. S. Info line for both: ☎ 206/628-3151. www.showbox online.com. Ticket prices vary by event; check website. Bus: 99, 113, 121, 122, 143. Map p 147.* ●

A performance of The Women *at ACT.*

Seattle **Lodging**

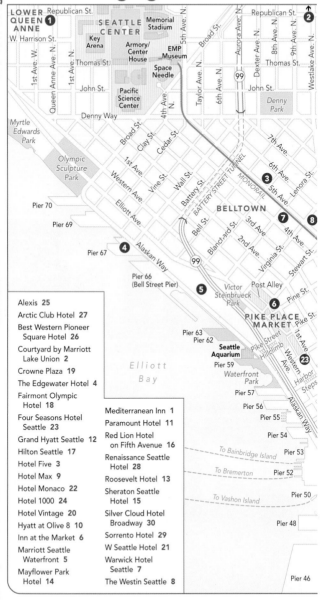

LOWER QUEEN ANNE ❶

Republican St.
W. Harrison St.
W. Thomas St.
John St.
Denny Way

SEATTLE CENTER
Key Arena
Armory/Center House
Pacific Science Center

Memorial Stadium
EMP Museum
Space Needle

Republican St. ❷
Thomas St.
John St.

Denny Park

Myrtle Edwards Park
Olympic Sculpture Park
Pier 70
Pier 69
Pier 67 ❹

Broad St.
Clay St.
Cedar St.
1st Ave.
Western Ave.
Vine St.
Wall St.
Battery St.
Elliott Ave.
Bell St.
Alaskan Way

BATTERY STREET TUNNEL
MONORAIL

BELLTOWN
3rd Ave.
2nd Ave.
Blanchard St.
Virginia St.
Stewart St.

7th Ave.
6th Ave.
5th Ave.
Lenora St.
4th Ave.

❸ ❼ ❽

Pier 66 (Bell Street Pier) ❺

Victor Steinbrueck Park
Post Alley
Pine St.

PIKE PLACE MARKET
Pike St.

❻

Elliott Bay

Pier 63
Pier 62
Seattle Aquarium
Pier 59
Waterfront Park
Pier 57
Pier 56
Pier 55
Pier 54

Pike Street Hillclimb
Western Ave.
Harbor Steps
Alaskan Way
❷❸

To Bainbridge Island   Pier 53
To Bremerton   Pier 52
To Vashon Island   Pier 50

Pier 48

Pier 46

Alexis **25**
Arctic Club Hotel **27**
Best Western Pioneer Square Hotel **26**
Courtyard by Marriott Lake Union **2**
Crowne Plaza **19**
The Edgewater Hotel **4**
Fairmont Olympic Hotel **18**
Four Seasons Hotel Seattle **23**
Grand Hyatt Seattle **12**
Hilton Seattle **17**
Hotel Five **3**
Hotel Max **9**
Hotel Monaco **22**
Hotel 1000 **24**
Hotel Vintage **20**
Hyatt at Olive 8 **10**
Inn at the Market **6**
Marriott Seattle Waterfront **5**
Mayflower Park Hotel **14**

Mediterranean Inn **1**
Paramount Hotel **11**
Red Lion Hotel on Fifth Avenue **16**
Renaissance Seattle Hotel **28**
Roosevelt Hotel **13**
Sheraton Seattle Hotel **15**
Silver Cloud Hotel Broadway **30**
Sorrento Hotel **29**
W Seattle Hotel **21**
Warwick Hotel Seattle **7**
The Westin Seattle **8**

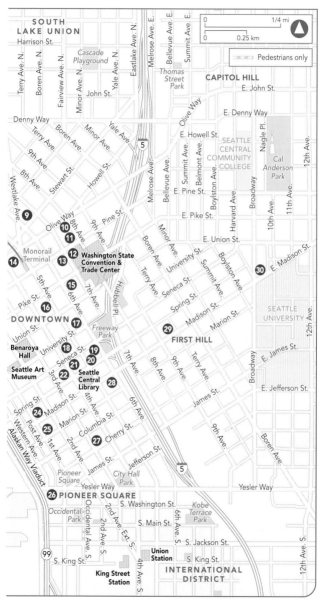

SOUTH LAKE UNION
Harrison St.

Cascade Playground

Thomas Street Park

CAPITOL HILL

Terry Ave. N.
Boren Ave. N.
Minor Ave. N.
Fairview Ave. N.
Yale Ave. N.
Eastlake Ave. N.
Melrose Ave. E.
Bellevue Ave. E.
Summit Ave. E.

E. John St.

John St.

Denny Way

Olive Way

E. Denny Way

Terry Ave.
Boren Ave.
Minor Ave.
Yale Ave.

E. Howell St.

9th Ave.
8th Ave.
Stewart St.
Howell St.

Minor Ave.

Melrose Ave.

Bellevue Ave.
Summit Ave.
Belmont Ave.
Boylston Ave.
Harvard Ave.
Broadway

SEATTLE CENTRAL COMMUNITY COLLEGE

E. Pine St.

E. Pike St.

Nagle Pl.

Cal Anderson Park

10th Ave.
11th Ave.
12th Ave.

Westlake Ave.

⑨

Olive Way

8th Ave.
9th Ave.
Pine St.

E. Union St.

⑩
⑪

Monorail Terminal

⑭

⑬

⑫ Washington State Convention & Trade Center

Hubbell Pl.

Minor Ave.
Boren Ave.
Terry Ave.
University St.
Seneca St.
Spring St.
Summit Ave.
Boylston Ave.
University Ave.

㉚ E. Madison St.

SEATTLE UNIVERSITY

5th Ave.
6th Ave.
7th Ave.

⑮

Pike St.

⑯

⑰

Freeway Park

Madison St.
Marion St.

㉙ FIRST HILL

12th Ave.

DOWNTOWN

Union St.
University St.
Seneca St.

Benaroya Hall

⑱
㉑
⑲
⑳

3rd Ave.
4th Ave.

7th Ave.
8th Ave.
9th Ave.
Terry Ave.

Broadway

E. James St.

Seattle Art Museum

㉒ Seattle Central Library

㉘

James St.

E. Jefferson St.

Spring St.
Madison St.
Marion St.

㉔

㉕

Columbia St.

6th Ave.
9th Ave.

Western Ave.
Post Ave.
1st Ave.
2nd Ave.

Alaskan Way Viaduct

㉗ Cherry St.

Jefferson St.

Boren Ave.

Pioneer Square
James St.

City Hall Park

5

Yesler Way

Yesler Way

㉖ PIONEER SQUARE

Occidental Park

Occidental Ave. S.
2nd Ave.

S. Washington St.

Kobe Terrace Park

2nd Ave. Ext. S.
4th Ave. S.

S. Main St.

S. Jackson St.

99

S. King St.

King Street Station

Union Station

S. King St.

INTERNATIONAL DISTRICT

12th Ave. S.

0   1/4 mi
0   0.25 km

Pedestrians only

Lodging **Best Bets**

Most **Authentic Seattle Experience**
★★★ The Edgewater Hotel $$$–$$$$ 2411 Alaskan Way (p 157)

Best **Panoramic City Views**
★★ The Westin Seattle $$–$$$$ 1900 5th Ave. (p 162)

Most **Romantic**
★★★ Inn at the Market $$$–$$$$ 86 Pine St. (p 160)

Most **Traditionally Elegant**
★★★ Fairmont Olympic $$$–$$$$ 411 University St. (p 157)

Most **Whimsical**
★★ Hotel Monaco $$–$$$$ 1101 4th Ave. (p 159)

Most **Elegant European Style**
★★★ Sorrento $$–$$$ 900 Madison St. (p 161)

Best **Location**
★★ Alexis $$–$$$$$ 1007 1st Ave (p 157)

Best **Choice for Wine-Lovers**
★★★ Hotel Vintage $$–$$$$ 1100 5th Ave. (p 159)

Greenest Hotel
★★ Hyatt at Olive 8 $$–$$$$ 1635 8th Ave. (p 160)

Hippest Hotel
Tie: ★★★ W Seattle Hotel $$–$$$$ 1112 4th Ave. (p 162); and ★★★ Hotel 1000 $$–$$$$$ 1000 1st Ave. (p 159)

Newest Hot Hotel
★★★ Arctic Club 700 $$–$$$ 3rd Ave. (p 157)

Most **Stunning Lobby**
★★★ Four Seasons Hotel $$–$$$$ 99 Union St. (p 158)

Artsiest Hotel
★★ Hotel Max $$–$$$ 620 Stewart St. (p 158)

Best **Seattle History**
★★ Best Western Pioneer Square Hotel Way $$–$$$ 77 Yesler (p 157)

Pool with the Best View
★★★ Seattle Marriott Waterfront $$–$$$$ 2100 Alaskan Way (p 161)

The Edgewater Hotel brings Seattle's unique style to each of its guest rooms.
Page 153: The W Seattle.

Seattle **Hotels A to Z**

★★ kids **Alexis** DOWNTOWN
Just north of Pioneer Square, this
cozy boutique hotel is luxurious
and romantic, pampering guests
with 300-thread count sheets,
comfy beds, flatscreen TVs, and a
spa. Jetted tubs and wood-burning
fireplaces are available in some
suites. Unwind and/or dine at the
Bookstore Bistro & Bar. *1007 1st
Ave. (at Madison).* ☎ *866/356-8894
or 206/624-4844. www.alexishotel.
com. 121 units. Standard doubles
$175–$485. AE, DC, DISC, MC, V.
Bus: 12, 16, 66, 99. Map p 154.*

★★★ **Arctic Club Hotel**
DOWNTOWN Once an exclusive
club for gold prospectors who
struck it rich, this historic building
now houses the luxurious Double-
tree Arctic Club Hotel. The period
warmth and glamour remains, from
the beautiful Alaskan marble to the
sculpted walruses that wrap around
the outside of the building. Ask to
see the dramatic Northern Lights
Dome Room, with its spectacular
restored stained-glass dome. *700
3rd Ave. (at Cherry St.).* ☎ *800/600-
7775 or 206/340-0340. www.arctic
clubhotel.com. 120 units. Standard
doubles $349–$429. AE, DC, DISC,
MC, V. Bus: 11, 15, 18, 121, 122,
Map p 154.*

★★ **Best Western Pioneer
Square Hotel** PIONEER SQUARE
Set in the midst of Seattle's charming historic district, this hotel brings
history to life in a century-old
Romanesque Victorian building. *77
Yesler Way.* ☎ *800/800-5514 or
206/340-1234. www.pioneersquare.
com. 72 units. Standard doubles
$125–$250 w/deluxe continental
breakfast. AE, DC, DISC, MC, V. Bus:
99, 143, 157, 158, 159. Map p 154.*

★ kids **Courtyard by Marriott
Lake Union** LAKE UNION This
hotel on Lake Union is not in the
heart of downtown, but a nearby
streetcar runs downtown every
15 minutes until 9pm (11pm on
weekends). Try to book a room
overlooking the lake with its houseboats, sailboats, steamers and kay-
aks. The hotel also has a pool. *925
Westlake Ave. N.* ☎ *800/321-2211
or 206/213-0100. www.courtyard
lakeunion.com. 250 units. Standard
doubles $169–$239. AE, DC, DISC,
MC, V. Bus: 26, 28. Map p 154.*

★★ **Crowne Plaza** DOWN-
TOWN Two blocks from the convention center and a few blocks
from Pike Place Market, this comfortable, inviting hotel is also near
the theaters and downtown shops.
1113 6th Ave. ☎ *800/770-5675 or
206/464-1980. www.cphotelseattle.
com. 415 units. Standard doubles
$209–$309. AE, DC, DISC, MC, V.
Bus: 3, 5, 16, 82. Map p 154.*

★★★ **The Edgewater Hotel**
WATERFRONT This landmark Seattle inn has the woodsy feel of a
mountain lodge, and it's the only
hotel in town directly on the waterfront. Perched over Elliott Bay, the
Edgewater affords stunning sunset
views. The Beatles once stayed
here, and fished in the sound from
their window. *2411 Alaskan Way,
Pier 67.* ☎ *800/624-0670 or 206/
728-7000. www.edgewaterhotel.com.
223 rooms. Standard doubles $202–
$449. AE, DC, DISC, MC, V. Bus: 19
24, 99. Map p 154.*

★★★ kids **Fairmont Olympic
Hotel** DOWNTOWN Traditional
elegance is the theme at this classic
luxury hotel. The rooms have down
pillows and duvets and have an

The lushly elegant lobby at the Fairmont Olympic.

old-fashioned comfort and graciousness. A welcome package is available for children. *411 University St.* ☎ *800/257-7544 or 206/621-1700. www.fairmont.com/seattle. 450 units. Standard doubles $249–$449. MC, V. Bus: 85, 143, 150, 157, 158. Map p 154.*

★★★ Four Seasons Hotel

DOWNTOWN One of Seattle's newest hotels, the chic and luxurious Four Seasons features floor-to-ceiling windows in its guest rooms, looking out on expansive bay or city views. The rooftop pool shimmers beside a toasty-warm fireplace, the lobby is a dream of basalt, wood, and marble. *99 Union St.* ☎ *206/749-7000. www.fourseasons.com/seattle. 149 rooms. Standard doubles $385–$635. Bus: 12, 99, 121, 122, 125. Map p 154.*

★★★ Grand Hyatt Seattle

DOWNTOWN This high-tech hotel has comfy beds and oversized bathrooms with soaking tubs. Check out the local art throughout the hotel, including a glass "waterfall" sculpture in the lobby. Adjacent to Ruth's Chris Steak House. *721 Pine St.* ☎ *888/591-1234 or 206/774-1234. www.grandseattle. hyatt.com/hyatt/hotels/index.jsp.*

Standard doubles $179–$369. AE, DC, DISC, MC, V. Bus: 10, 11, 14, 43, 49. Map p 154.

★ kids Hilton Seattle DOWN-

TOWN Conveniently connected by tunnel to both the convention center and 5th Avenue shopping area, the Hilton is especially popular with business travelers. The staff is multilingual. The rooms have great views, and they come with large HDTVs with music channels and Nintendo systems. *1301 6th Ave.* ☎ *800/HILTONS or 206/624-0500. www.seattlehilton.com. Standard doubles $219–$360. AE, DC, DISC, MC, V. Bus: 2, 250, 306, 312, 522. Map p 154.*

★ Hotel FIVE Seattle DOWN-

TOWN This former Ramada Inn, now with completely reimagined decor, is a reasonably priced choice. While not right in the shopping core, you can easily walk to downtown and Seattle Center. Max's Café serves breakfast and lunch. *2200 5th Ave. (at Blanchard St.).* ☎ *206/441-9785. www.hotel fiveseattle.com. Standard doubles $120–$235. AE, DC, DISC, MC, V. Bus: 56, 202. Map p 154.*

★★ Hotel Max DOWNTOWN

Don't have time to stop at the art

museum? At this unique hotel, where you get a menu of pillow choices, the original works of hundreds of local artists and photographers are showcased in the lobby and guestrooms. There a free, nightly craft-beer hour and Miller's Guild restaurant (p 129) is on site. *620 Stewart St. (at 6th Ave.).* ☎ *866/833-6299 or 206/728-6299. www. hotelmaxseattle.com. 163 units. Standard doubles $149–$389. AE, DISC, MC, V. S. Union Street Car 99, Bus: 25, 123, 250, 252, 257. Map p 154.*

★★ **kids** **Hotel Monaco** DOWN-TOWN The whimsical decor at this lovely boutique hotel makes it an inviting place for kids and adults. Kids get their own welcome gift and special programs, but there's ample pampering for grown-ups, too, including a complimentary evening wine hour. You can bring your dog—and even order dinner and a free pillow for him—or just borrow a goldfish overnight. The Sazerac restaurant (p 132) injects a dash of New Orleans to its dishes. *1101 4th Ave.* ☎ *800/715-6513 or 206/621-1770. www.monaco-seattle.com. 189 units. Standard doubles $149–$389. AE, DC, DISC, MC, V. Bus: 202, 210, 214, 215, 554. Map p 154.*

★★★ **Hotel 1000** DOWNTOWN This modern, sophisticated hotel offers sleek beauty and the latest technology, like 40-inch flatscreen TVs and free Wi-Fi everywhere. And check out the artsy tubs: They fill from the ceiling down. The technology is impressive, but excellent service is also part of the mix here. The BOKA Restaurant + Bar (p 124) offers creative cuisine and a lively lounge scene. *1010 1st Ave.* ☎ *877/315-1088 or 206/957-1000. www.hotel1000seattle.com. 120 units. $209–$729. AE, DC, DISC, MC, V. Bus: 12, 16, 66, 99. Map p 154.*

★★ **kids** **Hotel Vintage** DOWN-TOWN A facelift in 2014 refreshed the rooms in this romantic, wine-themed hotel where each room is named for a different Washington winery, and guests are treated like royalty. In-room spa services are available, and an elegant wine reception is held nightly. The wonderful Tulio Ristorante (p 134) excels at handmade pasta, and the Fifth Avenue Theatre and shops are steps away. *1100 5th Ave.* ☎ *800/853-3914 or 206/624-8000. www.hotel vintage-seattle.com. 125 units. $149–$349. AE, DC, DISC, MC, V. Bus: 12, 143, 157, 18, 159. Map p 154.*

The cozy Hotel Monaco is pet-friendly, so bring Fido.

Relax in the classy Urbane Restaurant and Bar at the Hyatt Olive 8.

★★ Hyatt at Olive 8 DOWN-TOWN One of Seattle's newest hotels, this is also one of the greenest—it's LEED-certified for energy efficiency (for example, the lights are activated only when your cardkey is in its slot). The rooms may be a bit smaller than at the Grand Hyatt around the corner, but the prices are lower and the service is excellent. Urbane (p 134) is a great choice for breakfast, brunch, lunch or dinner. *1635 8th Ave.* ☎ *206/695-1234. www.olive8.hyatt.com. Double $160–$369. Bus: 10, 11, 14, 43. 49. AE, DC, DISC, MC, V. Bus: 12, 21, 99, 120. Map p 154.*

★★★ Inn at the Market PIKE PLACE MARKET A romantic hideaway right across from Pike Place Market, this friendly hotel offers spectacular views of Elliott Bay and the mountains. Best-kept secret: the 5th-floor roof garden. Take a bottle of wine, a couple of glasses, and enjoy! Room service is from the nearby Café Campagne (p 124). *86 Pine St.* ☎ *800/446-4484 or 206/443-3600. www.innatthemarket. com. 70 units. Standard double $225–$350. AE, DC, DISC, MC, V. Bus: 10, 99, 113, 121, 122. Map p 154.*

★★ kids Mayflower Park Hotel DOWNTOWN This elegantly restored grand dame has been operating since 1927. A wine reception is served at 4:30 Wednesdays, and the rooms have lots of modern touches. It connects to Westlake Center shopping mall (and the monorail). Oliver's Lounge (p 141) and Andaluca restaurant (p 123) are located here. *405 Olive Way.* ☎ *800/426-5100 or 206/623-8700. www.mayflowerpark.com. 171 units. Double $189–$289. AE, DC, DISC, MC, V. Bus: 25, 79, 123, 202, 355. Map p 154.*

★ Mediterranean Inn QUEEN ANNE A sunny yellow building in a quiet neighborhood houses this moderately priced hotel. Rooms come with kitchenettes. A short stroll takes you to Seattle Center, where you can catch the monorail downtown. *425 Queen Anne Ave. N.* ☎ *866/525-4700 or 206/428-4700. www.mediterranean-inn.com. Doubles $159–$169. AE, DC, DISC, MC, V. Map p 154.*

★★ kids Paramount Hotel DOWNTOWN Across the street from the Paramount Theatre, this European-style hotel offers stylish, contemporary rooms and is also near the convention center and Pacific Place. Video games are available. *724 Pine St.* ☎ *800/663-1144 or 206/292-9500. www.paramount hotelseattle.com. 146 units. Standard doubles $268–$458. AE, DC, DISC, MC, V. Bus: 10, 11, 14, 43, 49. Map p 154.*

★★ Red Lion Hotel on Fifth Avenue DOWNTOWN The freshly refurbed Red Lion's location is just about perfect, an easy walk from Pike Public Market and downtown shops. There's a roomy outdoor dining patio and the Elephant & Castle pub downstairs. *1415 5th Ave.* ☎ *206/971-8000. www.seattleredlion fifthavenue.com. 297 units. Standard double $149–$300. AE, DC, DISC, MC, V. Bus: 143, 150, 157, 306, 312. Map p 154.*

★★ Renaissance Seattle Hotel DOWNTOWN This upscale luxury property offers great views and a homey Northwestern decor. Maxwells serves breakfast, lunch, and dinner on site. *515 Madison St.* ☎ *800/546-9184 or 206/583-0300. www.marriott.com/hotels/travel/ seasm-renaissance-seattle-hotel. 553 units. Standard doubles $229–$379. AE, DISC, MC, V. Bus: 12, 124, 250, 252, 257. Map p 154.*

★ Roosevelt Hotel DOWNTOWN This lovely old hotel has personality, and it's right across from Pacific Place, in the heart of downtown. Nice in-room extras include free Wi-Fi and Starbucks coffee. *1531 7th Ave.* ☎ *206/621-1200. www.roosevelthotel.com. 151 units. Standard doubles $169–$309. AE, DC, DISC, MC, V. Bus: 10, 11, 14, 43, 49. Map p 154.*

★★★ kids Seattle Marriott Waterfront WATERFRONT A short walk from Pike Place Market and across the street from the waterfront, this hotel was built with dramatic views in mind: water, cityscape, mountains. To showcase them, half the rooms have balconies, and the indoor/outdoor pool has a sweeping view of Elliott Bay and the Olympic Mountains. *2100 Alaskan Way.* ☎ *800/455-8254 or 206/443-5000. www.marriott.com/ hotels/travel/seawf-seattle-marriott-waterfront. 358 units. Standard doubles $239–$429. AE, DC, DISC, MC, V. Bus: 99. Map p 154.*

★★★ kids Sheraton Seattle Hotel DOWNTOWN One of the city's larges and greenest hotels, the Sheraton has a pool and workout center. Near the convention center and downtown shops, it offers both views and convenience. The beds are oh-so-comfy, and the Pike Street Cafe and Gallery Lounge are great for relaxing and dining. Cribs and video games are a help for families. *1400 6th Ave.* ☎ *206/621-9000. www.starwood hotels.com/sheraton/seattle. 1,258 units. Standard doubles $215–$289. AE, DC, DISC, MC, V. Bus: 306, 312, 522. Map p 154.*

★★ kids Silver Cloud Hotel Broadway CAPITOL HILL Situated in the funky Capitol Hill district, the Silver Cloud has its own indoor pool and fitness center. A shuttle gets you downtown. *1100 Broadway.* ☎ *800/590-1801 or 206/325-1400. www.silvercloud.com/seattle broadway. 179 units. Standard doubles $159–$259. AE, DC, DISC, MC, V. Bus: 12. Map p 154.*

★★★ Sorrento Hotel FIRST HILL This luxury boutique's first guest was Teddy Roosevelt, and it's been pampering travelers ever since with European style and service. Spacious bathrooms feature Italian marble, and rooms come with thoughtful extras like a French press for coffee. The hotel is located in a quiet neighborhood, walkable from downtown. The Hunt Club is one of Seattle's finest restaurants. *900 Madison St. (at Terry).* ☎ *800/426-1265. www.hotelsorrento.com. 76 units.*

The Inn at the Market has one of the best locations in town.

Doubles $197–$589. AE, DC, DISC, MC, V. Bus: 12. Map p 154.

★★★ W Seattle Hotel DOWNTOWN

Sleek, contemporary, and youthful, the W is trendy in a good way. The rooms are warmly inviting, and you can choose from a "Wonderful" room to an "Extreme Wow" suite (on the 24th floor with more than 1,000 square feet of space). Get a shiatsu massage in your room—or most anything (legal!) your heart desires, via the Whatever/Whenever service. Dine at the palate-pleasing Trace. *1112 4th Ave. ☎ 206/264-6000. www.Whotels.com/Seattle. 417 units. Doubles $189–$399. AE, DC, DISC, MC, V. Bus: 202, 210, 214, 215, 554. Map p 154.*

★★ kids Warwick Hotel Seattle BELLTOWN

This moderately priced, French-owned Belltown property is an easy walk from downtown and Pike Place Market. It features an indoor pool, accommodating staff, and a balcony on every room. Dine at the excellent Brasserie Margaux. *401 Lenora St. ☎ 206/443-4300. www.warwickhotels.com/seattle. 230 units. Doubles $169–$320. AE, DC, DISC, MC, V. Bus: 116, 118, 119, 120, 202. Map p 154.*

★★ kids The Westin Seattle DOWNTOWN

Located in landmark round towers, the 47-story Westin offers breathtaking views of the Space Needle, sound and cityscape. Rooms come with the Westin Heavenly Bed that makes you want to lounge in bed a little longer. Kids get a special welcome kit, and you can request a Heavenly Crib for the baby. Cool off in the roomy indoor pool; enjoy American comfort food at Relish Burger Bistro. *1900 5th Ave. ☎ 800/WESTIN or 206/728-1000. www.westin.com/seattle. 891 units. Doubles $249–$369. AE, DC, DISC, MC, V. South Lake Union Street Car 98, Bus: 25, 79, 123. Map p 154.* ●

Check out the Space Needle from your room—views from the Westin are spectacular.

10 The Best Day Trips & Excursions

Tacoma

1. Tacoma Art Museum
2. Hello, Cupcake
3. Tacoma Union Station
4. Washington State History Museum
5. Chihuly Bridge of Glass
6. Museum of Glass
7. Point Defiance Zoo & Aquarium

Greater Tacoma Convention & Trade Center

UNIV. OF WASHINGTON AT TACOMA

True, it has no Space Needle, but the town of Tacoma, 30 miles south of its glitzy northern neighbor, has spruced up its image by redeveloping its downtown into a charming area with free light rail, an esplanade along the Thea Foss Waterway, a convention center, and major cultural facilities as anchors. It's worth checking out. START: **1701 Pacific Ave.**

1 ★★ kids Tacoma Art Museum. The building is itself a work of art, with a ramp that spirals up through galleries, arranged around an atrium with a stone garden. The museum houses a fine collection of works by Northwest artists, including one of the world's largest collection of Tacoma native Dale Chihuly's glass. In addition to American art, you'll find European

Previous page: There's a good chance you'll spot an orca if you go on a whale watch in summertime.

and Asian works. ⏱ *1 hr. 1701 Pacific Ave.* ☎ *253/272-4258. www. tacomaartmuseum.org. $10 adults, $8 seniors & students, $25 family (2 adults & up to 4 children), free ages 4 & under, Wed–Sun 10am–5pm, 3rd Thurs 10am–8pm (free 5–8pm).*

2 Hello, Cupcake. Just look for the pink bicycle outside. This charming little spot serves the tastiest cupcakes around. Try the red velvet and the vanilla vanilla. Mmm! *1740 Pacific Ave.* ☎ *253/383-7772. $*

③ Tacoma Union Station. The former terminus of the Northern Pacific Railroad, this grand station was abandoned for many years, then renovated in the 1990s. There are no more trains, but it's worth a stop to admire the magnificent 90-foot-tall rotunda dome, now decorated with a splendid 20-foot Chihuly chandelier. ⏱ *15 min. 1717 Pacific Ave.* ☎ *253/863-5173, ext. 223. www.unionstationrotunda.org. Free to the public. Mon–Fri 8am–5pm.*

④ ★★★ kids Washington State History Museum. History comes to life here via high-tech interactive displays. Engaging for all ages, these exhibits make

World-famous glass artist Dale Chihuly designed the glass bridge that now connects downtown to the waterfront.

learning history not only painless but terrific fun. "Meet" characters from Washington's past—like Lewis & Clark—in the Great Hall of Washington history. ⏱ *1½ hr. 1911 Pacific Ave.* ☎ *253/272-3500. www. washingtonhistory.org. $8.75 adults, $76 seniors/ ages 6–17, $25 families (2 adults & up to 4 children), Wed– Sun 10am–5pm, third Thurs 10–8pm (free 2–8pm).*

⑤ ★★★ Chihuly Bridge of Glass. Connecting the revitalized downtown to Tacoma's waterfront is a spectacular 500-foot walking bridge by Chihuly. It rises 70 feet into the air as it crosses Interstate 705, and features a ceiling of "seaform" glass, blue crystal towers, and variety of glass sculptures. *1801 Dock St.*

⑥ ★★ Museum of Glass. Here you'll find works by world-famous contemporary glass artists, and you can stop at the hot shop to watch artisans at work. ⏱ *1hr. 1801 Dock St.* ☎ *253/284-4750. www.museum ofglass.org. $12 adults, $10 seniors, $5 ages 6–12, $36 families (2 adults & up to 4 children). Summer: Mon–Sat 10am–5pm, Sun noon–5pm, third Thurs 10am–8pm (free 5–8pm). Fall/ Winter/Spring: Wed–Sat 10am–5pm, Sun noon–5pm, third Thurs 10am– 8pm (free 5–8pm).*

⑦ ★★ Point Defiance Zoo & Aquarium. This terrific little zoo is best known for its marine exhibits, including its beluga whales. I once saw one retrieve a piece of litter thrown in its tank by a guest and deliver it to a docent. ⏱ *1½ hr. 5400 N. Pearl St.* ☎ *253/404-3689. www.pdza.org. $15 adults, $14 seniors, $13 ages 5–12, $8.75 ages 3–4. Daily 9:30am (8:30am July to early Sept), closing hours vary.*

San Juan Islands

1 Friday Harbor Ferry Dock
2 Whale Watch
3 San Juan Coffee Roasting Co.
4 Pelindaba Lavender Gallery
5 Whale Museum

Just a few hours from Seattle, these small islands feel much, much farther away. The quaint portside town of Friday Harbor, at the tip of San Juan Island, is lined with interesting shops, art galleries, and cafes. The islands are a popular getaway for both tourists and local residents. You won't need a car, unless you want to drive around the islands and do some exploring. Even then, you can rent bikes or mopeds when you get there. START: **Friday Harbor Ferry Dock.**

1 **kids Friday Harbor Ferry Dock.** This landing, with its stunning views of the surrounding hilly islands, is where your adventure begins. You can get here from the Seattle waterfront, via the *Victoria Clipper* (☎ **206/448-5000;** www. victoriaclipper.com), or you can drive up I-5 to Anacortes (about a 2-hr. trip), then follow the signs to the Washington State ferry dock. You can take your car on the boat, but it costs quite a bit more.

Long-term parking at the dock is cheaper, and you can walk right onto the boat. Car lines get long in the summertime. For Anacortes–San Juan Islands ferry schedules, check the website (www.wsdot. wa.gov/ferries). This 1½-hour ferry ride is arguably the prettiest in the world, winding its way among enchanting emerald islands. It's spectacular on a sunny day, but dreamy in the mist as well. ⏲ *2 hr., 45 min. each way on Victoria Clipper* from Seattle (round trip $75–$80 adults, $38 children; discounts if purchased in advance); or 2 hr. by car, then about 1½ hr. excluding wait time on Washington State ferry, each way (current Anacortes–Friday Harbor round-trip Washington State ferry fares: passenger-only $13 adults, $6.35 seniors/ages 6–18. For car under 22-ft. long, add $44, which includes driver's fare).

❷ ★★★ kids Whale Watch. A number of whale-watch cruises leave from Friday Harbor. If you get there via the Victoria Clipper, whale-watch tickets can be purchased as a package. Most companies won't guarantee you'll see sleek black-and-white orcas leaping out of the water, but chances are good in the summer. Most boats have knowledgeable guides who recognize the individual whales in the resident pods. *Victoria Clipper:* ⏱ *2½ hr. from the port. Friday Harbor Port.* ☎ *800/888-2535. www. clippervacations.com. Prices vary, depending on date, how far in advance purchased & whether purchased separately or as package from Seattle. Check website for options. Victoria Clipper round-trip with whale watch: $93–$138 adult, $47–$69 ages 1–11.*

❸ ★ Pelindaba Lavender Gallery. FRIDAY HARBOR Who knew there were so many uses for lavender—from cooking ingredients to pet-odor spray? Pelindaba grows its own lavender right on San Juan Island. *150 1st St., Friday Harbor.* ☎ *866/819-1911. www.pelindaba lavender.com. AE, MC, V.*

❹ kids San Juan Coffee Roasting Co. For a great cup of island-roasted coffee, made with estate-grown beans from around

Watch for the lighthouse as you head out to find whales.

the world, pop into San Juan Coffee and sample their smooth java. While you're there, give in to your sweet tooth; their chocolates are the melt-in-your-mouth variety. The shop is right beside the ferry dock. *18 Cannery Landing.* ☎ *800/624-4119. $*

❺ ★ kids Whale Museum. FRIDAY HARBOR Three blocks from the harbor, this unusual little museum is chock full of information on these huge sea mammals, especially the three orca pods that spend their summers around the San Juans. Exhibits include a whale skeleton. ⏱ *1 hr. 62 1st St. N.* ☎ *360/378-4710. www.whale museum.org. $6 adults, $5 seniors, $3 ages 5–18. Daily summer 10am–6pm, winter 10am–4pm.*

Bellevue

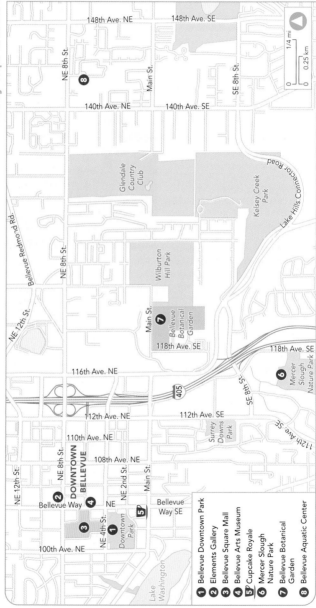

1 Bellevue Downtown Park
2 Elements Gallery
3 Bellevue Square Mall
4 Bellevue Arts Museum
5 Cupcake Royale
6 Mercer Slough Nature Park
7 Bellevue Botanical Garden
8 Bellevue Aquatic Center

Shooting for the stars across the lake from Seattle is the city of Bellevue, which has quietly boomed from a sleepy Eastside suburb into one of the richest towns in Washington, with an overall per capita income nearly twice that of Seattle. Along with a thriving population comes high-end shopping, skyscrapers teeming with shops and offices, and lots of great activities. As elsewhere in the Northwest, there is a reverence for all things outdoors: Bellevue boasts miles of beautiful parks and waterfront. Just a short drive from downtown Seattle—across Lake Washington on either of two floating bridges—Bellevue has its own personality: less eccentric and more well-heeled than its westside counterpart. START: **Bus 233, 234, or 249 to NE 10th Street & 110th Avenue, walk to 108th Avenue NE., or drive across SR 520 floating bridge, left on NE 12th Street, right on 108th Avenue NE, to 1116 108th Avenue NE.**

1 Bellevue Downtown Park. This 21-acre park in the heart of downtown Bellevue is a good spot to start your tour of Bellevue, a city that has experienced explosive growth in the last 20 years as a result of high-tech industries like Microsoft and a per capital income that is income is reputedly twice that of Seattle. Bellevue Downtown Park, with its circular promenade and encircling water channel that ends in a splashing waterfall, reflects something of Bellevue's nouveau upmarket aesthetic. Only a block from the legendary Bellevue Mall and close to new residential towers and rowhouses, the park is an oasis with a big green central lawn for volleyball and Frisbee, and plenty of benches for relaxing. ⏱ *30 min. 10201 NE Fourth St. Dawn to 11pm.*

2 Elements Gallery. Visitors can take home a treasured souvenir or just enjoy gazing at the exquisite art, much of it created in the Northwest. Brilliantly colored glass, elegant sculptures, gleaming carved wood, and stunning jewelry share the space here. ⏱ *30 min. 10500 NE 8th St.* ☎ *425/454-8242. www. elementsglassgallery.com.*

3 ★ kids Bellevue Square Mall. A shopping excursion at Bellevue Square is not your ordinary mall experience. With about 200 shops and restaurants to explore, I still occasionally get lost—which

Cupcake Royale will entice even the most reluctant cupcake converts.

usually translates into more shopping bags. Tenants now include a Microsoft outlet (giving the existing Apple store a little competition), Nordstrom, Crate & Barrel, Harry & David, Macy's, Once Upon a Time (quality toys), Something Silver, True Religion, Zumiez, and Tiffany & Co. If the little ones get antsy, head up to the Kids' Cove play area on the third floor. Mom and Dad can grab a latte while the tots scramble across a Washington ferryboat and other brightly colored climbing toys. Parking at the mall is free. Try to find *that* in Seattle. ⏱ *1 hr. 1086 Bellevue Sq.* ☎ *425/646-3660. www.bellevuecollection.com. Mon–Sat 9:30am–9:30pm, Sun noon–5pm.*

④ ★★ kids Bellevue Arts Museum.

With a focus on fine crafts and design, BAM is appropriately housed in an eye-catching red building by contemporary architect

Exhibits at the Bellevue Arts Museum are thought provoking and kid-friendly.

Steven Holl. Exhibits are inventive and thoughtful, showcasing Northwest and international artists. A favorite was Belgian artist's Isabelle de Borchgrave's collection of historic dresses made out of paper. The museum often hosts Saturday craft classes in conjunction with exhibits, so kids can create art of their own; check the schedule. Free docent tours are offered daily at 1pm. ⏱ *1 hr. 510 Bellevue Way NE.* ☎ *425/519-0770. www.bellevuearts.org. Admission $10 adults, $8 students & seniors, free for kids 5 & under. Hours: Tues–Sun. 11am–6pm.*

⑤ kids Cupcake Royale.

Seattle's first cupcake bakery, this Bellevue shop is one of seven locations. My favorites are lavender, with real flower buds stirred into the buttercream, and peppermint patty—but a case could also be made for the chocolate orange. Or save yourself the agonizing and get the baker's-choice dozen. ⏱ *15 min. 21 Bellevue Way NE.* ☎ *425/454-7966. www.cupcakeroyale.com. $3.65 each; $40 per dozen.*

⑥ kids ★ Mercer Slough Nature Park.

Explore 320 acres of hiking trails, wetlands, and wildlife habitat along beautiful Lake Washington. Be sure to stop by the environmental education center's visitor center, where you'll find interpretive displays, libraries for adults and children, trail maps and nature-inspired art exhibits. The treehouse offers a bird's-eye view of the park, and free nature walks leave from the center at 2pm every Saturday. From May to September, 3-hour guided canoe trips ($18 per person; ☎ **425/452-6885**) leave at 8:45am every Saturday from Enatai Beach Park, 3519 108th Ave. SE. Advance registration and canoeing

Mercer Slough Nature Park is an oasis of hiking trails and wildlife.

experience are required. ⏱ *1 hr. Environmental Education Center, 1625 118th Ave. SE. Daily 10am–4pm.*

❼ ★★★ kids Bellevue Botanical Garden. No one loves flowers like Northwesterners. It would be hard not to, surrounded as we are by an ever-changing natural palette: delicate cherry blossoms, outrageous azaleas, rhododendrons in every hue, tulips, daffodils, camellias . . . and let's not forget roses. The glorious Bellevue Botanical Garden has several display gardens, including a show-stopping perennial border. A well-paved trail winds through all the gardens and natural areas. From Thanksgiving through New Year, more than a half-million lights lend a festive glow to the garden from 5 to 10pm daily during Garden d'Lights. It is not to be missed. The garden

opened a new Visitor Center in 2014; stop in first for maps and info. ⏱ *1 hr. 12001 Main St.* ☎ *425/452-2750. www.bellevuebotanical.org. Admission free except $5 adults for Garden d'Lights. Daily dawn to dusk, Visitor Center daily 9am–4pm.*

❽ kids Bellevue Aquatic Center. With two large indoor pools, the Blue Lagoon and Warm Springs, this is a great place for a refreshing workout, rain or shine. You can also dive into the tank or head down the 10-foot slide. The Warm Springs is heated to a balmy 91 degrees for therapy, but it's often open to the public—and perfect for the younger set. *601 143rd Ave. NE.* ☎ *425/452-4444. www.ci.bellevue.wa.us/aquatic_center.htm. Open swim sessions $6 adults, $5 ages 12 & under. Mon–Fri 8am–8pm, Sat 8am–2pm, Sun 9am–2pm.*

Mount Rainier National Park

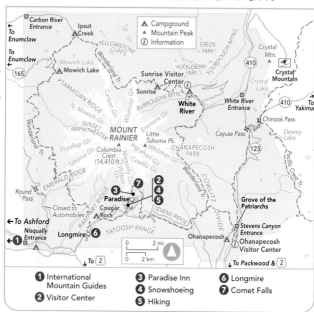

- ▲ Campground
- ▲ Mountain Peak
- ⓘ Information

① International Mountain Guides
② Visitor Center
③ Paradise Inn
④ Snowshoeing
⑤ Hiking
⑥ Longmire
⑦ Comet Falls

Seattleites can go for weeks without seeing the sun, and they're pretty OK with that. What gets them down is when the gray skies blanket their beloved Mount Rainier, which soars—on a clear day—a mile-and-a-half above the surrounding Cascade peaks. When it breaks through the clouds, you're likely to hear someone say, "The mountain's out!" Less than 3 hours from the city, Mt. Rainier is considered somewhat of a backyard by Seattle-ites, who love to hike it, climb it, picnic on it, and marvel at its wild-flowers. START: **The Nisqually Entrance.**

① ★ Go Mountain Climbing.
Several mountain-climbing organizations offer programs for various levels of climbers (including novices). A popular one is International Mountain Guides. *31111 S.R. 706, Ashford.* ☎ *360/569-2609. www.mountain-guides.com. Prices start at $180 for 1-day mountaineering school.*

② Paradise Jackson Visitor Center. From Seattle, drive south

on I-5, east on SR 512, south on SR 7 to Elbe, then east on SR 706 through Ashford to reach the Nisqually Entrance of Mount Rainier National Park. This entrance is open year-round, as is the ride along the Nisqually-Paradise Road to Paradise. The drive is spectacular, winding through old-growth forest as the road climbs the mountain. At Paradise, stop at the Visitor Center for maps of the park and its many trails. Free nature walks also leave from the center. *At Paradise.* ☎ *360/569-2211, ext. 3314.*

3 **The stunning Paradise Inn.** This national historic building, made of Alaskan cedar, is a beautiful hotel with a huge fireplace and the feel of a woodsy lodge. In the dining room (closed in the winter months), you can grab a buffalo burger or a smoked salmon Caesar salad. ☎ *360/569-2275. www. mtrainierguestservices.com. $*

4 ★★ **kids** **Try Snowshoeing.** Snowshoe-ing is a popular sport on Mount Rainier, and no wonder: The variety of trails is endless, from very easy to super challenging. Beginners might want to try the half-mile Myrtle Falls trail, which starts near the Paradise Inn and leads to a lovely view of Myrtle Falls and the Paradise Valley. From mid-December through March, rangers lead free 2-hour snowshoe walks for kids and adults, with snowshoes provided. ⏱ *2 hr. Visitors Center.* ☎ *360/569-2211, ext. 3314. Free. Walks leave from Visitors Center at 12:30pm & 2:30pm daily mid-Dec to early Jan; Sat–Sun early Jan to early April.*

5 ★★ **kids** **Take a Hike.** The park maps will help you decide which trails will suit you best. There are plenty of easy hikes, and lots of tougher ones as well. Watch for wildlife and dramatic mountain vistas. Or continue driving up the Nisqually-Paradise Road to Kautz Creek, where you can park and enjoy the view of Mount Rainier. You can also hike along the Kautz Creek trail to Indian Henry's Hunting Ground.

6 ★ **kids** **Longmire.** Nisqually-Paradise Road takes you next to Longmire, a town about 12 miles from Paradise, where you will find the Longmire Museum (☎ **360/ 569-2211,** ext. 3314; usually open year-round, daily 9am–4:30pm, free to all) with exhibits about the land's history and geology, the National Park Inn (☎ **360/569-2275**) and more trails near mineral springs, which are worth checking out even though you can no longer soak in them.

7 ★ **kids** **Comet Falls.** About 10 miles from the entrance to the park, Nisqually-Paradise Road takes you to a 300-foot waterfall, Comet Falls. You can hike there or drive to the viewing area, just past Christine Falls.

A view of Mt. Rainier.

Vancouver, B.C.

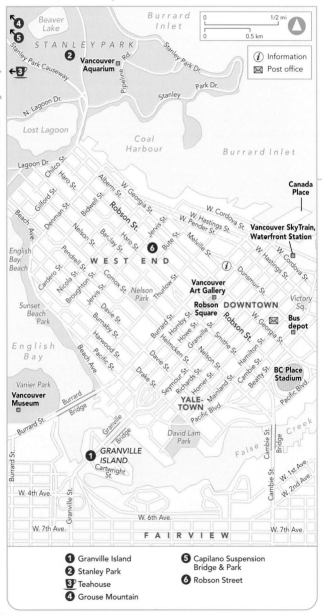

Burrard Inlet

Beaver Lake

STANLEY PARK

❷ Vancouver Aquarium

Stanley Park Causeway

Stanley Park Dr.

Pipeline Rd.

Park Dr.

Stanley

❹
❺
←❸

| 0 | 1/2 mi |
| 0 | 0.5 km |

ⓘ Information
✉ Post office

N. Lagoon Dr.

Lost Lagoon

Coal Harbour

Burrard Inlet

Lagoon Dr.

Chilco St.

Gilford St.

Haro St.

Denman St.

Bidwell St.

Alberni St.

W. Georgia St.

Robson St.

Haro St.

Jervis St.

Bute St.

W. Cordova St.

W. Hastings St.

W. Pender St.

Melville St.

Canada Place

Vancouver SkyTrain, Waterfront Station

W. Cordova St.

Beach Ave.

Barclay St.

Nelson St.

Comox St.

W E S T   E N D

Cardero St.

Pendrell St.

Nicola St.

Broughton St.

Jervis St.

Nelson Park

Thurlow St.

❻

ⓘ

Dunsmuir St.

W. Hastings St.

English Bay Beach

Davie St.

Burnaby St.

Harwood St.

Pacific St.

Beach Ave.

Vancouver Art Gallery

Robson Square

Burrard St.

Hornby St.

Howe St.

Granville St.

Smithe St.

Nelson St.

Robson St.

DOWNTOWN

W. Georgia St.

Victory Sq.

✉

Bus depot

Sunset Beach Park

English Bay

Helmcken St.

Davie St.

Seymour St.

Richards St.

Homer St.

Hamilton St.

Cambie St.

Beatty St.

BC Place Stadium

Pacific Blvd.

Vanier Park

Vancouver Museum

Burrard Bridge

Burrard St.

Granville

Drake St.

Mainland St.

YALE-TOWN

Pacific Blvd.

Cambie St.

Bridge

Creek

False

Burrard St.

Granville Bridge

❶ **GRANVILLE ISLAND**

Cartwright St.

David Lam Park

Cambie St.

Creek

W. 1st Ave.

W. 2nd Ave.

W. 4th Ave.

Granville St.

W. 6th Ave.

W. 7th Ave.

F A I R V I E W

W. 7th Ave.

❶ Granville Island
❷ Stanley Park
❸ Teahouse
❹ Grouse Mountain

❺ Capilano Suspension Bridge & Park
❻ Robson Street

So close to Seattle it's considered a neighbor, Vancouver is a sophisticated city with lots to offer. The people are friendly, the shopping and dining top-notch, the skyline dramatic. Set on the Pacific Ocean, with the majestic Coast Mountains looming in the background, this is breathtaking country. To get there, drive 2½ hours north from Seattle along I-5, over the Canadian border at Blaine or take the 4-hour Amtrak Cascades ride (☎ 800/USA-RAIL; www.amtrak.com). Passports are a must. Getting around town is a breeze—by light rail (The Vancouver Sky Train), bus, or ferry. START: **GRANVILLE ISLAND. Take the #50 False Creek bus from Gastown (downtown area), which stops just off Granville Island; walk toward the sign. Other city buses will take you to Granville & 5th Ave., and you can walk to the island. You can also take a ferry (continuous runs 7am to 10:30pm in the summer; until 8:30pm in the winter).**

The Public Market at Granville Island rivals Pike Place Market.

❶ ★★★ kids Granville Island. If you have time for only one stop, make it lively, picturesque Granville Island. The public market is an almost overwhelming sensory experience of colors, smells, and tastes (free samples!). The fish and produce are fresh and delicious. Meanwhile, entertainers of some sort are usually performing on the deck. Shops range from custom-made jewelry to magic kits. The Kids Market is an entire building of children's shops surrounding a three-story climbing ball pit. ⏱ *2 hr. www.granvilleisland.com/public-market.*

❷ ★★★ kids Stanley Park. One of the world's most magnificent parks, Stanley is a 1,000-acre paradise of meadows, forests, and gardens. As if the natural beauty weren't enough, there's plenty to do here. The **Vancouver Aquarium** is open daily (www.vanaqua.org; C$25 adults, C$18 ages 13–18, C$14 ages 4–12; daily 10am–6pm) The Variety Kids Water Park is free—and teeming with little ones cooling off in water sprays, from the end of May 'til Labor Day. For more water fun, take a plunge into the heated pool (late May through Labor Day) or bask on two bathing beaches. If you want to get around in style, take a horse and carriage—they run every day (C$33 adults, C$31 seniors and students with ID, C$17 children 3–12, free 2 & under). Enter the park on Georgia Street, and turn left. ⏱ *2 hr. Georgia St., north end.* ☎ *604/257-8400. www.stanleypark.com. Bus: 19.*

❸ Teahouse in Stanley Park. Elegant but never stuffy, the Teahouse serves lunch (grilled panini Provencal is a favorite), brunch, or dinner—or just a pick-me-up treat, like the gingerbread

Olympic Gains

Vancouver and environs spruced up to the tune of US$6 billion for the 2010 Winter Olympics. That included improvements to the Sea to Sky Highway (99), a formerly challenging—and sometimes scary!—route from Vancouver north to the breathtaking ski town of Whistler. Now wider and safer, the road takes you there in less than 2 hours. You'll need an early start to fit this into your day trip, but it's worth it for the spectacular alpine scenery.

cake with caramel sauce and lemon. Reservations recommended. *Ferguson Point, Stanley Park Drive.* ☎ *604/669-3281. $–$$$*

④ ★ kids Grouse Mountain. Just a 15-minute drive from the city, Grouse Mountain offers snowshoeing, ice skating, and sleigh rides in the winter. In the summer, take the SkyRide cable car (all-day admission: C$58 adults, C$45 seniors/youth13–18, C$25 ages 5–12) up to the top and enjoy the panoramic view. The price includes other activities, such as films about endangered animals, the Refuge for Endangered Wildlife, chairlift rides,

If you're afraid of heights, you may want to skip the Capilano Suspension Bridge, but the park is still worth checking out.

and—in season—sleigh rides. Work up an appetite, then enjoy fine dining at the Observatory Restaurant, or a casual bite at the cafe or bistro. ⏲ *2 hr. 6400 Nancy Greene Way.* ☎ *604/980-9311. www.grousemountain.com. Take Bus 232 from Phibbs Exchange or Bus 236 from Lonsdale Quay. Or drive north across Lions Gate Bridge, take the North Vancouver exit to Marine Drive, then 3 mi. up Capilano Road. Daily 9am to 10pm.*

⑤ ★ kids Capilano Suspension Bridge & Park. This 443-foot swinging bridge gives you a breathtaking view of the rainforest and the Capilano River rushing along below. In the park, you can watch First Nation carving demonstrations and go on the Treetops Adventure, which takes you far above the forest floor on a separate series of suspension bridges. ⏲ *1½ hr. 3735 Capilano Rd.* ☎ *604/985-7474. www.capbridge.com. C$32 adults, C$30 seniors, C$26 ages 13–16, C$12 ages 6–12. Open daily, but check website for times.*

⑥ ★ Robson Street. The Rodeo Drive of Vancouver, with upscale shopping and lots of cafes and coffee shops. *Btw. Burrard & Jervis sts.* ●

The
Savvy Traveler

Before You Go

Tourist Offices
Need more information about Seattle? You can get all the details your heart desires by contacting **Seattle's Convention and Visitors Bureau,** 701 Pike St., Suite 800, Seattle, WA 98101 (☎ 206/461-5800; www.visitseattle.org), which operates the Seattle Visitor Center and Concierge Services inside the Washington State Convention and Trade Center, 7th Avenue and Pike Street, Upper Pike Street Lobby (☎ 206/461-5840); and the Market Information Center, Southwest Corner of 1st Avenue and Pike Street in the Pike Place Market (☎ 206/461-5840). For information on other parts of Washington, contact **Washington State Tourism** (☎ 800/544-1800; www.experiencewa.com).

The Best Times to Go
Summer arrives with a bang in Seattle around the Fourth of July. From then through the end of September, the rain (for the most part) goes away and Seattleites come out to play. The picture-perfect weather means hotels and restaurants are crowded, so book as far in advance as possible. If you're not afraid of the rain—usually more of a mist than a downpour—come in the winter months, when rates are lower, crowds are thinner, and the theaters are churning out top-notch productions. With Seattle's temperate climate, it will probably be warmer than wherever you started out.

Festivals & Special Events
SPRING. April brings the **Skagit Valley Tulip Festival** (☎ 360/428-5959; www.tulipfestival.org), in and around La Conner. An hour north of Seattle, acres and acres of tulips

Previous page: A ride on the Bainbridge ferry.

and daffodils blanket the Skagit Valley with a living quilt for weeks, accompanied by festivities. May starts with a splash the first Saturday of the month, **Opening Day of Boating Season** (☎ 206/325-1000; www.seattleyachtclub.org). It's held on Lakes Union and Washington. Next comes the first big street fair, the **U District StreetFair** (☎ 206/547-4417; www.udistrictstreetfair.org), in the lively University District. Also in mid-May is Giant Magnet's **International Children's Friendship Festival** (☎ 206/684-7338), at Seattle Center, celebrating cultures from around the world. Then comes the world-famous **Seattle International Film Festival** (☎ 206/324-9996; www.seattlefilm.com), held at area theaters, mid-May through early June. On Memorial Day weekend, the **Northwest Folklife Festival** (☎ 206/684-7300; www.nwfolklife.org) at Seattle Center honors the many cultures that come together in the Northwest.

SUMMER. The third weekend in June is time for the wackiest festival of all, the **Fremont Fair** (☎ 206/694-6706; www.fremontfair.com), which welcomes the summer solstice with a quirky parade, complete with political satire and bicyclists in the buff. At the end of the month comes **Seattle Pride** (☎ 206/322-9561; www.seattlepride.org), a gay, lesbian, bisexual, and transgender festival. On the Fourth of July, head for **Lake Union** (☎ 206/281-7788; www.familyfourth.org) to ooh and ahhh at fireworks over the lake. The biggest event of the season is **Seafair** (☎ 206/728-0123; www.seafair.com), which starts in early July and lasts for a month. Highlights are the

SEATTLE'S AVERAGE TEMPERATURE & DAYS OF RAIN

	JAN	FEB	MAR	APR	MAY	JUNE
Temp. (°F)	46	50	53	58	65	69
Temp. (°C)	8	10	12	14	18	21
Rain (days)	16	17	14	10	9	5

	JULY	AUG	SEPT	OCT	NOV	DEC
Temp. (°F)	75	74	69	60	52	47
Temp. (°C)	24	23	21	16	11	8
Rain (days)	7	9	14	18	20	19

hydroplane boat races, the Navy's Blue Angels show and the Torchlight Parade. At **Bite of Seattle** in mid-July, crowds head to Seattle Center to hear live bands and sample treats and wine from local restaurants. Wrapping up the summer is **Bumbershoot, the Seattle Music & Arts Festival** (☎ 206/281-7788; www.bumbershoot.org), at Seattle Center on Labor Day weekend. It's a little bit crazy and a lot of fun.

FALL. Issaquah Salmon Days Festival (☎ 425/392-0661; www.salmon days.org) welcomes the salmon on their return to the lakes and streams. Issaquah, 15 miles east of Seattle, the first full weekend in October.

WINTER. Throughout December, the **Argosy Cruises Christmas Ships Festival** (☎ 888/623-1445 or 206/ 622-8687; www.argosycruises.com) takes place at various waterfront locations. Boats decked out with Christmas lights parade past a number of beaches. What better way to ring in the new year than with **New Year's at the Needle** (☎ 206/905-2100; www.space needle.com), Seattle Center, December 31?

In January, Seattle celebrates the Chinese New Year in a big way, with dragon kites, music and dance. The **Chinatown/International District Lunar New Year Celebration** (☎ 206/382-1197; www.cidbia.org), is held at Hing Hay Park (423 Maynard Ave. S.).The next month,

gardening buffs head to the **North-west Flower & Garden Show** (☎ 253/756-2121; www.garden show.com), at the Washington State Convention and Trade Center.

The Weather

Okay, so Seattle doesn't come to mind when you think of sunny destinations. But if you're here in July, August, or September, when those glorious summer days stretch lazily on 'til 10pm, you might think the city has an undeserved rap. Come back in November and you might change your mind. But even then, the rain is generally more drizzle than downpour. When they run the numbers, it turns out that Seattle gets 19 inches less rain every year than Miami—though it rains here 29 more days. Theirs is torrential downpour; ours is gentle mist. So Seattle has less rain but more gray days. No matter when you visit, bring an umbrella or hooded jacket for chilly nights. Winters seldom bring below-freezing temperatures in temperate Seattle, and snow is a rarity in the city.

Car Rentals

All the major car-rental agencies have offices in Seattle and at or near Seattle-Tacoma International Airport. These include the following:

• **Advantage** (☎ 800/777-5500 or 206/824-0161; www.advantage. com)

Useful Websites

- Seattle's Convention and Visitors Bureau (www.visitseattle.org)
- Seattle-Tacoma International Airport (www.portseattle.org/seatac)
- *Seattle Times* (www.seattletimes.com)
- *Seattle Weekly* (www.seattleweekly.com)
- Universal Currency Converter (www.xe.com/ucc)
- Visa ATM Locator (www.visa.com), MasterCard ATM Locator (www.mastercard.com)
- Washington State Ferries (www.wsdot.wa.gov/ferries)
- Weather (www.intellicast.com and www.weather.com)

- **Alamo** (877/905-5555 or 206/433-0182; www.goalamo.com)
- **Avis** (800/331-1212 or 206/433-5231; www.avis.com)
- **Budget** (800/527-0700 or 206/444-7510; www.budget.com)
- **Dollar** (800/800-3665 or 206/433-5825; www.dollar.com)
- **Enterprise** (800/261-7331 or 206/246-1953; www.enterprise.com)
- **Hertz** (800/654-3131 or 206/248-1300; www.hertz.com)
- **National** (877/222-9058 or 206/433-5501; www.nationalcar.com)

- **Thrifty** (800/847-4389 or 877/283-0898; www.thrifty.com)

Cellphones

It's a good bet that your phone will work in major cities, but take a look at your wireless company's coverage map on its website before heading out. If you need to stay in touch at a destination where you know your phone won't work, **rent** a phone that does from **InTouch USA** (800/872-7626; www.intouchglobal.com) or a rental car location, but beware that you'll pay by the minute for airtime.

Getting **There**

By Plane

The **Seattle-Tacoma International Airport** (206/433-5388; www.portseattle.org/seatac) is served by about 30 airlines.

International carriers that fly from Europe to Los Angeles and/or San Francisco (continue to Seattle on a domestic carrier) include **Aer Lingus** (0818/365-000 in Ireland; www.aerlingus.com) and **British Airways**

(0870/850-9850; www.british airways.com). The latter also flies directly to Seattle from London.

From New Zealand and Australia, there are flights to San Francisco and Los Angeles on **Qantas** (13-13-13 in Australia; www.qantas.com.au) and **Air New Zealand** (0800/737-000 in New Zealand; www.airnewzealand.co.nz).

From Los Angeles, you can continue on to Seattle on a regional domestic carrier.

Seaplane service between Seattle and the San Juan Islands; and Victoria, British Columbia, is offered by **Kenmore Air** (☎ 866/435-9524 or 425/486-1257; www.kenmoreair.com), which has its Seattle terminals at the south end of Lake Union and at the north end of Lake Washington.

By Car

There are two main exits from the airport: From the loading/unloading area, take the first exit if you're staying near the airport. Take the second exit (Wash. 518) if you're headed to downtown Seattle. Driving east on Wash. 518 will connect you to I-5, where you'll then follow the signs for Seattle. Generally, allow 30 minutes for the drive between the airport and downtown—45 minutes to an hour during rush hour.

By Taxi, Shuttle, or Bus

A taxi into downtown Seattle will cost you about $32 to $52. There are usually plenty of taxis around, but if not, call **Yellow Cab** (☎ 206/622-6500) or **Farwest Taxi** (☎ 206/622-1717). **Gray Line Airport Express** (☎ 800/426-7532 or 206/626-6088; www.graylineofseattle.com) is a good way to get downtown. They leave the airport every 30 minutes from 6:20am (5:30am from downtown) to 9pm. Passengers are picked up outside the baggage-claim area, on Level Three of the parking garage, Island Two. Airporter shuttles stop at the following downtown hotels: Madison Renaissance, Crowne Plaza, Fairmont Olympic, Seattle Hilton, Sheraton Seattle, Grand Hyatt, Westin, and Warwick. Fares are $18 one-way and $31 round-trip for adults, free for children under 17 accompanied by adult.

Shuttle Express

Shuttle Express (☎ 800/487-7433 or 425/981-7000; www.shuttleexpress.com) provides 24-hour service between Sea-Tac and Seattle and environs. Rates to downtown Seattle hotels are $18 for adults, children 17 and under ride free with paying adult. You need a reservation to get to the airport; to leave the airport, reservations are recommended, but walk-ups are welcome. Head to the Ground Transportation Center on the third floor of the parking garage.

Link Light Rail

The new **Link Light Rail Station** (☎ 800/201-4900 or 206/398-5000; www.soundtransit.org) is connected to the fourth floor of the parking garage. Trains run between the airport and downtown every 7½ to 15 minutes, from 5am to 1am Monday through Saturday, and 6am to midnight Sunday, $2 to $2.75. The trip takes about 35 minutes.

By Ferry

Seattle is served by **Washington State Ferries** (☎ 888/808-7977 within Washington, or 206/464-6400; www.wsdot.wa.gov/ferries). Car ferries travel between downtown Seattle and both Bainbridge Island and Bremerton from Pier 52. Car ferries also connect Fauntleroy (in West Seattle) with Vashon Island and the Kitsap Peninsula; Tahlequah (Vashon Island) with Point Defiance in Tacoma; Edmonds with Kingston (on the Kitsap Peninsula); Mukilteo with Whidbey Island; Whidbey Island at Keystone with Port Townsend; and Anacortes with the San Juan Islands and Sidney, British Columbia (near Victoria).

If you're traveling between Victoria, British Columbia, and Seattle, several options are available through **Victoria Clipper,** Pier 69,

2701 Alaskan Way (☎ **800/888-2535,** 206/448-5000, or 250/382-8100 in Victoria; wwwvictoriaclipper.com).

By Train
Amtrak (☎ **800/872-7245;** www.amtrak.com) service runs from Vancouver, British Columbia, to Seattle and from Portland and as far south as Eugene, Oregon. The train takes about 4 hours from Vancouver and 3½ to 4 hours from Portland. One-way fares from Vancouver or from Portland to Seattle run $30 to $60. There is also Amtrak service to Seattle from San Diego, Los Angeles, San Francisco, and from Spokane and points east. Amtrak also operates a bus between Vancouver and Seattle.

By Bus
Greyhound (☎ **800/231-2222;** www.greyhound.com) bus service provides connections to almost any city in the continental United States. Seattle's Greyhound bus station is at 811 Stewart St., a few blocks northeast of downtown.

Bolt Bus (☎ **877/BOLTBUS** [265-8287]; www.boltbus.com) offers an inexpensive, direct service between Portland and Vancouver, B.C., to Seattle several times a day, stopping in Seattle at King St. in the Chinatown/International District.

By Metro Bus King County's extensive **Metro** (☎ **206/553-3000;** http://metro.kingcounty.gov) bus system will get you anywhere you need to go in and around the city; adult fares range from $2.25 to $3, depending on distance and time of day. You need exact change; or a TAP card (www.taptodo.net), which allows you to load fares and purchase $5 day passes.

Getting **Around**

By Car
Seattle is 110 miles from Vancouver, British Columbia, 175 miles from Portland, 810 miles from San Francisco, 1,190 miles from Los Angeles, 835 miles from Salt Lake City, and 285 miles from Spokane. I-5 is the main north–south artery, running south to Portland and north to the Canadian border. I-405 is Seattle's eastside bypass and accesses Bellevue, Redmond, and Kirkland on the east side of Lake Washington. I-90, which ends at I-5, connects Seattle to Spokane in the eastern part of Washington. Wash. 520 connects I-405 with Seattle just north of downtown and also ends at I-5. Wash. 99, the Alaskan Way Viaduct, is another major north–south highway through downtown Seattle but it's slated to be removed by 2017 and replaced by a tunnel. All the major car-rental agencies have offices in Seattle and at or near Sea-Tac International Airport.

Keep in mind that Seattle traffic congestion is bad, parking is limited (and expensive), and streets are almost all one-way. You'll avoid frustration by leaving your car in your hotel parking garage. You might not need a car at all. The city center is well served by public transportation. Plus, Seattle is very walkable. However, to get north of Seattle Center, east of Lake Washington, west of Puget Sound or south of the sports stadiums is a bit tricky without a car (of course, you can take the foot ferry for a trip to Bainbridge Island). You could certainly have a very fun trip to Seattle without renting a car.

Parking

On-street parking in downtown Seattle is expensive and extremely limited. Most downtown parking lots charge $20 to $25 per day, though many offer early-bird specials. Some lots near the Space Needle charge less, and you can leave your car there, then take the monorail downtown. Some restaurants and Pike Place Market merchants validate parking permits.

By Streecar

The **Seattle Streetcar** (www.seattle streetcar.org) runs from downtown to Lake Union and will eventually have another line up First Hill and along Broadway. Fares are $2.50 for adults.

By Light Rail

The **Central Link Light Rail** (www. soundtransit.org) runs beneath 3rd Avenue from Westlake Station to Sea-Tac airport, making key downtown stops along the way. Adult fares range from $2 to $2.75 depending on distance traveled.

Fast **Facts**

AREA CODE   The area code is 206 in Seattle, 425 for the Eastside (including Kirkland and Bellevue), and 253 for south King County (near the airport).

ATMS   Bank and street ATMs are located all through downtown Seattle and at major tourist attractions.

BUSINESS HOURS   The following are general guidelines. Banks are open Monday through Friday from 9am to 5pm (some also on Sat 9am–noon). Stores are open Monday through Saturday from 10am to 6pm and Sunday from noon to 5pm (malls usually stay open until 9pm Mon–Sat). Bars can stay open until 2am.

CURRENCY   The most common bills are the $1 (a "buck"), $5, $10, and $20 denominations. Coins: 1¢ (1 cent, or a penny); 5¢ (5 cents, or a nickel); 10¢ (10 cents, or a dime); 25¢ (25 cents, or a quarter); 50¢ (50 cents, or a half dollar); the gold-colored Sacagawea coin, worth $1; and the rare silver dollar.

DENTIST   Contact the **Dental Referral Service** (☎ 800/510-7315).

DOCTOR   To find a physician, check at your hotel for a referral, contact **Swedish Medical Center** (☎ 800/833-8879; www.swedish.org), or call the referral line of the **Virginia Mason Medical Center** (☎ 888/862-2737; www.virginiamason.org).

DRINKING LAWS   The legal age for purchase and consumption of alcoholic beverages is 21; proof of age is required and often requested at bars and restaurants. Do not carry open containers of alcohol in your car or any public area that isn't zoned for alcohol consumption. And nothing will ruin your trip faster than getting a citation for DUI ("driving under the influence"), so don't even think about driving while intoxicated.

EMBASSIES & CONSULATES   All embassies are located in the nation's capital, Washington, D.C. and some consulates are located in major U.S. cities. If your country isn't listed below, call for directory information in Washington, D.C. (☎ 202/555-1212) or log on to www.embassy.org/embassies.

The embassy of **Australia** is at 1601 Massachusetts Ave. NW, Washington, DC 20036 (☎ 202/797-3000; www.usa.embassy.gov.au). There are consulates in New York, Atlanta, Chicago, Denver, Honolulu, Houston, Los Angeles, and San Francisco.

The embassy of **Canada** is at 501 Pennsylvania Ave. NW, Washington, DC 20001 (☎ 202/682-1740; www.canadianembassy.org). Other Canadian consulates are in cities including Buffalo (New York), Detroit, Los Angeles, New York, and Seattle.

The embassy of **Ireland** is at 2234 Massachusetts Ave. NW, Washington, DC 20008 (☎ 202/462-3939; www.embassyofireland.org). Irish consulates are in Boston, Chicago, New York, San Francisco, and other cities. See website for complete listing.

The embassy of **New Zealand** is at 37 Observatory Circle NW, Washington, DC 20008 (☎ 202/328-4800; www.nzembassy.com/usa). New Zealand consulates are in Los Angeles, Salt Lake City, San Francisco, and Seattle.

The embassy of the **United Kingdom** is at 3100 Massachusetts Ave. NW, Washington, DC 20008 (☎ 202/588-6500; www.ukinusa. fco.gov.uk/en). Other British consulates are in Atlanta, Boston, Chicago, Cleveland, Houston, Los Angeles, New York, San Francisco, and Seattle.

EMERGENCIES For police, fire, or medical emergencies, phone ☎ 911.

HOLIDAYS Banks, government offices, post offices, and many stores, restaurants, and museums are closed on the following legal national holidays: January 1 (New Year's Day), the third Monday in January (Martin Luther King, Jr., Day), the third Monday in February (Presidents' Day), the last Monday in May (Memorial Day), July 4 (Independence Day), the first Monday in September (Labor Day), the second Monday in October (Columbus Day), November 11 (Veterans' Day/Armistice Day), the fourth Thursday in November (Thanksgiving Day), and December 25 (Christmas). The Tuesday after the first Monday in November is Election Day.

HOSPITALS Hospitals convenient to downtown include **Swedish Medical Center,** 747 Broadway (☎ 206/386-6000; www.swedish. org), and **Virginia Mason Medical Center,** 1100 9th Ave. (☎ 206/583-6433 for emergencies or 206/624-1144 for information; www. virginiamason.org).

INTERNET ACCESS First, ask at your hotel to see if it provides Internet access. Alternatively, you can head to the **Seattle Central Library,** 1000 4th Ave. (☎ 206/386-4636), which has hundreds of online computer terminals.

LOST & FOUND Be sure to tell all of your credit card companies the minute you discover your wallet has been lost or stolen and file a report at a police precinct. Your credit card company or insurer may require a police report number or record of the loss. Most credit card companies have an emergency toll-free number to call if your card is lost or stolen. **Visa**'s U.S. emergency number is ☎ 800/847-2911. **American Express** cardholders and traveler's check holders should call ☎ 800/528-4800. **MasterCard** holders should call ☎ 800/627-8372. For other credit cards, call the toll-free number directory at ☎ 800/555-1212. You can have money wired to you via **Western Union** (☎ 800/325-6000; www. westernunion.com).

NEWSPAPERS & MAGAZINES The "Seattle Times" is Seattle's daily newspaper. "Seattle Weekly" is the city's free arts-and-entertainment weekly.

PHARMACIES   Conveniently located downtown pharmacies include **Rite Aid,** with branches at 319 Pike St. (☎ **206/223-0512**) and 2603 3rd Ave. (☎ **206/441-8790**). For 24-hour service, try **Bartell Drug Store,** 600 1st Ave. N. (☎ **206/284-1353**).

POLICE   For police emergencies, phone ☎ **911.**

RESTROOMS   There are public restrooms in Pike Place Market, Westlake Center, Pacific Place, Seattle Center, and the Washington State Convention and Trade Center. You'll also find restrooms in most hotel lobbies and coffee bars in downtown Seattle.

SAFETY   Although Seattle is a relatively safe city, it has its share of crime. The most questionable neighborhood you're likely to visit is the Pioneer Square area. By day, this area is quite safe (though it has a large contingent of street people), but when the bars are closing, stay aware of your surroundings. Also take extra precautions with your wallet or purse when you're in the crush of people at Pike Place Market. Try to park your car in a garage at night. If you must park on the street, make sure there are no valuables in view.

SMOKING   Smoking is banned in public indoor spaces throughout the state of Washington, even in bars.

TAXES   Seattle has a 9.5% sales tax. In restaurants, there's an additional .5% food-and-beverage tax. The hotel-room tax in the metro area ranges from around 10% to 16%. On rental cars, you pay an 18.6% tax, plus, if you rent at the airport, a 10% to 12% airport concession fee (plus other fees for a whopping total of around 45%!).

TELEPHONES   Hotel surcharges can be astronomical, so use your cellphone. Many convenience groceries sell prepaid calling cards; for international visitors these can be the least expensive way to call home. For calls within the United States and to Canada, dial 1 followed by the area code and the seven-digit number. For other international calls, dial 011 followed by the country code, city code, and the number you are calling.

Calls to area codes 800, 888, 877, and 866 are toll-free. For local directory assistance ("information"), dial 411; for long-distance information, dial 1, then the appropriate area code and 555-1212.

TIME   Seattle is in the Pacific Standard Time (PST) zone, making it 3 hours behind the East Coast of the U.S.

Daylight Saving Time is in effect from 1am on the second Sunday in March to 1am on the first Sunday in November. Daylight Saving Time moves the clock 1 hour ahead of standard time.

TIPPING   Tips are the standard way of showing appreciation for services provided. In hotels, tip bellhops at least $1 per bag ($2–$3 if you have a lot of luggage) and tip the cleaning staff $1 to $2 per day (more if you've left a disaster area). Tip the doorman or concierge only if he or she has provided you with some specific service. Tip the valet-parking attendant $1 every time you get your car. In restaurants, bars, and nightclubs, tip service staff 15% to 20% of the check, tip bartenders 10% to 15%, tip checkroom attendants $1 per garment, and tip valet-parking attendants $1 per vehicle. Tip cab drivers 15% of the fare; tip skycaps at airports at least $1 per bag ($2–$3 if you have a lot of luggage); and tip hairdressers and barbers 15% to 20%.

TRANSIT INFO For 24-hour information on Seattle's **Metro bus system,** call ☎ 206/553-3000 or go to http://metro.kingcounty.gov. For information on the **Washington State Ferries,** call ☎ 888/808-7977 within Washington, or 206/464-6400; www.wsdot.wa.gov/ferries.

TRAVELERS WITH DISABILITIES For anyone using a wheelchair, the greatest difficulty of a visit to Seattle is dealing with the city's steep hills. One solution for dealing with downtown hills is to use the elevator at Pike Place Market to get between the waterfront and 1st Avenue. There's also a public elevator at the west end of Lenora Street (just north of Pike Place Market). This elevator connects the waterfront with the Belltown neighborhood.

Organizations that offer assistance to disabled travelers include **MossRehab** (☎ 800/CALL-MOSS; www.mossresourcenet.org); the **American Foundation for the Blind (AFB)** (☎ 800/232-5463; www.afb.org); and **SATH (Society for Accessible Travel & Hospitality)** (☎ 212/447-7284; www.sath. org). AirAmbulanceCard.com is now partnered with SATH and allows you to preselect top-notch hospitals in case of an emergency.

WEATHER Check the "Seattle Times" or "Seattle Post-Intelligencer" newspapers for forecasts. If you want to know what to pack before you depart, go to www.wrh. noaa.gov/seattle, www.cnn.com/weather, or www.wunderground. com/US/WA.

A Brief **History**

1792 British Capt. George Vancouver explores and names Puget Sound.

1851 The Denny party makes land at Alki Point (now West Seattle) and endures a harsh first winter with the help of local Indian tribes.

1852 Denny and gang move their town to the more temperate east side of the Puget Sound; "Doc" Maynard names the town after Chief Sealth of the local Duwamish tribe.

1853 The Washington Territory is officially created; it includes what is now Idaho and part of Montana.

1853 Henry Yesler opens the first of many sawmills to be built in the Puget Sound area.

1855 The U.S. government signs treaties with several Native-American tribes in the

Washington Territory, giving much of their land to the federal government.

1861 The University of Washington (then called Territorial University) opens its doors to students.

1863 Idaho Territory is separated from the Washington Territory.

1863 The "Gazette," later to become the "Seattle Post-Intelligencer," publishes its first newspaper.

1864 Cross-country Western Union telegraph line reaches Seattle.

1869 The City of Seattle incorporates.

1871 The Indian Appropriations Act says Indians are no longer sovereign but federal "wards."

1878 Seattle gets its first telephones.

1885 Chinese immigrants are forced out of Seattle.

1889 Twenty-five blocks of Seattle burn to the ground in the Great Fire, prompting a frenzy of building—several feet higher than the original shops had been.

1889 Washington becomes the nation's 42nd state.

1893 Transcontinental Great Northern Railway reaches Seattle.

1893 Great Panic delivers a punch to Washington's economy.

1896 Col. Alden Blethen buys "The Seattle Daily Times." (The Blethen family still owns "The Seattle Times.)"

1897–1899 Seattle booms as a stopping-off point for Klondike gold-seekers.

1901 John Nordstrom opens his first shoe store.

1907 Pike Place Market brings farmers and customers directly together.

1910 Seattle women win their on-again-off-again right to vote once and for all.

1914 Smith Tower is completed in Seattle, becoming the tallest building west of Ohio.

1915 William Boeing goes for his first flight.

1916 A long, violent longshore-men's strike takes place.

1917 Construction is complete on the Lake Washington Ship Canal.

1917 Boeing Airplane Co. is launched.

1919 The nation's first general strike causes mayhem in Seattle.

1919 First international airmail delivery by Boeing and Hubbard.

1919 Eddie Bauer's first store opens.

1921 The Alien Land Law is passed in Washington, restrict-ing Asian immigrants' rights to own or lease property.

1924 Native Americans are made U.S. citizens.

1926 Seattle elects the first woman mayor of any major U.S. city.

1940 Lake Washington Floating Bridge becomes the first of its kind in the world.

1940 Sen. Henry "Scoop" Jackson wins election to Congress, and later to the U.S. Senate.

1942 FDR signs order sending Japanese Americans from the West Coast to internment camps; thousands in the Seattle area are forced to abandon their homes and businesses.

1942 Seattle native Jimi Hendrix is born.

1949 Sea-Tac International Airport is opened.

1951 Washington State Ferries begin service on Puget Sound.

1954 First successful passenger jet, Boeing 707, takes off.

1962 Seattle builds Space Needle and monorail for the World's Fair.

1966 Boeing builds 747 assembly plant.

1970S Boeing layoffs devastate the local economy.

1971 Starbucks opens its first shop, and the rest is history.

1975 Microsoft is founded by Bill Gates and Paul Allen in Albuquerque; three years later it moves to Seattle area.

1976 First woman governor of Washington, Dixy Lee Ray, is elected.

1976 The new Seahawks football team plays its first game.

1977 The new Mariners baseball team throws its first pitch.

1979 The Seattle SuperSonics win the NBA Championship.

1999 A World Trade Organization conference in downtown Seattle prompts riots, property damage, and accusations of police misconduct.

2001 The Nisqually Earthquake causes extensive damage to many older Seattle buildings.

2004 Washington elects Christine Gregoire in tightest governor's race in U.S. history, giving Washington state three women in its powerful political positions—two U.S. senators and the governor.

2005 Smoking is banned in all public places in Washington.

2006 Starbucks CEO Howard Schultz sells the Seattle SuperSonics team to an Oklahoma group after the city refuses to expand the basketball arena or build a new one. This leaves the Sonics' future in Seattle in doubt.

2007 The Washington state Legislature legalizes same-sex domestic partnerships.

2008 Seattle voters approve $73 million worth of renovations to their beloved but aging Pike Place Market.

2009 The Link light rail station opens at Sea-Tac Airport, providing rapid mass transportation from downtown Seattle to the airport.

2010 A new law makes it a primary offense to text-message or hold a cellphone to your ear while driving.

2010 The Seattle Storm women's basketball team win their second WNBA championship.

2012[Washington State legalizes same-sex marriage and possession of small amounts of marijuana for recreational use.

2013 Works begins on the demolition of Alaskan Way, a 1960s-era freeway that blights the downtown waterfront; a new tunnel will carry traffic and street adjacent to Seattle's waterfront will eventually be transofmred into a park.

2014 Seattle Seahawks beat the Denver Broncos and win the Super Bowl. An estimated 700,000 people celebrate the event at a downtown parade.

Index

See also Accommodations and Restaurant indexes, below.

A

Accommodations, 154–162. *See also* Accommodations Index
  best bets, 156
ACT (A Contemporary Theatre), 32, 151
Aer Lingus, 180
Agate Designs, 91
AirAmbulanceCard.com, 186
Air New Zealand, 180
Airpark, 22
Air travel, 180–181
Akanyi African & Tribal Art Gallery, 87
Alibi Room, 139
Alki Bakery and Cafe, 18
Alki Beach, 5, 17–18
Allen, Paul, 13, 105
Alphabet Soup, 75
Amazon.com, 105
American Express emergency number, 184
American Foundation for the Blind (AFB), 186
Amtrak, 182
Antiques, 87
Antiques at Pike Place, 87
A Piece of Cake, 72
Aquarium
  Point Defiance Zoo & Aquarium (Tacoma), 165
  Seattle, 11, 35, 99–100
  Vancouver, B.C., 175
Archie McPhee, 75
Architecture, 43–48
Arctic Building, 45
Area codes, 183
Argosy Cruises, 25, 100, 105
  Christmas Ships Festival, 179
Art museums and galleries, 87
  Bellevue Arts Museum, 170
  Elements Gallery (Bellevue), 169
  First Thursday Gallery Walk, 53
  Frye Art Museum, 28
  Henry Art Gallery, 29
  Museum of Glass (Tacoma), 165
  Seattle Art Museum, 11, 27, 46, 65
  Seattle Asian Art Museum, 28
  Tacoma Art Museum, 164
Arts and entertainment, 146–152
Artusi, 139
ATMs (automated teller machines), 183
Australian embassy and consulates, 184
Azalea Way, 111

B

Bad Woman Yarn, 76
Bainbridge Island, 18
Ballet, 29
Baltic Room, 143
Banana Republic, 47
Barnes & Noble, 87–88
Bars and lounges, 139–144
Bathhouses (sentos), 73
Bathtub Gin and Co., 139
Bauhaus Books & Coffee, 41
Bay Pavilion, 99–100
Bellevue, 168–171
Bellevue Aquatic Center, 171
Bellevue Arts Museum, 170
Bellevue Botanical Garden, 171
Bellevue Downtown Park, 169
Bellevue Square Mall, 169–170
Benaroya Hall, 65
Bigfoot (Sasquatch), 69
Bite of Seattle, 101, 179
Black Bottle Gastro-Tavern, 140
Blake Island, 5
Boating (boat rentals)
  Argosy Cruises Christmas Ships Festival, 179
  Green Lake Park, 109
  Lake Union, 103
  Mercer Slough Nature Park (Bellevue), 170
  Opening Day of Boating Season, 178
Boat tours and cruises, 100
  Harbor Tour, 17
  Queen of Seattle Paddlewheel Cruises, 105
  Sunday Ice Cream Cruise (Lake Union), 104
BOKA Restaurant + Bar, 140

Bolt Bus, 182
Bookstore Bar, 140
Bookstores, 87–88
Botanical gardens
  Bellevue Botanical Garden, 171
  Carl S. English, Jr. Botanical Garden, 106–107
  Japanese Garden, 111
  Woodland Park Rose Garden, 112–113
Bottleworks, 75
Bourgeois, Louise, 28
British Airways, 180
Bumbershoot, 5, 101
  the Seattle Music & Arts Festival, 179
Burke Museum of Natural History and Culture, 24
Business hours, 183
Bus travel, 182–183

C

Caffe Ladro Espresso Bar & Bakery, 41
Caffe Umbria, 15, 40
Caffe Vita, 40–41
Calder, Alexander, 28
Canada, embassy and consulates, 184
Can Can, 149
Candy, 88
Canoeing, Mercer Slough Nature Park (Bellevue), 170
Capilano Suspension Bridge & Park (Vancouver, B.C.), 176
Capitol Hill, 6
  neighborhood walk, 66–69
Carl S. English, Jr. Botanical Garden, 107
Car rentals, 179–180
Car travel, 181–182
Cellphones, 180
Center for Wooden Boats, 36, 104
Central Link Light Rail, 183
The Central Saloon, 140
CenturyLink Field, 44
Cha Cha Lounge, 140
Chihuly, Dale, 28
Chihuly Bridge of Glass, 165
Chihuly Garden and Glass, 27–28, 115
Children's Museum, Seattle, 13, 36, 115
Children's Theatre, Seattle, 35–36, 116

Chinatown/International District, Lunar New Year Celebration, 179
Chinatown/International District, neighborhood walk, 70–73
Chinese Gate, 73
Chocolate, 126
Chopstix, 144
Chop Suey, 143
Cinemas, 31–33
Cinerama, 33
City Centre, 64, 94
CityPass, 11
Classical music, 148
The Clog Factory, 96
Coffee, 6, 39–41, 126
San Juan Coffee Roasting Co. (San Juan Island), 167
Comedy clubs, 148
The Comedy Underground, 148
Comet Falls, 173
Concert venues, 148
Consulates, 184
Contour, 143
Credit cards, lost or stolen, 184
Crossroads Trading Co., 89
Cruise terminals, 99
The Cuff Complex, 143
Cupcake Royale (Bellevue), 170
Currency, 183
Cutty Sark Nautical Antiques, 87

D

Daily Dozen Doughnuts, 10
Dance clubs, 142–143
Dance Footsteps, 68
Dance performances, 149
Daylight Saving Time, 185
Dentists, 183
Department stores, 89
Dilettante Mocha Café, 41, 88–89
Dimitriou's Jazz Alley, 144, 150
Dining, 118–134. See also Restaurants Index
best bets, 118
food courts, 36, 63, 71
Dinner theater, 149–150
Disabilities, travelers with, 186
Discount/consignment shopping, 89
Doctors, 183
Dotcom economy, 63

Downtown, neighborhood walk, 60–65
Dragon's Toy Box, 96
Drinking laws, 183
Driscoll Robbins Fine Carpets, 95
Drugstores, 185

E

Easy Street Records and CDs, 94
Economy Building, 57
Eddie Bauer, 90
E.E. Robbins, 94
Egyptian Theatre, 31
88 Keys Dueling Piano Sports Bar, 144
Elements Gallery (Bellevue), 169
Elliott Bay, 25
Elliott Bay Book Company, 5, 15, 69, 88
Elliott's Oyster House, 18
Elysian Brewing Company, 140
Embassies and consulates, 183–184
Emergencies, 184
The Erotic Bakery, 76
Espresso Vivace, 41, 68
Experience Music Project (EMP), 13–14, 47–48, 116, 148

F

Facèrè, 94
Fado Irish Pub, 140
Fall, 179
Families with children, 35–37
The Farm Boat, 105
Farmers' market, The Farm Boat, 105
Farwest Taxi, 181
Fashion (clothing), 89–91
consignment apparel shops, 68
Ferries, 4, 182
Bainbridge Island, 18
San Juan Island, 166–167
Festivals and special events, 101, 178–179
5th Avenue Theatre, 32, 151
Fireside Room, 140
Fireworks, 91
First and Pike News, 88
First Thursday Gallery Walk, 53
Fish Ladder, 107
Fish 'n chips, stands selling, 10

Flanagan & Lane Antiques, 87
Flowers, 91
Floyd's Place, 144
Food courts, 36, 63, 71
Foster/White, 93
Fourth of July fireworks, 101
Fremont Fair, 178
Fremont neighborhood walk, 78–80
Fremont Rocket, 80
Fremont Troll, 4, 78–79
Friday Harbor Ferry Dock (San Juan Island), 166
Frye Art Museum, 28–29, 69
Fuel Coffee, 75–76
Furniture, 91

G

GameWorks, 61
Garden d'Lights (Bellevue), 171
Gasworks Park, 77
Gasworks Park Kite Shop, 77
Gays and lesbians
nightlife, 143
Seattle Pride, 178
Gelato, 15
Gem Heaven, 91
Gems, 91
G. Gibson Gallery, 87
Ghost Tour, Pike Place Market, 56
Gifts, 91–93
Glass, 93
Glasshouse Studio, 52–53, 93
Globe Bookstore, 53, 88
Graham Visitors Center, Washington Park Arboretum, 111
Grand Central Bakery, 53
Granville Island (Vancouver, B.C.), 175
Gray Line Airport Express, 181
Green Lake Park, 37, 108–109
Green Lake Path, 108
Greyhound, 182
Grouse Mountain (Vancouver, B.C.), 176
Guild 45th, 76

H

Harbor Tour, 17
Harvard-Belmont Landmark District, 68
Harvard Exit, 31
Hello, Cupcake (Tacoma), 164
Hendrix, Jimi, 13

Henry Art Gallery, 29
Hiking
    Mercer Slough Nature
        Park (Bellevue), 170
    Mount Rainier National
        Park, 173
    Washington Park Arbo-
        retum, 111
Hing Hay Park, 71–72
Hiram M. Chittenden Locks,
    4–5, 106–107
Historic Panama Hotel Bed
    & Breakfast
    bathhouse, 73
    Tea & Coffee House, 72
Historic sights and attrac-
    tions, 22–25
History of Seattle, 186–188
Holidays, 184
Hospitals, 184
Hotels, 154–162. See also
    Accommodations Index
    best bets, 156
Housewares, 93

I
Information Booth (Pike
    Place Market), 55
International Children's
    Festival, 178
International District/China-
    town neighborhood walk,
    70–73
International Fountain, 116
Internet access, 184
Intiman Theatre, 33, 151
InTouch USA, 180
Ireland, embassy and
    consulates, 184
Issaquah Salmon Days
    Festival, 179
Izilla Toys, 96

J
Japanese Garden, 111
Jazz and blues, 143–144, 150
Jeffrey Moose Gallery, 87
Jewelry, 94

K
Karma Martini Lounge &
    Bistro, 141
Kayaking, Lake Union, 103
Kells Irish Restaurant & Pub,
    141
Kenmore Air, 181
King Street Station, 44
Kites, 77
Klondike Gold Rush
    National Historical Park,
    22–23, 52

Kobo at Higo, 72
Kobo Capitol Hill, 92

L
Lake Union, 6, 102–105
    Fourth of July fireworks,
        178
Left Bank Books, 88
Lenin, Statue of, 79
Link Light Rail Station, 181
Lodging, 154–162. See also
    Accommodations Index
    best bets, 156
Longmire, 173
Longmire Museum, 173
Lost and found, 184–185
Lunar New Year Celebration,
    179
LUSH, 95

M
Macy's, 63–64, 89
Made in Washington, 92
Madison Pub, 143
Magic Mouse Toys, 96
Malls, 94
Marion Oliver McCaw
    Hall, 28
Mario's, 90
Market Ghost Tour, 56
Market Heritage Tour, 59
Market Magic & Novelty
    Shop, 96
Market Spice, 56
MasterCard, emergency
    number, 184
Mercer Slough Nature Park
    (Bellevue), 170
Merry Tails, 92
Metro Bus, 182
The Metro Clothing Co., 90
Microsoft, 63
Millstream, 92
MOHAI (Museum of History
    & Industry), 24, 69
Molly Moon's Ice Cream, 75
Monorail, 6, 9
Monorail Espresso, 40
The Moore Theatre,
    151–152
MossRehab, 186
Mountain climbing, Mount
    Rainier National Park, 172
Mount Rainier National Park,
    172–173
Movies at the Mural, 115
Mud Bay Granary, 95
Museum of Flight, 22
Museum of Glass (Tacoma),
    165
Museum of History & Indus-
    try (MOHAI), 24, 103

Museums
    art. See Art museums
        and galleries
    Burke Museum of
        Natural History and
        Culture, 24
    Longmire Museum, 173
    Museum of Flight, 22
    Museum of History &
        Industry (MOHAI),
        24, 103
    Nordic Heritage
        Museum, 24
    Seattle Children's
        Museum, 13, 115
    Washington State His-
        tory Museum
        (Tacoma), 165
    Whale Museum (Friday
        Harbor), 167
    Wing Luke Asian
        Museum, 23, 72–73
Music, 15
    classical, 148
    Experience Music Proj-
        ect (EMP), 13–14,
        47–48, 115–116
    jazz and blues, 143–144,
        150
    popular, 152
Music stores, 94–95

N
Neighborhood walks, 49–80
    Capitol Hill, 66–69
    Chinatown/Interna-
        tional District, 70–73
    downtown, 60–65
    Fremont, 78–80
    Pike Place Market,
        54–59
    Pioneer Square, 50–53
    Wallingford, 74–77
Neighbours, 143
New Orleans, 144
Newspapers and magazines,
    184–185
New Year's, 5
New Year's at the Needle,
    179
New Zealand, embassy and
    consulates, 184
Nightlife, 136–144
    bars and lounges,
        139–144
    best bets, 136
    dance clubs, 142–143
    gay and lesbian, 143
    live jazz and blues,
        143–144
    piano bars, 144
    sports bars, 144

Niketown, 96
Noble Horse Gallery, 92
Nordic Heritage Museum, 24
Nordstrom, 62, 89, 96
Nordstrom Rack, 89–90
Northwest Fine Wood-working, 91
Northwest Flower & Garden Show, 179
Northwest Folklife Festival, 101, 178
Northwest Puppet Center, 36

O

Occidental Park and Pedestrian Walkway, 11
Oliver's Lounge, 141
Olympic Sculpture Park, 28
Opera, 150–151
Outdoor activities, 98–116
Owl 'N Thistle, 141

P

Pacific Northwest Ballet, 29, 149
Pacific Place, 61–62, 94
Pacific Science Center, 13, 36, 116
Palace Rug Gallery, 96
Panache, 90
Panama Hotel, 72
Paradise Inn (Mount Rainier National Park), 173
Paradise Jackson Visitor Center (Mount Rainier National Park), 172
Paramount Theatre, 31, 152
Parking, 183
PCC Natural Markets, 80
Pegasus Coffee House and Gallery (Winslow), 18
Pelindaba Lavender Gallery, 95, 167
Perennial Tearoom, 59
Pets, 95
Pharmacies, 185
Piano bars, 144
Pike Place, 58
Pike Place Flowers, 91
Pike Place Market, 4
   Down Under, 58–59
   Information Booth, 55
   Main Arcade, 9–10, 56–57
   neighborhood walk, 54–59
   restaurants, 58
   South Arcade, 57
   tours, 56, 59

The Pike Pub & Brewery, 141
The Pink Door Cabaret, 149
Pioneer Building, 44, 51
Pioneer Square, neighborhood walk, 50–53
Pioneer Square Park, 51
Pioneer Square Pergola, 45
Pirates Plunder, 92
Playground, Green Lake Park, 108–109
Point Defiance Zoo & Aquarium (Tacoma), 165
Polar Bar, 141
Police, 185
Popular music, 152
Post Alley, 59
Purple Café and Wine Bar, 141
Pyramid Alehouse, 142

Q

Qantas, 180

R

Rachel the Pig, 55–56
Ragazzi's Flying Shuttle, 90
Raygun Lounge, 142
Re-bar, 143
Red Barn, 22
Restaurants, 118–134. See also Restaurants Index
   best bets, 118
   food courts, 36, 63, 71
Restrooms, 185
Robson Street (Vancouver, B.C.), 176
Rocky Mountain Chocolate Factory, 89
Rugs, 95–96

S

Safeco Field, 43
Safety, 185
Salmon
   Hiram M. Chittenden Locks, 4–5, 107
   Issaquah Salmon Days Festival, 179
   at Tillicum Village, 5
San Juan Coffee Roasting Co. (San Juan Island), 167
San Juan Islands, 166–167
Sasquatch (Bigfoot), 69
SATH (Society for Accessible Travel & Hospitality), 186
Seafair, 6, 101, 178–179
Seafood, 126
Seaplane flights, 104
Seasons, 178

Seattle Aquarium, 11, 35, 99–100
Seattle Architecture Foundation, 47
Seattle Art Museum, 11, 27, 46, 65
Seattle Asian Art Museum, 29
Seattle Center, 114–116
Seattle Center House, 115
Seattle Center House Food Court, 36
Seattle Center Skatepark, 36
Seattle Central Public Library, 46–47, 65
Seattle Children's Museum, 13, 36, 115
Seattle Children's Theatre, 35–36, 116
Seattle Fudge, 116
Seattle Gilbert & Sullivan Society, 150–151
Seattle Glassblowing Studio, 93
Seattle Great Wheel, 99–100
Seattle International Film Festival, 31, 178
Seattle Mystery Bookshop, 51, 88
Seattle Opera, 29, 151
Seattle Pride, 178
Seattle Pride Festival, 101
Seattle Public Theater at the Bathhouse, 109
Seattle Repertory Theatre, 33, 152
Seattle's Best Coffee, 40
Seattle's Convention and Visitors Bureau, 178
Seattle Streetcar, 183
Seattle Symphony, 148
Seattle-Tacoma International Airport, 180
See's Candies, 89
See Sound Lounge, 142
Shoes, 96
Shopping, 82–96
   antiques, 87
   art galleries, 87
   best bets, 82
   bookstores, 87–88
   candy, 88
   department stores, 89
   fashion, 89–91
   flowers, 91
   gems, 91
   gifts, 91–93
   glass, 93
   housewares, 93
   jewelry, 94
   malls, 94
   music/CDs, 94–95

Pacific Place, 62
perfume/skincare/
    herbal products, 95
pet store, 95
rugs, 95–96
shoes, 96
toys and novelties, 96
Showbox, 152
Shuttle Express, 181
Silver Platters, 94
Simo Silk, 90
The Sitting Room, 142
Sixth Avenue Wine Seller, 62
Skagit Valley Tulip Festival
    (La Conner), 178
Skatepark, Seattle Center, 36
Slugger's, 144
Smith, 142
Smith Tower, 45, 52
Smoking, 185
Snowshoeing, Mount Rainier
    National Park, 173
The Sock Monster, 76
South Lake Union, 105
Space Gallery, 22
Space Needle, 4, 5, 9, 48,
    115
Special events and festivals,
    101, 178–179
Spitfire, 144
Sport Restaurant & Bar, 144
Sports bars, 144
Spring, 178
Stanley Park (Vancouver,
    B.C.), 175–176
Starbucks, 39
Summer, 178
    festivals and special
    events, 101
Sunday Ice Cream Cruise
    (Lake Union), 104
Sur La Table, 93
Swedish Medical Center,
    184
Swimming, Bellevue Aquatic
    Center, 171
Swimming pools, Green
    Lake Park, 108

T
Tacoma, 164–165
Tacoma Art Museum, 164
Tacoma Union Station, 165
Tap House Grill, 142
Taxes, 185
Taxis, 181
Teatro ZinZanni, 150
Telephones, 185
Temple Billiards, 144
Tennis, Green Lake Park,
    109

Tenzing Momo & Company,
    95
Theater, 33, 35–36, 109,
    151–152
    dinner, 149–150
Theo Chocolate, 126
Tillicum Village, 5, 25
Time zones, 185–186
Tin Cup Espresso, 41, 104
Tipping, 185
TNT Espresso, 41
Top Ten Toys, 62
Torchlight Parade, 6
Tourist information, 178
Town Hall, 148
Toys and novelties, 96
Train travel, 182
Transit info, 186
Transportation, 181–183
Traveling to Seattle,
    180–181
Trendy Wendy, 90
Trinity Nightclub, 143
The Triple Door, 144, 150
Tugboat Storytime, 36
Tula's, 144
Tully's Coffee, 39
Twice Sold Tales, 88
Twist, 92–93
Two Bells, 142

U
U District StreetFair, 178
Underground Tour, 4, 14
Union Station
    Seattle, 44
    Tacoma, 165
United Kingdom embassy
    and consulates, 184
Uptown Espresso, 41
Utilikilts, 90–91
Uwajimaya, 71
UW World Series, 149

V
Vancouver, BC, 174–176
Vancouver Aquarium, 175
Victoria Clipper, 166–167,
    181–182
Victor Steinbrueck Park, 99
Vintage apparel shops, 68
Virginia Mason Medical
    Center, 184
Visa, emergency number,
    184
Visitor information, 178
Volunteer Park, 67
Von Trapp's, 142
Von's 1000 Spirits, 142

W
Waiting for the Interurban
    (sculpture), 80
Walking tours, architectural
    highlights, 47
Wallingford, neighborhood
    walk, 74–77
Wallingford Playfield, 76
Wall of Sound, 95
Washington Park Arbore-
    tum, 110–111
Washington State Conven-
    tion & Trade Center, 61
Washington State Ferries,
    181
Washington State Ferry Ter-
    minal, 101
Washington State History
    Museum (Tacoma), 165
Washington State Tourism,
    178
Waterfall Garden Park, 52
The waterfront, 10
Waterfront Park, 10, 99
Watson Kennedy Fine
    Home, 93–94
W Bar, 142
Weather, 179
Weather forecasts, 186
Websites, useful, 180
Westlake Center, 63, 94
    food court at, 63
Whale Museum (Friday
    Harbor), 167
Whale-watch cruises, Friday
    Harbor (San Juan Island),
    167
The Wild Rose, 143
Wine World & Spirits, 77
Wing Luke Asian Museum,
    23, 72–73
Winslow, 18
Winter, 179
Winterfest, 115–116
Woodland Park, 112–113
    Rose Garden, 112–113
Woodland Park Zoo, 37,
    112, 113, 148

Y
Yellow Cab, 181
Ye Olde Curiosity Shop,
    100–101
Young Flowers, 91

Z
Zeitgeist Coffee, 39, 52
ZigZag Café, 142

Index

Zoos
  Point Defiance Zoo & Aquarium (Tacoma), 165
  Woodland Park, 37, 112, 113, 148
Zootunes, 113, 149

Accommodations

Alexis, 157
Arctic Club Hotel, 157
Best Western Pioneer Square Hotel, 157
Courtyard by Marriott Lake Union, 157
Crowne Plaza, 157
The Edgewater Hotel, 157
Fairmont Olympic Hotel, 157–158
Four Seasons Hotel, 158
Grand Hyatt Seattle, 158
Hilton Seattle, 158
Hotel FIVE Seattle, 158
Hotel Max, 158–159
Hotel Monaco, 159
Hotel 1000, 159
Hotel Vintage, 159
Hyatt at Olive 8, 160
Inn at the Market, 160
Mayflower Park Hotel, 160
Mediterranean Inn, 160–161
Paramount Hotel, 160
Red Lion Hotel on Fifth Avenue, 160
Renaissance Seattle Hotel, 161
Roosevelt Hotel, 161
Sheraton Seattle Hotel, 161
Silver Cloud Hotel Broadway, 161
Sorrento Hotel, 161
Warwick Hotel Seattle, 162
The Westin Seattle, 162
W Seattle Hotel, 162

Restaurants

Alki Bakery and Cafe, 18
Ambrosia Cafe, 73
Andaluca, 123
Aqua, 123
Assaggio, 123
The Athenian Inn, 57
Bastille, 123
Blueacre, 124
BOKA Kitchen + Bar, 124
Café Campagne, 124
Café Paloma, 124
Caffe Umbria, 15
Canlis, 124
Charlie's Bar & Grill, 69
Cherry Street Coffee House, 27
Compass Cafe, 103–104
Cutters Crabhouse, 124–125
Dahlia Lounge, 125
Daniels' Broiler, 105
Dick's Drive-In, 125
El Gaucho, 125
Elliott's Oyster House, 125
Etta's Seafood, 125–126
Hello, Cupcake (Tacoma), 164
The Herbfarm, 133
Hunt Club, 126
Il Fornaio, 127
Irwin's Neighborhood Bakery and Cafe, 77
Ivar's Acres of Clams, 127
Ivar's Seafood Bar, 100
Jade Garden, 127
Joey Lake Union, 105
Joule, 127
Julia's on Broadway, 31
Kabul, 127
La Carta de Oaxaca, 127
Lark, 127
Larsen's Danish Bakery, 25
La Spiga, 127–128
Le Pichet, 128
List, 128
Lockspot Café, 107
Lola, 128
Marco's Supperclub, 129

Marrakesh Moroccan Restaurant, 128
Matt's in the Market, 128
Maximilien, 129
McCormick & Schmick's, 105, 129
Merchants Cafe, 51
Metropolitan Grill, 129
MistralKitchen, 129–130
Morton's The Steakhouse, 130
O'Asian Kitchen, 130
Pagliacci Pizza, 130
Palisade, 130
Perennial Tearoom, 59
Place Pigalle, 130
Poppy, 130–131
Purple Café and Wine Bar, 131
Racha Thai & Asian Kitchen, 131
Ray's Boathouse, 131
Royal Grinders, 79
Salty's on Alki, 131–132
Sazerac, 132
Serious Pie, 132
72nd Street Café, 109
Shiro's, 132
Sitka & Spruce, 132
Six Seven, 132
SkyCity at the Needle, 133
Soups!, 64
Specialty's Café & Bakery, 46
Steelhead Diner, 133
Tavolata, 133
Teahouse in Stanley Park (Vancouver, B.C.), 175–176
Ten Mercer, 133–134
Tilth, 134
Traveler Montlake, 111
Tulio Ristorante, 134
Urbane, 134
Volterra, 134
Wild Ginger, 134
Zeek's, 134

Photo **Credits**